THE RED BOOK OF UNITED STATES COINS

———————— *1974* ————————

A GUIDE BOOK
of
UNITED STATES COINS

27th Revised Edition

Fully Illustrated
Catalog and Valuation List — 1616 to Date

By R. S. YEOMAN

Including . . .

A BRIEF HISTORY OF AMERICAN COINAGE
EARLY AMERICAN COINS AND TOKENS
EARLY MINT ISSUES • REGULAR MINT ISSUES
PRIVATE, STATE AND TERRITORIAL GOLD
SILVER AND GOLD COMMEMORATIVE ISSUES
PROOFS

Edited by Kenneth Bressett

 Whitman Coin Products

THE SPANISH MILLED DOLLAR
The Coin of Our Nation's Founders

The Spanish milled dollar valued at 8 *reales,* otherwise known as the "pillar dollar" or "piece of eight," has been given a place in romantic fiction unequaled by any other coin.

This time-honored piece and its fractional parts of ½ and 1 *real,* 2 and 4 *reales* were the principal coins of the American colonists, and were the forerunners of our own silver dollar and its fractional divisions.

The coin shown above bears the M̃ mint mark for Mexico City. Similar pieces with other mint marks were struck in Bolivia, Chile, Colombia, Guatemala and Peru. For details see listings in Whitman's *Coins of the World 1750-1850* by W. D. Craig and *Silver Dollars of North and South America* by Wayte Raymond. Average value for an 8 *reales* of common date and mint is $25 to $35 in Fine condition. Dates range from 1732 to 1772.

Note: Many modern copies of the 8 *reales* exist. These are produced mostly as souvenirs and have little or no value.

THE PURPOSE OF THIS BOOK

Coin values listed in the Guide Book are averaged from data supplied by contributors several months before publication. The coin market is so active in some categories that values can easily change during this period. Prices are shown as a guide and are not intended to serve as a price-list for any dealer's stock.

Prices rise because: 1. The trend of our economy is inflationary. 2. The number of collectors is increasing rapidly, while coin supplies remain stationary. 3. Dealers can procure their stock of coins only from collectors or other dealers, who expect a profit over and above what they originally paid.

Prices decline because: 1. Speculators buy and sell in large quantities, drawing in thousands of unwary persons looking for quick profits. When the average collector stops buying, the prices drop. 2. Hoards of coins suddenly are released from estates of deceased collectors or Federal Reserve vaults (as in the case of silver dollars) and the like. Such conditions usually adjust themselves within months or a few years.

Those who edit, contribute to, and publish this book advocate the collecting of coins for pleasure and educational benefits. A secondary consideration is that of investment, the profits from which are realized over the long term based on intelligent purchases of the best grades of coins.

The *Handbook of United States Coins* by R. S. Yeoman, containing average prices dealers will pay for these coins, is obtainable at hobby dealers for $1.50. A companion book, *Buying and Selling U.S. Coins* by Ken Bressett (paperback edition, $1.00), gives a capsule comparison of Guide Book and Handbook prices for coins in average grades.

Neither the publisher nor the editor of this book deals in coins; therefore, the values shown here are not offers to sell but are included only as general information.

CONTRIBUTORS TO THE TWENTY-SEVENTH EDITION
KENNETH E. BRESSETT, Coordinating Editor
Neil Shafer and Holland Wallace, Editorial Assistants

Robert F. Batchelder	Abner Kreisberg
A. E. Bebee	Kenneth W. Lee
Philip E. Benedetti	John B. Love
George H. Blenker	Raymond N. Merena
Q. David Bowers	Lester Merkin
Walter Breen	Bill Mertes
Dan Brown	Roy A. Miller
Malcolm O. E. Chell-Frost	Ken Nichols
Alan R. Cohen	Jerome Nusbaum
Jerry Cohen	Dean Oakes
Carl Curcio	Walter R. Perschke
B. M. Douglas	Joe Person
Ben Dreiske	Richard Picker
Kurt Eckstein	Elmer B. Ray
Charles F. French	Joel D. Rettew
Dorothy Gershenson	James F. Ruddy
Bernard Gimelson	F. K. Saab
Ira M. Goldberg	Earl C. Schill
Lawrence S. Goldberg	Norman Shultz
Gene L. Henry	Mulford B. Simons, Jr.
Curtis Iversen	Sidney W. Smith
Floyd O. Janney	Benjamin Stack
Robert R. Johnson	Harvey G. Stack
A. M. Kagin	Norman Stack
Donald Kagin	Leonard W. Stark
Paul Kagin	Maurice A. Storck
Mike Kliman	R. E. Wallace
Abe Kosoff	Gary L. Young

Special credit is due to the following for data and service in connection with this book.

Herbert Bergen, Harry X Boosel, Hy Brown, Ronnie Carr, Ted F. Clark, William L. Clark, George Fuld, James A. Haxby, Robert W. Julian, Warren A. Lapp, Raymond D. Munde, Hubert L. Polzer, Max M. Schwartz, Arlie Slabaugh, Jack H. Tod, Stewart P. Witham and Leo A. Young.

Those now deceased, but whose contributions have been a part of this book since early editions, include:

David M. Bullowa, Charles E. Green, Richard D. Kenney, Steve Kosoff, Franklyn H. Miller, Stuart Mosher, Gen. M. S. Newton, Al C. Overton, Earl Parker, Lewis M. Reagan, Herbert E. Rowold, Walter Thompson and Farran Zerbe.

CONDITION OF COINS

FAIR. Coin has sufficient design and letters to be easily identified. Excessive wear.

G. or GOOD. All of design, every feature and legend must be plain and date clear.

V. G. or VERY GOOD. Features all clear and bold. Better than good, but not quite fine.

F. or FINE. Obviously a circulated coin but little wear. Mint luster gone. All letters in LIBERTY and mottoes clear.

V. FINE or VERY FINE. Shows enough wear on high spots to be noticeable. Still retains enough luster to be desirable.

EX. FINE or EXTREMELY FINE. Slightly circulated with some luster but faint evidence of wear.

UNC. or UNCIRCULATED. New. Regular mint striking, but never placed in circulation. Older pieces may be tarnished or "toned."

PF. or PROOF. Coins with mirrorlike surface, specially struck for coin collectors. Also sandblast and matte proof. See Pages 59 and 60.

Pre-1968 branch mint coins having a mirrorlike surface are not proofs but are first strikings of new dies.

IMPORTANT: Coins in any condition with defects, such as those which are bent, corroded, scratched, holed, nicked, stained, oxidized, mutilated, or have other imperfections, are worth less than if free of these defects. Flawless uncirculated coins are generally worth more than values quoted in this book. Slightly worn coins which have been cleaned and conditioned to simulate uncirculated luster are worth considerably less than perfect pieces.

Brief guides to grading are placed before each major coin type in this book. For those readers who desire more detailed descriptions of all coin grades, we recommend A GUIDE TO THE GRADING OF UNITED STATES COINS, by Martin R. Brown and John W. Dunn.

QUANTITIES OF COINS STRUCK

Collectors are cautioned that mint reports are not always reliable for estimating the rarity of coins. In the early years of the mint, dies of previous years were often used until they became worn or broken.

It should also be emphasized that quantities reported, particularly for gold and silver, cover the number of coins struck and have no reference to the quantity reaching actual circulation. Many issues were deposited in the treasury as backing for paper currency and were later melted. There are other similar examples.

The rarity of gold pieces struck before 1834, particularly half eagles, can be traced to the fact that the gold content was reduced in 1834, making previous issues greater in value than face, causing melting and reminting.

The quantities reported by the mint of three dollar gold pieces from 1873 to 1877 and half cents from 1832 to 1836 are subject to doubt.

Coinage figures shown for 1964 through 1966 are for coins bearing those dates. Some of them were struck in more than one year and at various mints, both with and without mint marks.

Mint quantities are shown adjacent to each date throughout the book.

PROOF TOTALS ARE SHOWN IN PARENTHESES

AN INTRODUCTION TO UNITED STATES COINS

Money of the Early Americans

The story of American money, which occupies a period of about three centuries, began when the early settlers in New England carried on their fur trade with the Indians through the use of wampum, which had been fashioned from mussel shells in the form of "beads." Beaver skins, wampum, and in Virginia, tobacco, soon became the common accepted media of exchange for all other available commodities. The immigrants, in fact, had little use for coined money at first, but when traders arrived from foreign lands, coins were usually demanded in payment for goods. Any foreign coins were usually accepted, such as French louis, English guineas, German thalers, Dutch ducats, and various Spanish coins, including doubloons and particularly the Spanish milled dollar, or piece of eight. The coin last mentioned remained as a standard money unit throughout the entire colonial period. Even after the Revolutionary War, the Spanish dollar and its fractional parts continued to circulate in this country with official sanction until 1857. One *real* equaled 12½ cents and was known as a "bit." A quarter of the dollar thus became known as "two bits," a term still in common use.

England consistently ignored the plight of the colonists and made no effort to provide gold or silver coins, or a small-change currency for them. Although coins known as "Hogge Money" were provided for the Sommer Islands, now known as the Bermudas, about the year 1616, the first coins minted in America were minted by John Hull in the Massachusetts Bay Colony. The General Court of the colony granted him authority to begin coinage. Starting in 1652 the Boston mint provided the famous N.E., pine tree, and similar shillings, with their fractional parts, for the hardpressed colonists. Other colonies tried similar projects but failed.

As time went on coins and tokens of many types were introduced and employed by the colonists in their daily course of business. Lord Baltimore in Maryland was responsible for a series of silver pieces, which were probably struck in England in 1659. Mark Newby introduced a piece known as St. Patrick's Halfpence into the province of New Jersey in 1682. Coins dated 1722 to 1724, known as Rosa Americana and Hibernia coppers, were produced by William Wood in England and were widely circulated in America. The Carolina and New England Elephant tokens were current in the years following 1694. There were also a few issues of uncertain date and origin, such as the New Yorke Token, which circulated among the Dutch settlers and was probably sent over from Holland.

Enterprising American individuals were responsible for some of the copper pieces that circulated during the eighteenth century. The Gloucester Token, about which little is known, was one of these. John Higley of Granby, Connecticut, made an interesting series of threepence pieces during the period from 1737 to 1739. J. Chalmers, a goldsmith in Annapolis, Maryland, issued silver shillings, sixpence, and threepence pieces in 1783. In 1787 Ephraim Brasher, a New York goldsmith, struck a gold piece of the value of a doubloon (about $16.00). Standish Barry of Baltimore, Maryland, made a curious silver token threepence in 1790.

Still other tokens, struck in England, reached our shores in Revolutionary times and were for the most part speculative ventures. These much-needed, small-denomination coppers were readily circulated because of the great scarcity of fractional coins. Included in this category were the Nova Constellatio coppers and the Bar cent.

During the period of confederation following the War of Independence, still more English tokens were added to the great variety of coins and tokens employed in the new nation. In 1787 the Nova Eboracs, known as New York

Coppers, the Georgius Triumpho, the Auctori Plebis, and later the Kentucky, Myddelton and Franklin Press tokens were introduced.

Another interesting series, important because of its close association with our first president, comprises those tokens bearing the portrait of Washington. They circulated during and after the Confederation.

Coinage of the States

The Articles of Confederation, adopted July 9, 1778, provided that Congress should have the sole right to regulate the alloy and value of coin struck by its own authority or by that of the respective states.

Each state, therefore, had the right to coin money, but Congress served as a regulating authority. New Hampshire was the first state to consider coinage, but few if any coins were placed in circulation. The only specimens known bear the date 1776.

Vermont, Connecticut, and New Jersey granted coining privileges to companies or individuals. Massachusetts erected its own mint in which copper coins were produced. A number of interesting varieties of these state issues, most of which were struck in fairly large quantities, can still be easily acquired, and form the basis for many present day collections of early American coins.

The Beginnings of United States Coinage

Throughout the Colonial years, Americans had become accustomed to the use of the Spanish dollar and its fractional parts, the *real,* the medio (half-*real),* etc. It was only natural, therefore, that when a national coinage was under consideration the dollar was mentioned most frequently. In earlier years currency statutes in many of the colonies had given first consideration to the Spanish dollar. Connecticut, Massachusetts, and Virginia, particularly, passed laws making Spanish coins a legal tender. The first issue of Continental paper money May 10, 1775, offers further evidence that the dollar was to be our basic money unit, for it provided that the notes should be payable in "Spanish Milled dollars or the value thereof in gold or silver."

The Assistant Financier of the Confederation, Gouverneur Morris, proposed a decimal coinage ratio, and his plan was incorporated in a report presented by Robert Morris, Superintendent of Finance, to the Congress, January 15, 1782. Plans for a mint were advanced, and a uniform national currency to relieve the confused money conditions was outlined. Morris's unit, 1/1440 of a dollar, was calculated to agree without a fraction with all the different valuations of the Spanish milled dollar in the various States. Although a government mint was approved February 21, 1782, no immediate action was taken. During 1784 Thomas Jefferson, then a member of the House of Representatives, brought in a report concerning the plan, and expressed disagreement with Morris' complicated money unit. He advocated the simple dollar unit because he believed the dollar was already as familiar and convenient a unit of value as the British pound. He favored the decimal system and remarked that, "The most easy ratio of multiplication and division is that of ten. President George Washington referred to it as 'a measure, which in my opinion, has become indispensibly necessary.'"

The Grand Committee in May 1785 recommended a gold five-dollar piece; a dollar of silver with fractional coins, of the same metal, in denominations of half, quarter, tenth, and twentieth parts of a dollar; and copper pieces valued at one-hundredth and one two-hundredth of a dollar.

In 1783 Robert Morris submitted a series of pattern pieces in silver which were designed by Dudley to carry out the decimal idea for United States money. These are known as the Nova Constellatio Patterns and consist of the "Mark" or 1,000 units, the "Quint" or 500 units, and the "Bit" or 100 units. The unit was to be a quarter grain of silver. This was not the first

[6]

attempt at a dollar coin, for the Continental currency piece of dollar size, dated 1776, had been struck in such metals as brass, pewter, and silver. The variety in silver probably saw limited service as a dollar.

Congress gave formal approval to the basic dollar unit and decimal coinage ratio in its resolution of July 6, 1785, but other more pressing matters delayed further action. Not until the Constitutional Convention had placed the country on firm ground and the new nation had elected George Washington President, did the Congress again turn attention to the subject of currency, a mint, and a coinage system.

The Massachusetts cents and half-cents struck in 1787 and 1788 were the first official coins to bear a stated value in terms of decimal parts of the dollar unit in this country. The cent represented a hundredth part of a Spanish dollar.

The first federally authorized coin was the Fugio Cent, sometimes called the Franklin Cent, as he was supposed to have supplied the design and composed the legends. This piece, similar in design to the Continental Currency dollar of 1776, was privately struck in 1787 by contract with the Government.

Alexander Hamilton, then Secretary of the Treasury, reported his views on monetary matters January 21, 1791. He concurred in all essentials with the decimal subdivisions and multiples of the dollar contained in the earlier resolutions and urged the use of both gold and silver in our standard money.

Congress passed a resolution March 3, 1791, that a mint be established, and authorized the President to engage artists and procure machinery for the making of coins. No immediate steps were taken, but when Washington delivered his third annual address, he recommended immediate establishment of a mint.

On April 2, 1792, a bill was finally passed providing "that the money of account of the United States should be expressed in dollars or units, dismes or tenths, cents or hundredths, and milles or thousandths; a disme being the tenth part of a dollar, a cent the hundredth part of a dollar, a mille the thousandth part of a dollar . . ."

Denominations specified in the act were as follows:

	Value of	Grains Pure	Grains Standard
Gold Eagle	$10.00	247 - 4/8	270
Gold Half Eagle	5.00	123 - 6/8	135
Gold Quarter Eagle	2.50	61 - 7/8	67 - 4/8
Silver Dollar	1.00	371 - 4/16	416
Silver Half-Dollar	.50	185 - 10/16	208
Silver Quarter-Dollar	.25	92 - 13/16	104
Silver Disme (dime)	.10	37 - 2/16	41 - 3/5
Silver Half-Disme	.05	18 - 9/16	20 - 4/5
Copper Cent	.01	11 pennyweights	
Copper Half-Cent	.005	5½ pennyweights	

The word "pure" meant unalloyed metal; "standard" meant, in the case of gold, 11/12 fine or 11 parts pure metal to one part alloy, which was mixed with the pure metal to improve the wearing qualities of the coins. The fineness for silver coins was 1485/1664 or approximately 892.43 thousandths, in contrast with the gold coins of 22 karats, or 916⅔ thousandths fine.

The law also provided for free coinage of gold and silver coins at the fixed ratio of 15 to one, and a token coinage of copper cents and half-cents. Under the free coinage provision no charge was to be made for converting gold or silver bullion into coins "weight for weight." At the depositor's option, however, he could demand an immediate exchange of coins for his bullion, for which privilege a deduction of one-half of one per cent was to be imposed.

Washington appointed David Rittenhouse, a well-known philosopher and scientist, as the first Director of the Mint. A mint building was started nearly four months after the passage of the Act of April 2, 1792. It was located on Seventh Street near Arch in Philadelphia.

The first coin struck at the new mint was the half-disme. Fifteen hundred of these pieces were produced during the month of July 1792 before the mint was completed. Washington supplied some of his own silverware to the value of about one hundred dollars for these first mint coins. Dismes also were probably struck at this time or a short while later. The portrait on these pieces is presumed to have been modeled by Martha Washington.

Copper for cents and half-cents was covered in the Act of May 8, 1792 when the purchase of not over 150 tons was authorized. On September 11, 1792, six pounds of old copper were purchased, this being the first purchase of copper for coinage, which was probably used for the striking of patterns.

Planchets with upset rims for cents and half-cents were purchased from Boulton of Birmingham, England from 1798 to 1838.

Several pattern coins were prepared in 1792 before regular mint operations commenced. These included the silver center cent by Voigt, a smaller piece than that of regular issue. The small plug of silver, worth about three-quarters of a cent, was evidently intended to bring the intrinsic value of the coin up to the value of one cent and permit production of a coin of more convenient size. Alexander Hamilton had mentioned a year before that the proposed "intrinsic value" cent would be too large, and suggested that the amount of copper could be reduced and a trace of silver added. This pattern cent with a silver center may have been designed to conform to this recommendation.

The cents by Robert Birch are equally interesting. These patterns are identified by their legends which read "LIBERTY PARENT OF SCIENCE AND INDUSTRY" and "TO BE ESTEEMED BE USEFUL." The cent with an eagle on the reverse side belongs among the early patterns devised before regular issues were struck.

The first depositor of silver was the bank of Maryland, which sent $80,715.73½ in French coins to the mint July 18, 1794. Moses Brown, a Boston merchant, deposited the first gold in the form of ingots, February 12, 1795, amounting to $2,276.22, receiving silver coin in payment. The first coins transferred to the Treasurer consisted of 11,178 cents on March 1, 1793. The first return of coined silver was made on October 15, 1794, and the first gold coins were delivered July 31, 1795, 744 half-eagles.

File marks on early U. S. coins are a mint process of weight adjustment.

Regular Mint Issues

Cents and half-cents exclusively were coined during the year 1793, and by 1799 approximately $50,000 in these coins had been placed in circulation. This amount proved insufficient for the requirements of commerce, and small denomination coins of the states and of foreign countries continued in use during the first few years of the nineteenth century.

One of the most serious problems confronting the commercial interests during the early years was the failure of the government to provide a sufficient volume of circulating coins. The fault, contrary to popular opinion at the time, did not lie with any lack of effort on the part of the mint. Other circumstances tended to interfere with the expected steady flow of new coinage into the channels of trade.

Free circulation of United States gold and silver coins was greatly hindered by speculators. For example, worn Spanish dollars of reduced weight and value were easily exchanged for U. S. silver dollars, which meant the export of most of the new dollars as fast as they were minted, and a complete loss to American trade channels.

Gold coins failed to circulate for similar reasons. The ratio of 15 to 1 between gold and silver was close to the world ratio when Hamilton recommended it, but by 1799 the ratio in European commercial centers had reached 15¾ to 1. At this rate the undervalued gold coins tended to flow out of the country, or were reduced for bullion. After 1800, therefore, United States gold coins were rarely seen in general circulation. As no remedy could be found, coinage of the Eagle and the silver dollar was suspended by President Jefferson in 1804 and 1806 respectively. It is generally conceded that the silver dollar was discontinued in 1804, although the last coins minted for the period were dated 1803.

Lacking gold coins and silver dollars, the half-dollar became the desirable coin for large transactions, bank reserves, and foreign payments. Until 1830, in fact, half-dollars circulated very little as they were mainly transferred from bank to bank. This will account for the relatively good supply of half-dollars of this period which are still available to collectors in better than average condition. A senate committee of 1830 reported that United States silver coins were considered so much bullion and were accordingly "lost to the community as coins."

There was only a negligible coinage of quarters, dimes, and half-dimes from 1794 to 1834. It has been estimated that there was less than one piece for each person in the country in the year 1830. This period has been described as one of nondescript currency made up of banknotes, underweight foreign gold coins, foreign silver coins of many varieties, and domestic fractional silver coins. Notes of "wildcat banks" flooded the country before 1830 and were much more common than silver coins.

On June 28, 1834, a new law was passed reducing the weight of standard gold, which had the effect of placing our money on a gold standard. Trade and finance were greatly benefited by this act, which also proved a boon to the gold mines of Georgia and North Carolina. Branch mints in Dahlonega, Georgia, and Charlotte, North Carolina, were established two or three years later to handle the newly-mined gold at the source. The Templeton Reid and Bechtler issues of private gold coins were struck in this area.

The law of January 18, 1837, completely revised and standardized the mint and coinage laws. Legal standards, mint charges, legal tender, mint procedure, tolerance in coin weights, accounting methods, a bullion fund, standardization of gold and silver coins to 900 thousandths fine, and other desirable regulations were covered by the new legislation. Results of importance to the collector were the changes in type for the various coin denominations and the resumption of coinage of the Eagle and silver dollar shortly thereafter.

The political and financial elements underwent a crisis at about this time. The familiar "Jackson Tokens" and fractional notes of banks and commercial establishments completely eclipsed the circulation of metallic currency. This was the era of "shinplasters."

The California gold discovery in 1848 was responsible for an interesting series of private, state, and territorial gold issues in the Western states, culminating in the establishment of a branch mint at San Francisco in 1854.

Two new regular gold issues were adopted in 1849. In that year the double Eagle and gold dollar joined our American family of coins. The California gold fields greatly influenced the world gold market, making the exportation of silver profitable. For example, the silver in two half-dollars was worth $1.03½ in gold. The newly introduced gold dollars soon took over the burden and hastened the disappearance of silver coins from trade channels. This was the situation when the new three-cent postage rate brought about the bill authorizing the coinage of the silver three-cent piece in 1851. This was our country's first subsidiary coin, for its value was intrinsically 86% of its face value, an expedient designed to prevent its withdrawal from circulation.

The three-dollar gold piece was authorized by the act of February 21, 1853. Never a popular or necessary coin, it nevertheless was issued regularly until 1889.

On February 21, 1853, fractional silver coins were made subsidiary resulting from the fact that the weight of all silver pieces, excepting the dollar, was reduced. As the coins were now worth less than their face value free coinage of silver was prohibited, and the mint was authorized to purchase its silver requirements on its own account using the bullion fund of the mint, and, according to law, "the profit of said coinage shall be, . . . transferred to the account of the treasury of the United States."

Arrows were placed at the date on all silver coins except three-cent pieces and dollars, and on the quarters and half-dollars rays were added on the reverse side to denote the change of weight. In 1854 the rays were removed, and in 1856 the arrows disappeared. Production of silver coins in large quantities during this period greatly relieved the demands on gold dollars and three-cent pieces. Consequently for the first time in our nation's history there was a sufficient supply of fractional coins in general circulation.

The law of 1857 was designed primarily to reform the copper coinage. No matter how interesting and valuable the large cents and half-cents may have become in the eyes of the modern collector, they were very unpopular with the people and cost the mint too much to produce.

The new law abolished the half-cent piece, and reduced the size and changed the design of the cent. The new Flying Eagle cent contained 88% copper and 12% nickel. Several hundred experimental cents were stamped from dies bearing the date 1856 although no authority for the issue existed before 1857. Other important effects of the law were the retirement of the Spanish silver coins from circulation, and dispersal of the new cents in such excessive quantities as to create a nuisance to business houses, particularly in the eastern cities. The Indian head device replaced the Eagle in 1859, and in 1864 the weight of the cent was further reduced and its composition changed to a proportion of 95% copper and 5% tin and zinc. This bronze composition has been standard for our cent except for the years 1943, 1944 and 1945. In 1962 the alloy was changed to 95% copper and 5% zinc.

Both Jefferson and Hamilton had contended in their day that the currency of money of small value benefits society. The history of our cent and its daily use proves the soundness of this principle.

Abundance turned to scarcity following the outbreak of the Civil War. Anticipation of a scarcity and depreciation of the paper money was sufficient to induce hoarding. The large volume of greenbacks in circulation caused a premium on gold, and subsidiary silver as a result of the sudden depreciation quickly vanished in the North. Resort was soon made to postage stamps for small change. All types of fractional notes were put out at this time by municipalities and the Government. "Postage currency" became widely used, and in 1863 a great variety of tokens appeared to help fill the vacuum. Like the tokens of 1837 they were of two general classes, tradesmen's coins and imitations of legal cents. The latter were usually produced at a profit, many of which were political or patriotic in character, with slogans typical of the times.

The Law of 1864, which effected changes in the cent, provided also for the new bronze two-cent piece. The act, moreover, provided legal tender status for these two coins up to ten times their value. The two-cent piece was the first coin to bear the motto IN GOD WE TRUST. The new coin was readily accepted by the people but proved an unnecessary denomination, going out of fashion and being discontinued only nine years later.

Secretary Chase had issued a great many currency notes of three-cent denomination early in 1865. The nickel interests seized upon this circumstance to fight for a new three-cent coin for redemption of the paper money. A law was quickly passed and signed by the president as of March 3, 1865, providing for a three-cent coin of 75-25 copper-nickel composition. Our country now possessed two types of three-cent pieces. The nickel three-cent piece was struck continuously until 1889; the three-cent silver until 1873.

The new copper-nickel alloy ratio was selected for the five-cent coin, adopted May 16, 1866, to be thereafter known as a "nickel." Again the people had a coin value available in two forms. The silver half-dime, like the three-cent piece, was retired from service in 1873.

The Carson City Mint was established in 1870 as a convenient depository for the miners in that area and operated until 1893.

The Law of March 3, 1871, was a redemption measure and was passed to provide a means for the disposal to the United States Treasury of millions of minor coins which had accumulated in the hands of postmasters, newsdealers, and others. Small-denomination coins as a result of this new law were placed on an equal footing and could be redeemed when presented in lots of twenty dollars.

There was a general revision of the coinage laws in 1873. Several years of study and debate preceded the final enactment. The legislative history of the bill occupies hundreds of pages of the Congressional Globe, and the result was considered by many a clumsy attempt and a failure. The law has sometimes been referred to as the "Crime of '73." One consequence of the bill, which achieved final enactment February 12, 1873, was the elimination of the silver dollar. In its stead the Trade dollar of greater weight was provided for use in commerce with the Orient in competition with the Mexican dollar. The legal tender provision, which unintentionally gave the trade dollar currency within our borders, was repealed the following year.

The charge for converting standard gold bullion into coin was reduced by the act to one-fifth of one per cent. The same rate was imposed on silver bullion for coining trade dollars only.

It may be a surprise to some collectors to learn that the silver dollar had not circulated to any great extent in the United States after 1803. The coin had been turned out steadily since 1840, but for various reasons such as exportation, melting, and holding in bank vaults, the dollar was virtually an unknown coin. The Law of 1873 in effect demonetized silver and committed our country to a gold standard. The silver mining interests came to realize what had occurred a little later, and the ensuing quarter century of political and monetary history was filled with their voluble protests. There was a constant bitter struggle for the return to bimetallism.

From an economic point of view the inadequate supply of gold was responsible for a gradual decline in prices throughout the world. This brought about a gradual business depression in our country, particularly in the South and Middle-West. Private silver interests influenced great sections of the West for bimetallism as a remedy for the failing price level. Authorities have concluded that a world-wide adoption of bimetallism would have improved economic conditions, but the United States alone proceeding to place its money on a double standard at the old 16 to 1 ratio would have led only to a worse situation.

Of particular importance to collectors, however, were those features of the Law of 1873 which affected the status and physical properties of the individual coins. The weight of the half-dollar, quarter, and dime, was slightly changed and arrows were placed at the date for the ensuing two years to indicate the difference in weight. Silver three-cent pieces, half-dimes, and two-cent pieces were abolished by the act, and the manufacture of minor coins was restricted to the Mint at Philadelphia.

The short-lived twenty-cent piece was authorized March 3, 1875. It was created for the Western states where the Spanish "bit" had become equivalent to a U. S. dime. The five-cent piece did not circulate there, so when a quarter was offered for a "bit" purchase, only a dime change was returned. However, it was confused with the quarter-dollar and was discontinued after 1878.

The Bland-Allison Act of February 28, 1878, gave the Secretary authority to purchase two to four million dollars worth of silver bullion each month to be coined into silver dollars. The coin, never popular, was produced in minimum quantities. This was not a bimetallic law, nor was it a free coinage act. Strictly speaking it was a subsidiary coinage law, called by some "a wretched compromise."

The North and East so disliked the silver dollars that they did not actively circulate there and eventually found their way back to the Treasury, mostly through tax payments. Secretary Manning transferred ownership to the people and removed them from Treasury holdings by the simple expedient of issuing silver certificates in small bills to effect a wide circulation.

The Bland-Allison Act was repealed in 1890 and the Sherman Act took its place. Under this new law 4,500,000 ounces of silver per month could be paid for with Treasury Notes that were to be legal tender, and redeemable in gold or silver dollars coined from the bullion purchased. Important in this case was the fact that the notes were constantly being redeemed for gold which was mainly exported. The measure was actually a government subsidy for the silver miners and as such it was marked for failure, and was hastily repealed. The Bland-Allison Act and the Sherman Act gave a total of 570 million silver dollars to our monetary stocks.

The "Gold Standard Act" of 1900 gave our country a single standard, but reaffirmed the fiction that the silver dollar was a standard coin. It still enjoyed unlimited, legal tender, but was as much a subsidiary coin, practically speaking, as the dime, for its value in terms of standard gold, even before the gold surrender executive order, was far below its face value.

The lapse in coinage after 1904 and until 1921 was due to lack of bullion. Legislation authorizing further metal supplies for silver dollars was not forthcoming until 1918 when the Pittman Act provided silver for the new dollars.

Before the first World War the value of gold was equal to the value of gold coined into money. In order to encourage a steady flow of gold to the mints the government (with the exception of the period 1853-1873) had adopted a policy of gratuitous coinage. The cost of converting gold into coin had generally been considered an expense chargeable to the government.

In practice the mint made fine bars for commercial use or mint bars for coinage at its discretion. The bars in later years were stored in vaults and gold or silver certificates issued in place of the coins.

On March 6, 1933 an order was issued by the President prohibiting banks from paying out gold and gold certificates without permission, and gold currency was thus kept for reserve purposes. Gold imports and newly mined domestic gold must now be sold to the government. Gold bullion may not be hoarded, and there is no free domestic gold bullion market.

Under the Coinage Act of 1965, the composition of dimes, quarters and half dollars was changed to eliminate or reduce the silver content of these coins. The "clad" dimes and quarters were composed of an outer layer of copper-nickel (75% copper and 25% nickel) bonded to an inner core of pure copper. The clad half dollar had an outer layer of 80% silver bonded to an inner core of 21% silver, with a total content of 40% silver. Starting 1971 the half dollar composition was changed to that of the dime and quarter.

By the Law of September 26, 1890, changes in designs of United States coins cannot be made oftener than once every twenty-five years. Since that date, there have been design changes in all denominations and there have been many gold and silver commemorative issues. These factors are largely responsible for the ever increasing interest in coin collecting.

COINS AND TOKENS OF THE
ENGLISH-AMERICAN COLONIES

★ Star Throughout Colonial Section Indicates That Struck Copies Exist.

Copies of certain early American issues were made to provide facsimiles of rare issues that would otherwise be unobtainable. A star, together with the fabricator's name, has been placed adjacent to those pieces of which copies exist. Many crude imitations have also been cast in recent years. The specimens illustrated are genuine.

SOMMER ISLANDS (Bermuda)

This coinage, the first struck for the English-American colonies, was issued about 1616. The coins were known as "Hogge Money" or "Hoggies."

The pieces were made of brass or a similar substance lightly silvered, in four denominations; shilling, sixpence, threepence and twopence, represented by Roman numerals. The hog is the main device and appears on the obverse side of each. SOMMER ISLANDS is inscribed within beaded circles. The reverse shows a full-rigged galleon with the flag of St. George on each of four masts.

The islands were named, during this early period, for Sir George Somers who was shipwrecked there in 1609 while enroute to the Virginia Plantation. Shakespeare's "The Tempest" was supposedly based on this incident.

The Bermuda Islands, as they are known today, were named for Juan Bermudez who is believed to have stopped there in 1515. A few hogs which he carried for delivery to the West Indies were left behind. When Somers and his party arrived many years later, the islands were overrun with the beasts, and they served as a welcome source of food for the members of the expedition.

Twopence   Threepence

Sixpence   Large Portholes   Small Portholes

Shilling   ★Dickeson

Twopence —
Fair: $400 G.: $700 F.: $1,500
Threepence —
_____ _____ _____

Sixpence: Small portholes—
_____ _____ _____

Sixpence: Large portholes —
Fair: $375 G.: $600 F.: $1,300
Shilling: Small sail —
Fair: $400 G.: $700 F.: $1,500
Shilling: Large sail —
_____ _____ _____

MASSACHUSETTS
"New England" Coinage (1652)

The earliest medium of exchange in the New England settlements was wampum. The General Court of Massachusetts in 1637 ordered "that wampampege should passe at 6 a penny for any sume under 12 d." Wampum consisted of shells of various colors ground to the size of a grain of corn. A hole was drilled through each piece so they could be strung on leather thongs for convenience and adornment.

Corn, pelts and bullets were frequently offered in lieu of coins, which were almost nonexistent. Currency brought over from England, Holland and other countries tended to flow back across the Atlantic for much needed supplies. The colonists thus thrown on their own resources dealt with the friendly Indians in kind. In 1661 the law authorizing wampum as legal tender was repealed.

Agitation for a standard coinage reached its height in 1651. England, with a civil war between the Puritans and Royalists on her hands, ignored the colonists, who took matters into their own hands in 1652.

The General Court in 1652 ordered the first metallic currency in the English Americas (the Spaniards had established a mint in Mexico City in 1535), the silver N.E. shillings, and fractional denominations. Silver bullion was procured principally from the West Indies. Joseph Jenks made the punches for the first coins at his Iron Works (Saugus, Massachusetts), just outside of Boston where the mint was located. John Hull was appointed mintmaster; his assistant was Robert Sanderson (or Saunderson). Mintmaster Hull received one shilling threepence for every twenty shillings coined as his compensation. This fee was adjusted several times during his term as mintmaster.

NE Threepence (1652)   NE Sixpence (1652)   ★Wyatt

Note: Early American coins in select condition (V. Fine, Ex. Fine, etc.) are much higher priced as these coins are scarce in these higher grades.

NE Shilling (1652)   ★Wyatt

	Good	Fine
NE Threepence (2 known)	——	——
NE Sixpence (6 known)	——	——
NE Shilling	$1,400	$3,750

MASSACHUSETTS
Willow Tree Coinage (1653-1660)

The simplicity of the design on the N.E. coins invited counterfeiting and clipping of the edges. Therefore, they were soon replaced by the Willow, Oak and Pine Tree series. The Willow Tree coins were struck from 1653 to 1660, the Oak Trees 1660 to 1667, and the Pine Trees 1667 to 1674. All of them (with the exception of the Oak Tree twopence) bore the date 1652, however. This evasion was to give them the appearance of having been struck during the English civil war, when authorization of such coinage by the King would not have been required.

The coinage was abandoned in 1682; a proposal to renew coinage in 1686 was rejected by the General Court.

Threepence   Sixpence

Shilling

	Fair	Good	Fine
Willow Tree Threepence 1652 (3 known)	——	——	——
Willow Tree Sixpence 1652	——	——	——
Willow Tree Shilling 1652	$650.00	$1,200	$4,000

Oak Tree Coinage (1660-1667)

★ Wyatt
Twopence   Threepence

Oak Tree Twopence 1662...................	100.00	225.00	400.00
Oak Tree Threepence 1652	120.00	250.00	460.00

MASSACHUSETTS

	Sixpence		Shilling ★Wyatt		
			Fair	Good	Fine
Oak Tree Sixpence 1652			$125.00	$250.00	$475.00
Oak Tree Shilling 1652			115.00	235.00	450.00

Pine Tree Coinage (1667-1674)

The first pine tree coins were stamped on wide thin planchets. The later
issues were narrower and thicker in imitation of English coins.

Threepence ★Wyatt

Sixpence ★Wyatt

Shilling,
Large Planchet
(1667-1674)

★Tatham

Shilling,
Small Planchet
(1675-1682)

	Fair	Good	Fine	V. Fine
Pine Tree Threepence 1652	$85.00	$170.00	$325.00	$485.00
Pine Tree Sixpence 1652	100.00	200.00	375.00	550.00
Pine Tree Shilling, large planchet 1652 .	100.00	200.00	400.00	575.00
Pine Tree Shilling, small planchet 1652 .	85.00	180.00	340.00	500.00

MARYLAND

In 1658 Cecil, the second Lord Baltimore and "Lord Proprietor of Maryland," began an issue of coinage. These pieces were made in England.

There were four denominations: shillings, sixpence, fourpence (groat) in silver, and the small copper penny (denarium). The silver coins show the bust of Cecil Calvert (Lord Baltimore) on the obverse, and the Baltimore family arms with the values in Roman numeral form and the legend CRESCITE ET MULTIPLICAMINI (Increase and be multiplied) on the reverse. The obverse of the penny is similar, but the reverse has a ducal coronet with two pennants and the inscription DENARIUM, TERRAE-MARIAE (Penny, Maryland). Numerous die varieties and patterns exist in this series.

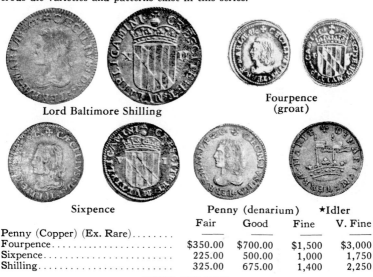

Lord Baltimore Shilling

Fourpence (groat)

Sixpence   Penny (denarium)   ★Idler

	Fair	Good	Fine	V. Fine
Penny (Copper) (Ex. Rare)........				
Fourpence.......................	$350.00	$700.00	$1,500	$3,000
Sixpence........................	225.00	500.00	1,000	1,750
Shilling........................	325.00	675.00	1,400	2,250

NEW JERSEY
St. Patrick or Mark Newby Coinage

Mark Newby, who came from Dublin, Ireland, in November 1681, brought some halfpenny pieces believed by numismatists to have been struck in Dublin in 1678. These were called St. Patrick Halfpence.

The coin received wide currency in the New Jersey Province, having been authorized to pass as legal tender by the General Assembly in May 1682.

These have a brass insert at the crown so that when the coin was struck it would appear as though it were a golden crown. On some pieces this insert has been removed or does not show.

The smaller piece, known as a farthing, was never authorized for circulation in the Colonies. The obverses show a crowned king kneeling playing a harp. The legend FLOREAT REX (May the King prosper) is separated by a crown. The reverse side of the halfpence shows St. Patrick with a crozier in his left and a trefoil in his right hand, surrounded by people. At his left is a shield. The legend is ECCE GREX (Behold the flock).

The farthing reverse shows St. Patrick driving away reptiles and serpents, as he holds a Metropolitan cross in his left hand. The legend reads QUIESCAT PLEBS (May the people be at ease). Numerous die variations exist.

NEW JERSEY

St. Patrick
Farthing

St. Patrick
Halfpenny

	Good	Fine
St. Patrick Farthing	$60.00	$135.00
St. Patrick Farthing, Silver	500.00	950.00
St. Patrick Halfpenny	110.00	225.00

COINAGE OF WILLIAM WOOD
ROSA AMERICANA AND HIBERNIA COINS

William Wood, an Englishman, obtained a patent from George I to make copper tokens for Ireland and the American Colonies.

The first pieces struck were undated; others bear the dates 1722, 1723, 1724 and 1733. The Rosa Americana pieces were issued in three denominations, halfpenny, penny and twopence, and were intended for America. This type had a full-blown rose on the reverse with the words ROSA AMERICANA UTILE DULCI (American Rose — the useful with the pleasant).

The obverse, common to both Rosa Americana and Hibernia pieces, shows the head of George I and the legend GEORGIUS D:G: MAG: BRI: FRA: ET. HIB: REX. (George, by the Grace of God, King of Great Britain, France and Ireland). Rosa Americana tokens, however, were rejected by the American Colonists.

	Good	Fine	Ex. F.
Twopence (No Date)	$45.00	$110.00	$200.00
Twopence (No Date) Motto without Label (3 known)	——	——	——

ROSA AMERICANA

	Good	Fine	Ex. F.
1722 Halfpenny D. G. REX ROSA AMERI. UTILE DULCI	$45.00	$100.00	$200.00
1722 Halfpenny DEI GRATIA REX UTILE DULCI	35.00	67.50	175.00
1722 Halfpenny VTILE DVLCI	—	—	—

1722 Penny UTILE DULCI	35.00	82.50	175.00
1722 Penny VTILE DVLCI	27.50	70.00	160.00

1722 Twopence, period after REX	45.00	115.00	200.00
1722 Twopence, no period after REX	45.00	115.00	200.00

1723 Halfpenny	30.00	75.00	160.00
1723 Halfpenny, uncrowned rose	—	—	—

ROSA AMERICANA

	Good	Fine	Ex. F.
1723 Penny...........................	$30.00	$75.00	$150.00
1723 Twopence (Illustrated)	40.00	115.00	200.00

1724 Penny...........................	——	——
1724 Penny (Undated) ROSA: SINE: SPINA. (3 known)	——	——

1724 Twopence (Pattern).....................   ——   ——

★A. S. Robinson

1733 Twopence (Pattern) Proof......................   ——   ——

The 1733 twopence is a pattern piece and bears the bust of George II facing to the left. Issued by the successors to the coinage patent, since William Wood had died in 1730.

HIBERNIA OR WOOD'S COINAGE

The type intended for Ireland had a seated figure with a harp on the reverse side and the word HIBERNIA. Denominations struck were halfpenny and farthing with dates 1722, 1723 and 1724. Hibernia coins were unpopular in Ireland, so most of them were sent to the American Colonies.

	First Type	Second Type	1723 over 22	
		Good	Fine	Ex. F.
1722 Farthing, D: G: REX (Ex. Rare)............		—	$200.00	$300.00
1722 Halfpenny, D: G: REX (Ex. Rare).........		—	—	—
1722 Halfpenny, First Type, harp at left........		$15.00	50.00	95.00
1722 Halfpenny, Second Type, harp at right.....		15.00	60.00	110.00
1723 over 22 Halfpenny......................		15.00	60.00	125.00
1723 Halfpenny.............................		10.00	25.00	65.00

1723 Hibernia Farthing	**1724 Hibernia Halfpenny**		
1723 Hibernia Farthing — DEI. GRATIA. REX.....	15.00	35.00	75.00
1723 Hibernia Farthing — D.G.REX. (Ex. Rare)...		200.00	300.00
1723 Hibernia Farthing — Silver..............			900.00
1724 Hibernia Farthing......................	25.00	60.00	125.00
1724 Hibernia Halfpenny.....................	15.00	55.00	105.00

PITT TOKENS

William Pitt, who endeared himself to America, is the subject of these pieces, probably intended as commemorative medalets. The halfpenny served as currency during a shortage of regular coinage. The reverse legend refers to Pitt's efforts to have the stamp act repealed. The Pitt farthing-size token, found in brass or copper, is rare.

1766 Farthing................................	—	—	—
1766 Halfpenny.............................	50.00	120.00	250.00

[21]

COINAGE OF THE STATES

NEW HAMPSHIRE

New Hampshire was the first of the states to consider the subject of coinage following the Declaration of Independence.

William Moulton was empowered to make a limited quantity of coins of pure copper authorized by the State House of Representatives in 1776. Although patterns were prepared, it is generally believed that they were not approved. Little of the proposed coinage was ever actually circulated.

Other purported patterns are of doubtful origin. These include a unique engraved piece and a rare struck piece with large initials WM on the reverse.

★Betts

	V. Good
1776 New Hampshire copper	——

VERMONT

Reuben Harmon, Jr., of Rupert, Vermont, was granted permission to coin copper pieces on June 15, 1785. The well-known Vermont coppers were first produced in that year.

Harmon's mint was located in the northeast corner of Rupert near a stream known as Millbrook. Col. William Cooley, a New York goldsmith, made the dies.

	Good	Fine		Good	Fine
1785 Copper IMMUNE COLUMBIA......	$500.00	$1,200	1785 Copper VERMONTS......	$55.00	$185.00

VERMONT

Good Fine | Good Fine

1785 Copper
  VERMONTIS..... $80.00 $250.00

1786 Copper
  Bust Left...... $55.00 $175.00

1786 Copper VERMON-
  TENSIUM....... 50.00 170.00

1787 Copper
  Bust Left...... ——— ———

1786 Copper
  Baby Head.... 100.00 325.00

1787 Copper (Several
  varieties)...... 35.00 100.00

1787 Copper
  BRITANNIA.... 30.00 100.00
←

Reverse of this coin is always
weak.

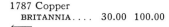

*Typical 1788 Variety

1788 Copper (Several
  varieties*)..... 35.00 90.00
1788 Copper VERMON
  AUOTORI....... ——— ———
1788 Copper *ET LIB*
  *INDE......... 100.00 250.00

VERMONT

	Good	Fine
1788 Copper GEORGIVS III REX	$75.00	$200.00

Most Vermont pieces are struck on poor and defective planchets. Well struck coins on clean planchets command higher prices.

NEW YORK

There are no records to show that coinage was authorized for New York following the Revolutionary War. The only coinage laws passed were those regulating coins already in use.

A firm composed of ten individuals became associated in 1787 for the purpose of striking copper coins, at Newburgh. The establishment was called a "Manufactory of hardware," but the operations there were conducted in secret and looked upon as illegal.

Members of the firm included Reuben Harmon, Jr., who operated the mint at Rupert, Vermont; James F. Atlee, a die engraver and others.

Reuben Harmon and William Cooley were listed as copartners "in such trades and merchandizing and in the coinage of copper for the state of Vermont, Connecticut and New York, for their most benefit advantage and profit."

Many of the pieces classified as Connecticut coins, the Vermon Auctori with the Britannia reverse and the counterfeit George III halfpence were products of this "hardware manufactory" known as Machin's Mill.

1786 NON VI VIRTUTE VICI

(Believed to be the head of Washington.)

	Good	Fine	V. Fine
Copper .	$500	$1,000	$1,750

*Robinson

*Bolen

	Good	Fine	V. Fine
1787 Excelsior copper, eagle on globe facing right............................	$300.00	$800.00	$1650.00
1787 Excelsior copper, eagle on globe facing left.............................	275.00	600.00	1250.00

[24]

NEW YORK

1787 Copper
Large Eagle on Reverse

Arrows and Branch
Transposed (Ex. Rare) ———

★Bolen

1787 George Clinton
Copper

Good   Fine   V.Fine
Copper..$600 $1,500 $2,500

1787 Indian
N.Y. Arms

Good   Fine   V. Fine
Copper:..$550 $1,300 $2,300

★Bolen

★Bolen

1787 Indian Copper
Reverse Eagle
on Globe

Good.............$600.00
Fine............... 1,500
V. Fine............ 2,500

1787 Indian Copper
with George III
Reverse (2 known)

Machin's Mill Coinage

The most prevalent Machin's Mill coins are lightweight imitations of the British halfpenny, with bust obverse and Britannia seated reverse. These can be distinguished by their crude die work, single outline in the crosses

NEW YORK

of Britannia's shield, and fictitious dates, which include 1771, 1772, 1774, 1776, 1778, 1787, and 1788. These pieces are not to be confused with the English made George III counterfeits, some of which have identical dates, or regular George III British halfpence, which were dated from 1770 to 1775.

Machin's Mill Copper, various dates	Good	Fine
GEORGIUS III REX/BRITANNIA	$25.00	$50.00

1787 IMMUNIS COLUMBIA
Eagle Reverse

Good	$100.00
Fine	165.00
V. Fine	325.00
Ex. Fine	600.00

THE NOVA EBORACS

1787
NOVA EBORAC
Reverse Seated
Figure Facing Left

Fair	$12.00
Good	45.00
Fine	100.00
V. Fine	175.00

1787
NOVA EBORAC
Reverse Seated
Figure Facing Right

Fair	$12.50
Good	50.00
Fine	125.00
V. Fine	200.00

1787 NOVA EBORAC
Small Head

Good	$200.00
Fine	450.00
V. Fine	800.00

1787 NOVA EBORAC
Large Head

Fair	$25.00
Good	110.00
Fine	250.00
V. Fine	425.00

CONNECTICUT

Authority for establishing a mint was granted to Samuel Bishop, Joseph Hopkins, James Hillhouse and John Goodrich in 1785.

Available records indicate that the Connecticut Coppers were turned out under a sub-contract by Samuel Broome and Jeremiah Platt, former New York merchants. Abel Buel and James Atlee were the principal die-sinkers.

1785 Copper
Bust Facing Right

Good $15.00
Fine 40.00
V: Fine 80.00

1785 Copper
African Head

Good $22.50
Fine 60.00
V. Fine 120.00

1785 Copper
Bust Facing Left

Good $75.00
Fine 160.00
V. Fine 275.00

1786 Copper
ETLIB INDE

Good $35.00
Fine 75.00
V. Fine 150.00

1786 Copper
Large Head Facing Right

Good $37.50
Fine 100.00
V. Fine 175.00

CONNECTICUT

1786 Copper
Mailed Bust Facing Left

Good............. $20.00
Fine.............. 45.00
V. Fine........... 100.00

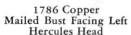

1786 Copper
Mailed Bust Facing Left
Hercules Head

Good........... $25.00
Fine............ 60.00
V. Fine........ 150.00

1786 Copper
Draped Bust

Good........... $35.00
Fine............ 80.00
V. Fine........ 170.00

The Connecticut coppers, especially those dated 1787 and 1788, were usually crudely struck and on imperfect planchets.

1787 Copper
Small Head Facing Right
ETLIB INDE

Good............. $40.00
Fine.............. 90.00
V. Fine........... 180.00

1787 Copper
Mailed Bust Facing Left
IND ET LIB

Good............. $40.00
Fine.............. 90.00
V. Fine........... 180.00

1787 Copper
Muttonhead
Variety

Good............. $35.00
Fine.............. 90.00
V. Fine........... 165.00

[28]

CONNECTICUT

	Good	Fine	V. Fine
1787 Mailed Bust facing left	$13.00	$35.00	$75.00
1787 Similar, Laughing Head Variety	14.00	37.50	80.00
1787 Similar, Hercules Head (see 1786).........	130.00	260.00	450.00
1787 Similar, dated 1787 over 1788	30.00	100.00	200.00

1787 Similar, Horned Bust Variety.............	13.00	35.00	75.00
1787 Similar, CONNECT Variety	35.00	100.00	170.00

1787 Draped Bust facing left (many varieties) ...	10.00	25.00	50.00
1787 Similar, AUCIORI Variety.................	15.00	40.00	80.00
1787 Similar, AUCTOPI Variety.................	15.00	40.00	80.00
1787 Similar, AUCTOBI Variety.................	17.00	45.00	100.00
1787 Similar, CONNFC Variety.................	13.00	35.00	75.00
1787 Similar, CONNLC Variety.................	35.00	90.00	135.00
1787 Similar, FNDE Variety...................	15.00	40.00	80.00
1787 Similar, ETLIR Variety..................	15.00	40.00	80.00
1787 Similar, ETIIB Variety..................	17.00	45.00	100.00

1788 Mailed Bust facing right	17.50	50.00	100.00
1788 Similar, small head.....................	50.00	125.00	200.00

CONNECTICUT

	Good	Fine	V. Fine
1788 Mailed Bust facing left	$18.00	$45.00	$100.00
1788 Mailed Bust left CONNLC.	22.50	55.00	115.00

1788 Draped Bust facing left	18.00	45.00	100.00
1788 Similar, CONNLC Variety	35.00	80.00	130.00
1788 Similar, INDL ET LIB Variety	25.00	60.00	120.00

MASSACHUSETTS

MASSACHUSETTS PINE TREE COPPER

Nothing is known regarding the origin of the Pine Tree pattern dated 1776. The obverse has a crude pine tree with an animal resembling a dog at its base; Inscription, MASSACHUSETTS STATE. The reverse has a figure probably intended to represent the Goddess of Liberty, seated on a globe and holding a liberty cap and staff. A dog sits at her feet. The legend LIBERTY AND VIRTUE surrounds the figure.

★Copley

1776 Pattern (Unique) . . . . ———

MASSACHUSETTS
MASSACHUSETTS HALFPENNY

This pattern piece is sometimes called the "Janus Copper." There are three heads facing left, front and right on the obverse with the inscription STATE OF MASSA. ½ D. The reverse shows the Goddess of Liberty, seated resting against a globe facing right, inscribed GODDESS LIBERTY 1776.

★Copley

1776 Halfpenny, 3 Heads on Obverse (Unique).................... ———

An "Act for establishing a mint for the coinage of gold, silver and copper" was passed by the Massachusetts General Court October 17, 1786. The next year the Council directed that the design should incorporate "the figure of an Indian with a bow and arrow and a star at one side, with the word 'Commonwealth,' the reverse, a spread eagle with the words 'of Massachusetts A.D. 1787'."

A Mr. Joshua Witherle was placed in charge of the mint, where he soon began coining the Massachusetts cents. There resulted many varieties, the rarest being that with arrows in the right talon. Half cents with similar devices and legends were also struck in 1787 and 1788.

Most of the dies for these coppers were made by Joseph Callender. Jacob Perkins of Newburyport probably engraved some of the dies.

The mint was abandoned early in 1789 as the venture was unprofitable to the Commonwealth.

1787 Half Cent

Good..................	$20.00
Fine..................	35.00
V. Fine...............	75.00
Ex. Fine..............	130.00

Obverse　　Arrows in Eagle's Right Talon　　in Left Talon

	Good	Fine	V. F.	E. F.
1787 Cent, Arrows in Right Talon (Ex. Rare)	———	———	———	———
1787 Cent, Arrows in Left Talon............	$16.50	$30.00	$60.00	$110.00
1787 Cent, "horn" (die break) from eagle's head........................	16.50	32.50	65.00	125.00

[31]

MASSACHUSETTS

1788 Half Cent

Good............	$25.00
Fine............	45.00
Very Fine........	80.00
Ex. Fine.........	150.00

★Evanson

1788 Cent
Period after Massachusetts

Good.............	$15.00
Fine.............	30.00
V. Fine..........	60.00
Ex. Fine..........	110.00

No period after Massachusetts

Good.............	$19.00
Fine.............	40.00
V. Fine..........	75.00
Ex. Fine..........	125.00

★Evanson

NEW JERSEY

On June 1, 1786, the New Jersey Colonial legislature granted to Thomas Goadsby, Albion Cox and Walter Mould authority to coin some three million coppers weighing six pennyweight and six grains apiece, not later than June 1788, on condition that they delivered to the Treasurer of the State, "one-tenth part of the full sum they shall strike and coin," in quarterly installments. These coppers were to pass current at 15 to the shilling.

In an operation of this kind the contractors purchased the metal and assumed all expenses of coining. The difference between these expenses and the total face value of the coins issued represented the profit.

Later Goadsby and Cox asked authority to coin two-thirds of the total independently. Their petition was granted November 22, 1787. Mould was known to have produced his coins at Morristown, while Cox (and probably Goadsby) operated in Elizabethtown.

The series offers many varieties. The obverse shows a horse's head with plow and the legend NOVA CAESAREA (New Jersey). The reverse has a United States shield and legend E PLURIBUS UNUM (One composed of many).

1786 IMMUNIS COLUMBIA Obverse Eagle Reverse	1786 IMMUNIS COLUMBIA Obverse Shield Reverse
Good....—— Fine....——	Good...—— Fine...——

[32]

NEW JERSEY

1786 (No Date) Washington obverse.................... ——— ———
1786 Eagle Obverse.................................... ——— ———
1786 Washington obv., Eagle rev. (Unique)............. ——— ———

1786 Date **Under Draw Bar**	**1786** **No Coulter**
Good... —— Fine... ——	Good... $85.00 Fine... $200.00

Narrow Shield

Wide Shield

	Good	Fine	V. Fine
1786 Narrow Shield.........................	$17.00	$42.50	$75.00
1786 Wide Shield............................	27.50	55.00	100.00
1786 Similar, Bridle Variety.................	22.50	50.00	90.00

Pluribs Variety Large Planchet	Small Planchet	Outlined Shield

1787 Pronounced Outline to Shield.............	15.00	35.00	60.00

NEW JERSEY

	Good	Fine	V. Fine
1787 Small Planchet, Plain Shield..............	$15.00	$35.00	$60.00
1787 Large Planchet, Plain Shield..............	16.00	37.50	65.00
1787 Similar, PLURIBS Variety................	30.00	70.00	125.00

Serpent Head		Fox Variety	
1787 Serpent Head Variety...................	27.50	65.00	125.00
1788 Horse's Head facing right................	15.00	35.00	60.00
1788 Similar, running fox before legend........	27.50	65.00	125.00
1788 Horse's head facing left.................	55.00	125.00	180.00

TOKENS AND PATTERN COINS
THE CONTINENTAL DOLLAR

The Continental Dollars were probably a pattern issue only and never reached general circulation. It was the first silver dollar size coin ever proposed for the United States. The dies were engraved by someone whose initials were E. G. (possibly Elisha Gallaudet). Some of them have his signature "EG FECIT" on the obverse. The coins were probably struck in Philadelphia.

Varieties are caused by differences in the spelling of the word CURRENCY and the addition of EG FECIT. These coins were struck in silver, pewter and brass, those in silver probably having done service as a dollar. Pewter coins in original bright uncirculated condition are worth an additional premium.

"CURRENCY"

"CURENCY"

★Dickeson

CONTINENTAL DOLLAR

Copies were struck in various metals for the 1876 Centennial Exposition in Philadelphia and also restruck from hubbed dies circa 1960.

	Good	Fine	Ex. F.	Unc.
1776 CURENCY — Brass (2 Varieties)....	—	—	—	—
1776 CURENCY — Pewter..............	$240.00	$500.00	$925.00	$1,700
1776 CURENCY — Silver...............	—	—	—	—
1776 CURRENCY — Pewter.............	270.00	525.00	1,000	1,850
1776 CURRENCY — Pewter, EG FECIT....	300.00	550.00	1,100	1,950
1776 CURRENCY — Silver, EG FECIT.....	—	—	—	—
1776 CURRENCEY — Pewter............	—	—	—	—

NOVA CONSTELLATIO PATTERNS (Silver)

These Nova Constellatio pieces undoubtedly represent the first patterns for a coinage of the United States. They were designed by Benjamin Dudley for Gouverneur Morris to carry out his ideas for a decimal coinage system. The 1000 unit designation he called a "mark," the 500 a "quint." These denominations, together with the smaller 100 unit piece, were designed to standardize the many different coin values among the several states. These pattern pieces represent the first attempt at a decimal ratio, and were the forerunners of our present system of money values. Neither the proposed denominations nor the coins advanced beyond the pattern stage. The pieces are all dated 1783 and are extremely rare. There are two types of the "quint."

★Sets of
Mickley
Electrotypes
Exist

Bit 100 Units

QUINT Type 1   Reverse   QUINT Type 2

MARK

1783 (Bit) "100," Silver	2 known
1783 (Quint) "500," Silver — Type 1	Unique
1783 (Quint) "500," Silver — Type 2	Unique
1783 (Mark) "1000," Silver	Unique

NOVA CONSTELLATIO COPPERS

The Nova Constellatio pieces were struck supposedly by order of Gouverneur Morris who had been Assistant Financier of the Confederation. The tokens were turned out in fairly large quantities in the years 1783 and 1785. Evidence indicates that they were struck in Birmingham from dies made there by Thomas Wyon, and imported for American circulation as a private business venture by Gouverneur Morris.

1783
"CONSTELLATIO"
Pointed Rays
Small U.S.

Good...............	$17.50
Fine...............	40.00
Ex. Fine...........	100.00

1783
"CONSTELLATIO"
Pointed Rays, Large U.S.

Good...............	$20.00
Fine...............	50.00
Ex. Fine...........	125.00

1783
"CONSTELATIO"
Blunt Rays

Good...............	$17.50
Fine...............	40.00
Ex. Fine...........	110.00

1785
"CONSTELATIO"
Blunt Rays

Good...............	$22.50
Fine...............	50.00
Ex. Fine...........	150.00

1785 "CONSTELLATIO"
Pointed Rays

Good...............	$15.00
Fine...............	35.00
Ex. Fine...........	90.00
1786 (Similar).......	——

IMMUNE COLUMBIA COPPERS

These are considered experimental or pattern pieces. No laws describing them are known. There are several types with the seated figure of Justice device. These dies were possibly the work of James F. Atlee.

1785 Copper............. ——
1785 Silver.............. ——

★Edwards

1785 Extra Star in Border
Copper, CONSTELLATIO
G. . .$450 Fine. .$900 V.F. .$1,500
Copper, CONSTELATIO,
Blunt Rays.......(2 known) ——
Gold.............(Ex. Rare) ——
A gold specimen in the National Coin Collection was acquired from Stickney in exchange for an 1804 dollar.

1785
George III Obverse
Good. . .$500.00   Fine. . .$1,200
1785
Vermon Auctori Obverse
Good. . .$500.00   Fine. . .$1,200

CONFEDERATIO COPPERS

The Confederatio Coppers are usually classed as experimental or pattern pieces. This will explain why the die with the CONFEDERATIO legend was combined with other designs such as bust of George Washington, Libertas et Justitia of 1785, Immunis Columbia of 1786, the New York "Excelsiors," Inimica Tyrannis Americana and others. There were in all thirteen dies struck in fourteen combinations. Some of the dies were believed to have been made by Thomas Wyon of Birmingham, England, whereas others may have been the work of James Atlee, or the New Jersey coiners.

There are two types of the Confederatio reverse. In one instance the stars are contained in a small circle; in the other larger stars are in a larger circle.

★Bolen

1785 Stars in Small Circle
Fine............... ——
V. Fine........... ——

1785 Stars in Large Circle
Fine............... ——
V. Fine........... ——

Reverse

CONFEDERATIO COPPERS

Typical Obverses
For Type with Stars in
Large Circle

THE FRENCH COLONIES

None of the coins of the French regime is strictly American. They were all general issues for the French colonies of the New World. The coinage of 1670 was authorized by an edict of Louis XIV dated February 19, 1670, for use in New France, Acadia, the French settlements in Newfoundland, and the French West Indies. The copper of 1717 to 1722 was authorized by edicts of 1716 and 1721 for use in New France, Louisiana, and the French West Indies.

Issue of 1670

The coinage of 1670 consisted of silver 5 and 15 sols. A copper 2 deniers was also authorized but never struck. A total of 200,000 of the 5 sols was struck, and 40,000 of the 15 sols, at Paris. Nantes was to have coined the copper, but did not; the reasons for this may never be known, since the archives of the Nantes mint before 1700 were destroyed. The only known specimen is a pattern struck at Paris. The silver coins were raised in value by a third in 1672 to keep them circulating, but in vain. They rapidly disappeared, and by 1680 none was to be seen. Later they were restored to their original value.

	V. Good	Fine	V. Fine	Ex. Fine	Unc.
5 sols 1670	$100.00	$200.00	$300.00	$450.00	$600.00
15 sols 1670	1,500	2,000	3,000	4,000	6,000

Coinage of 1717-1720

The copper 6 and 12 deniers of 1717 were authorized by an edict of Louis XV dated December 1716, to be struck at Perpignan. The order could not be carried out, for the supply of copper was too brassy. A second attempt in 1720 also failed, probably for the same reason. All these coins are extremely rare, the 6 deniers of 1720 probably being unique.

FRENCH COLONIES

Copper

	V.G.	Fine
6 deniers 1717...	$1,000	$1,500
6 deniers 1720...		Unique
12 deniers 1717..	1,500	2,000

Billon Coinage

The piece of 30 deniers was called a *mousquetaire,* and was coined at Metz and Lyons. The 15 deniers was coined only at Metz. The sou marque and half were coined at almost every French mint, those of Paris being commonest. Only Paris coined the half sou after 1748. Specimens of the sou marque dated after 1760 were not used in North America.

30 Deniers

Sou Marque

	V. Good	Fine	V. Fine	Ex. Fine
15 deniers 1710-1713AA................	$100.00	$150.00	$200.00	$250.00
30 deniers 1709-1713AA................	80.00	120.00	160.00	200.00
30 deniers 1709-1713D.................	80.00	120.00	160.00	200.00
Half sou marque 1738-1754............	50.00	70.00	90.00	125.00
Sou marque 1738-1760................	20.00	30.00	40.00	60.00

Coinage of 1721-1722

The copper coinage of 1721-1722 was authorized by an edict of Louis XV dated June 1721. The coins were struck on copper blanks imported from Sweden. Rouen and La Rochelle struck pieces of 9 deniers in 1721 and 1722. New France received 534,000 pieces, mostly from the mint of La Rochelle, but only 8,180 were successfully put into circulation as the colonists disliked copper. In 1726 the rest of the issue was sent back to France.

Copper Sou or Nine Deniers

	V. Good	Fine
1721-B (Rouen)....	$60.00	$90.00
1721-H (La Rochelle)....	27.50	40.00
1722-H............	30.00	45.00
1722-H, 2 over 1....	60.00	90.00

FRENCH COLONIES

	Good	Fine	Ex. Fine
1767 French Colonies, Sou.....................	$25.00	$60.00	$120.00
1767 French Colonies, Sou. Counterstamped RF for République Française.................	10.00	30.00	70.00

COPPER COMPANY OF UPPER CANADA

The reverse of this piece, according to S. S. Crosby, properly belongs upon another token and was apparently intended for Canadian circulation, or it was used to give the coin creditability. See Myddelton token, page 48.

	Proof
1796 Copper	$400.00

NORTH AMERICAN TOKEN

This piece was struck in Dublin, Ireland. The obverse shows the seated figure of Hibernia facing left. The date of issue is believed to have been much later than that shown on the token.

Like many Irish tokens, this issue found its way to America in large quantities and was readily accepted owing to a scarcity of small change.

	V. Good	Fine	V. Fine
1781 . . .	$10.00	$15.00	$25.00

NORTH WEST COMPANY TOKEN

These tokens were probably valued at one beaver and struck in Birmingham in 1820 by John Walker & Co. All but one known specimen are holed, and all have been found in the region of the lower Columbia River valley in Oregon.

	V. Good
1820 Brass	$300.00
1820 Copper	325.00

BRASHER'S DOUBLOONS

Perhaps the most famous piece brought out before the establishment of the mint at Philadelphia was that produced by a well-known goldsmith and jeweler, Ephraim Brasher, next door neighbor of George Washington, in New York.

Brasher produced a gold piece weighing about 408 grains, approximately equal in value to a Spanish doubloon (about $16.00).

The punch-mark EB appears in either of two positions as illustrated. This mark is found on coins of other countries as well, and probably was so used by Brasher as evidence of his approval of their value.

★Robinson

V. Fine

1787 Doubloon, Punch on Breast, Gold (Unique).................. ———
1787 Doubloon, Punch on Wing, Gold.......................... ———

AMERICAN TOKENS

Struck in America or England by Order of American Merchants
GLOUCESTER TOKENS

According to S. S. Crosby, in his book "The Early Coins of America" this piece appears to have been intended as a pattern for a shilling, a private coinage by Richard Dawson of Gloucester (county?), Virginia. The only specimens known are struck in brass, none in silver.

The denomination XII indicates that a silver coinage (one shilling) was planned but never issued. Known specimens are imperfect and a full description cannot be given.

The building may represent a warehouse or some public building, possibly a court house. The legend on the reverse may have been designed to read GLOUCESTER COURT HOUSE VIRGINIA.

1714 Shilling (2 known) Brass.................................... ———

HIGLEY OR GRANBY COPPERS

John Higley owned a private copper mine near Granby, Connecticut. He worked the mine as an individual, smelting his own ore and making his own dies for the coins that he issued.

The Higley coppers were never officially authorized. All the tokens were made of pure copper. There were seven obverse and four reverse dies. The first issue, in 1737, bore the legend THE VALUE OF THREEPENCE. After a time the quantity exceeded the local demand, and a protest arose against the value of the piece. Higley, a re-sourceful individual, promptly created a new design, still with the Roman III, but with the in-scription VALUE ME AS YOU PLEASE. On the reverse appeared the words I AM GOOD COPPER.

(Electrotypes and Casts Exist)

★Bolen

		Good	V. Good
1737 THE • VALVE • OF • THREE • PENCE. — 3 Hammers — CONNECTICVT		$1,000	$1,500
1737 THE • VALVE • OF • THREE • PENCE. — 3 Hammers — I • AM • GOOD • COPPER		1,000	1,500

1737 VALUE • ME • AS • YOU • PLEASE — 3 Hammers — I • AM • GOOD • COPPER		950.00	1,400
1737 VALVE • ME • AS • YOU • PLEASE — 3 Hammers — I • AM • GOOD • COPPER		(Ex. Rare)	

(1737) VALUE • ME • AS • YOU • PLEASE — Broad Axe — J • CUT • MY • WAY • THROUGH		1,250	1,750
1739 VALUE • ME • AS • YOU • PLEASE — Broad Axe — J • CUT • MY • WAY • THROUGH		1,500	——

J. CHALMERS
Annapolis, Maryland

J. Chalmers, a goldsmith, struck a series of silver tokens at Annapolis in 1783. The shortage of change and the refusal of the people to use underweight cut Spanish coins, or "bits," prompted the issuance of these pieces.

The shilling with rings on the reverse is very rare. The common type shilling has two clasped hands on the obverse. The reverse shows two doves pulling what appears to be a worm.

The sixpence has a star within a wreath on the obverse, and a cross with hands clasped on the reverse. The threepence has the clasped hands on the obverse side, and the reverse shows a branch encircled by a wreath.

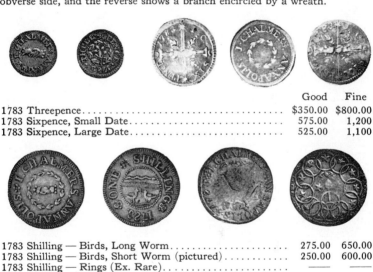

	Good	Fine
1783 Threepence	$350.00	$800.00
1783 Sixpence, Small Date	575.00	1,200
1783 Sixpence, Large Date	525.00	1,100

	Good	Fine
1783 Shilling — Birds, Long Worm	275.00	650.00
1783 Shilling — Birds, Short Worm (pictured)	250.00	600.00
1783 Shilling — Rings (Ex. Rare)	——	——

STANDISH BARRY, BALTIMORE, MARYLAND

Standish Barry, a Baltimore silversmith, circulated a silver threepence in 1790. He was a watch and clockmaker, engraver and later a silversmith. The tokens were believed to have been an advertising venture at a time when small change was scarce. The precise date, July 4, 90, on this piece may indicate that Barry intended to commemorate Independence Day, but there are no records to substantiate this belief. The head shown on the obverse is probably that of George Washington. The legend BALTIMORE TOWN JULY 4, 90 appears in the border. STANDISH BARRY THREE PENCE is on the reverse.

1790 Threepence	——	——

THE BAR "CENT"

The Bar "Cent" is undated and of uncertain origin.

It has thirteen parallel and unconnected bars on one side. On the other side is the large roman USA monogram.

The significance of the design is clearly defined by its extreme simplicity. The separate thirteen states (bars) unite into a single entity as symbolized by the interlocking letters (USA).

This coin is believed to have been issued at the same time as the Nova Constellatio coppers by Thomas Wyon at Birmingham, England, for America. It first circulated in New York during November, 1785. The design was supposedly copied from an old Continental button.

★Bolen (A is under S)

	V. Good	Fine	Ex. Fine
Undated (about 1785) Bar "Cent"..............	$225.00	$350.00	$650.00

THE MOTT TOKEN

This was one of the first tradesman's tokens issued in America. Manufactured in England, they were issued by Messrs. Mott of New York in 1789. The firm was composed of William and John Mott, located at 240 Water Street, a fashionable section of New York at that time.

	V. Good	Fine	Ex. Fine
1789 Mott Token, thick planchet...............	$60.00	$85.00	$185.00
1789 Mott Token, thin planchet................	70.00	100.00	250.00
1789 Mott Token, entire edge engrailed.........	——	——	——

TALBOT ALLUM & LEE CENTS

Talbot, Allum & Lee, engaged in the India trade and located at 241 Pearl Street, New York, placed a large quantity of English-made coppers in circulation during 1794 and 1795. ONE CENT appears on the 1794 issue, and the legend PAYABLE AT THE STORE OF—— on the edge. The denomination is not found on the 1795 reverse but the edge legend was changed to read: WE PROMISE TO PAY THE BEARER ONE CENT.

TALBOT ALLUM & LEE CENTS

1794 Cent NEW YORK
V. Good.............. $20.00
V. Fine............... 60.00
Unc.................. 150.00

1794 Cent without NEW YORK
V. Good.............. 140.00
V. Fine.............. 425.00
Unc................. ——

1795 Cent

V. Good............ $10.00
V. Fine............ 40.00
Unc............... 100.00

ANGLO-AMERICAN TOKENS
Supposedly of English Origin — Speculative Ventures
CAROLINA and NEW ENGLAND ELEPHANT TOKENS

Although no law is known authorizing coinage for Carolina, two very interesting pieces known as Elephant Tokens were current with the date 1694. These copper coins were of halfpenny denomination. The reverse reads GOD PRESERVE CAROLINA AND THE LORDS PROPRIETERS. 1694.

The second and more common variety has the last word spelled PROPRIETORS. The correction was made on the original die, for the E shows plainly beneath the O. The elephant's tusks nearly touch the milling on the second variety.

The Elephant Pieces were probably struck in England and perhaps intended only as tokens, or, as we might say today, as an advertising stunt to enliven interest in the Carolina Plantation.

Like the Carolina Tokens, the New England Elephant Tokens were believed to have been struck in England as a promotional piece to increase interest in the American Colonies. Some of these tokens were said to have been struck in brass.

NEW ENGLAND

★Robinson

1694 NEW ENGLAND...(Ex. Rare)

[45]

CAROLINA ELEPHANT TOKENS

Good   Fine

1694 PROPRIETERS (Ex. Rare)..........................

★Bolen

1694 PROPRIETORS, O over E.......................... $500.00 $1,000

The London Token, an early historian states, was produced during the great plague raging in London. The legend on this piece relates directly to that crisis. It has also been stated that the London Token was to have been current in Tangier, Africa, but was never used in that locality. No date appears on this coin.

	V. Good	V. Fine	Ex. Fine
(1694) Halfpenny GOD PRESERVE LONDON (Thick Planchet)......................	$50.00	$100.00	$160.00
(1694) Halfpenny GOD PRESERVE LONDON (Thin Planchet).......................	75.00	130.00	200.00
(1694) Halfpenny GOD PRESERVE LONDON (Diagonals in center of shield)...........	110.00	200.00	375.00
(1694) Halfpenny, similar. Variety with sword in second quarter of shield instead of first ...	——	——	——
(1694) Halfpenny LON DON....................	175.00	300.00	500.00

[46]

VIRGINIA HALFPENNY

In 1773, George III issued this halfpenny. There are also known to have been a few specimens struck on a larger planchet with a wide milled border, known as pennies.

The Virginia piece of 1774 known as a shilling may have been a pattern piece for a halfpenny.

Halfpenny   Penny

	Good	Fine	Unc.
1773 Halfpenny, Period after GEORGIUS.........	$10.00	$35.00	$100.00
1773 Halfpenny, No period after GEORGIUS......	17.50	60.00	175.00
1773 "Penny"..	Proof	1,000	

Virginia
Shilling
1774

1774 Shilling...Proof ——

ALBANY CHURCH PENNY

The First Presbyterian Church of Albany, New York authorized an issue of one thousand copper uniface tokens in 1790. These passed at twelve to a shilling and were used to stop contributions of worn and counterfeit coppers. Two varieties were made, one with the addition of a large D above the word CHURCH.

	V. Good
(1790) Albany Church Penny, without D......................	$700.00
(1790) Albany Church Penny, with D added..................	750.00

AUCTORI PLEBIS TOKEN

This token is sometimes included with the coins of Connecticut as it greatly resembles issues of that state. The coin was struck in England, maker unknown, for use in America.

1787 AUCTORI PLEBIS

Good..............	$35.00
Fine..............	90.00
V. Fine...........	150.00

KENTUCKY TOKEN

These tokens were struck in England about 1792-94. Each star in the triangle represents a state, identified by its initial letter. These pieces are usually called Kentucky Cents because the letter K (for Kentucky) happens to be at the top. Some of the edges are plain; others are engrailed with an oblique reeding, and some have the edge lettered: "PAYABLE IN LANCASTER LONDON OR BRISTOL," or "PAYABLE AT BEDWORTH NUNETON OR UNKIET."

	V. Good	V. Fine	Unc.
Cent, (1792-96) Plain Edge....................	$27.50	$50.00	$150.00
Cent, Engrailed Edge.........................	85.00	200.00	485.00
Cent, Lettered Edge PAYABLE AT BEDWORTH, etc.	——	——	——
Cent, Lettered Edge PAYABLE IN LANCASTER, etc.	40.00	65.00	160.00
Cent, Lettered Edge PAYABLE BY I. FIELDING, etc.	——	——	——

MYDDELTON TOKENS

These tokens were from the establishment of Boulton and Watt near Birmingham, England. They are unsurpassed in beauty and design by any piece issued for American circulation.

1796 Myddelton Token (Copper)...Proof $1,500

1796 Myddelton Token (Silver)....Proof $1,250

MISCELLANEOUS TOKENS
THE NEW YORKE TOKEN

Although only three or four specimens of this piece were known to S. S. Crosby, the authority on early American coins, a number have since been discovered. From an account in the Historical Magazine for 1861, he infers that this token is of Dutch origin. The following is quoted from the magazine article mentioned.

"The style in which it is executed is more Dutch than English; and as the only existing specimen has been preserved in Holland, it is probable that the dies were originally cut there. . . . There is no date upon the token; but it evidently belongs to the period between 1664, when the name New Yorke was first adopted, and 1710, after which it was rarely spelled with an e. It should probably be referred to the latter part of this period, for the currency of the colonies was then in a very unsettled state, and the amount in circulation was not adequate to the wants of trade. . . .

"Without venturing to claim that this coin contains the earliest display of the American eagle, we think it unquestionably deserves to be considered the earliest·New York token."

	Good	Fine
UNDATED Brass	$500.00	$900.00
Pewter	——	——

AMERICAN PLANTATIONS TOKEN

These tokens struck in nearly pure tin were the first authorized coinage for the British colonies in America. Bright, unblemished specimens are more valuable. Restrikes were made about 1828 from original dies.

(1688) James II Plantation Token,	Good	Fine	Unc.
1/24 PART REAL — Tin	$40.00	$90.00	$275.00
1/24 PART REAL — Tin. Sidewise 4 in 24	——	——	——
Restrike	30.00	70.00	200.00

FRANKLIN PRESS

This piece is an English token but has often been associated with Benjamin Franklin, and has accordingly been placed in American collections.

1794 Franklin Press Token

Good	Fine	Unc.
$25.00	$60.00	$125.00

HIBERNIA-VOCE POPULI

These coins, struck in the year 1760, were prepared by one Roche, of King Street, Dublin, who was at that period engaged in the manufacture of buttons for the army, for which he held a contract with home government. Like other Irish tokens, some of these pieces found their way to Colonial America. The piece dated 1700 is probably a die-cutter's error. It no doubt circulated in Colonies with numerous other counterfeit halfpence and "Bungtown Tokens."

| 1760 Farthing | Halfpenny 1700 |

| Halfpenny 1760 | VOOE POPULI |

	Good	Fine
1760 Farthing, large letters (pictured)	$80.00	$200.00
1760 Farthing, small letters............................	——	——
1700 Halfpenny.......................................	——	——
1760 Halfpenny.......................................	17.50	45.00
1760 Halfpenny VOOE POPULI...........................	30.00	75.00

NEW YORK THEATRE TOKEN

Token penny issued by Park Theatre, New York circa 1797.

	Ex. Fine	Unc.
Penny, THE • THEATRE • AT • NEW YORK • AMERICA.......	$950.00	$1,200

RHODE ISLAND SHIP TOKEN

Although this medal has a Dutch inscription, the spelling and design indicate an English or Anglo-American origin. Specimens are known in brass, copper, tin and pewter.

1778-1779 Rhode Island Ship Token

Wreath below ship......
V.F. $170.00 E.F. $310.00

No Wreath below ship...
V.F. $140.00 E.F. $280.00

VLUGTENDE below
ship. V.F. —— E.F. ——

★Grant

[50]

THE CASTORLAND MEDAL

This piece is dated 1796 and relates to a settlement of Frenchmen known as Castorland in Carthage, New York, at the time of the French Revolution.

1796 Silver Original (Reeded edge) .... ——
1796 Copper Original (Reeded edge, unbroken dies)................ ——

Copy dies are still available and have been used for restriking throughout the years. Above illustration is a modern restrike.

WASHINGTON PIECES

An interesting series of coins and tokens dated from 1783 to 1795 bear the portrait of George Washington. The likenesses in most instances were faithfully reproduced and were designed to honor Washington. Most of these pieces were of English origin and made in the 1810 to 1820 period.

The legends generally signify a strong unity among the states and a marked display of patriotism which pervaded the new nation during that period. We find among these tokens an employment of what were soon to become our official coin devices, namely, the American eagle, the United States shield and stars. The one cent value is used in several instances, while on some of the English pieces the halfpenny value will be found. Several pieces were intended to be patterns for half dollars.

Georgius Triumpho Token

Although the head shown on this token bears a strong resemblance to that upon some coins of George III, many collectors consider the Georgius Triumpho (Triumphant George) a token intended to commemorate the successful termination of the Revolutionary War — a triumph justly claimed for Washington.

The reverse side shows the Goddess of Liberty behind a framework of thirteen bars and fleur de lis. She holds an olive branch in her right hand and staff of liberty in her left. VOCE POPOLI (By the Voice of the People) 1783.

	Good	Fine	V. Fine
1783 GEORGIUS TRIUMPHO.....................	$45.00	$100.00	$165.00

WASHINGTON PIECES

Large Military Bust
Point of Bust Close to W

	Fine	V. Fine	Ex. Fine
1783 Large Military Bust.....................	$22.50	$40.00	$85.00
1783 Small Military Bust, plain edge...........	30.00	60.00	120.00
1783 Small Military Bust, engrailed edge........	40.00	90.00	150.00

1783 Draped Bust, no button.................	25.00	45.00	100.00
1783 Draped Bust, with button................	60.00	110.00	175.00
1783 Draped Bust, Copper Restrike, plain edge.............Proof			150.00
1783 Draped Bust, Copper Restrike, engrailed edge...........Proof			60.00
1783 Draped Bust, Silver Restrike, engrailed edge............Proof			200.00

UNITY STATES

V. Good............	$25.00
V. Fine............	70.00
Ex. Fine..........	125.00

Undated (1783)
Double Head
Cent

Fine...............	$45.00
V. Fine............	60.00
Ex. Fine..........	110.00

Ugly Head

1784 Ugly Head.....(Ex. Rare)
Presumably of American origin.

WASHINGTON PIECES

Edge lettered: UNITED STATES OF AMERICA

	Fine	Ex. Fine	Unc.
1791 Cent, Small Eagle	$85.00	$175.00	$275.00
1791 Cent, Large Eagle	75.00	150.00	250.00

1791 Liverpool Halfpenny

Lettered edge

Fine	$500.00
Ex. Fine	825.00
Unc.	1,100

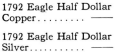

1792 Eagle Half Dollar
Copper........ ——

1792 Eagle Half Dollar
Silver........... ——

1792 Eagle Half Dollar
Gold........... ——

1792 Cent "WASHINGTON PRESIDENT"
    Plain edge........Fine $900.00   Lettered edge........ ——
(1792) Undated Cent "WASHINGTON BORN VIRGINIA"
    Copper.........Fine $900.00   Silver.............. ——
    (Restrike of obverse by Albert Collis, 1960.)

WASHINGTON PIECES

★ Idler

	Good	Fine
1792 Half Dollar, small eagle. Silver....................	——	——
1792 Half Dollar, small eagle. Copper...................	$600.00	$1,500
1792 Same, ornamented edge (circles and squares)........	——	——
1792 Same, Silver......................................	——	——
1792 Half Dollar, large eagle. Silver...................	(Unique)	

1792 Cent
Roman Head

Lettered edge —
**UNITED STATES OF
AMERICA**

Proof........ $3,000

1793 Ship
Halfpenny

Lettered Edge

Fine............	$60.00
V. Fine.........	110.00
Ex. Fine........	180.00
Plain edge (Rare).	——

1795 Halfpenny
Grate Token

(Large coat buttons
variety pictured)

	V. Fine	Ex. Fine	Unc.
1795 Large Buttons, lettered edge..............	$275.00	$400.00	$550.00
1795 Large Buttons, reeded edge...............	50.00	100.00	150.00
1795 Small Buttons, reeded edge...............	110.00	200.00	300.00

WASHINGTON PIECES
LIBERTY AND SECURITY HALFPENNY

	V. Good	Fine	Ex. F.
1795 Halfpenny, plain edge....................	$65.00	$100.00	$275.00
1795 Halfpenny, LONDON edge	40.00	70.00	150.00
1795 Halfpenny, BIRMINGHAM edge	50.00	85.00	250.00
1795 Halfpenny, ASYLUM edge	100.00	225.00	375.00

LIBERTY AND SECURITY PENNY
Undated (1795)

Fine............	$90.00
V. Fine..........	135.00
Ex. Fine........	190.00
Unc.	285.00
Dated 1795......	——

SUCCESS MEDALS

	Fine	V. Fine	Ex. F.
SUCCESS Medal, large. Plain or Reeded Edge ..	$100.00	$150.00	$200.00
SUCCESS Medal, small. Plain or Reeded Edge ..	100.00	150.00	200.00

NORTH WALES HALFPENNY

	Good	Fine
1795 NORTH WALES Halfpenny...	$50.00	$130.00
Lettered edge.....	——	——
Two stars at each side of harp....	——	——

THE FUGIO CENTS

The first coins issued by authority of the United States were the "Fugio" cents. Entries in the Journal of Congress supply interesting information about proceedings relating to this coinage.

"Saturday, April 21, 1787. . . .

"That the board of treasury be authorized to contract for three hundred tons of copper coin of the federal standard, agreeable to the proposition of Mr. James Jarvis, ... That it be coined at the expense of the contractor, etc."

On Friday, July 6, 1787, there was "Resolved, that the board of treasury direct the contractor for the copper coinage to stamp on one side of each piece the following device, viz: thirteen circles linked together, a small circle in the middle, with the words 'United States,' round it; and in the centre, the words 'We are one'; on the other side of the same piece the following device, viz: a dial with the hours expressed on the face of it; a meridian sun above on one side of which is the word 'Fugio,' (The meaning is, 'time flies') and on the other the year in figures '1787' below the dial, the words 'Mind Your Business.' "

The legends have been credited to Benjamin Franklin by many, and the coin, as a consequence, has been referred to as the Franklin Cent.

These cents were coined in New Haven, Conn., and it has been suggested, also in New York City, Rupert, Vt. and elsewhere. Most of the copper used in this coinage came from military stores. It is believed to have been the copper bands which held together the powder kegs sent to us by the French. The dies were made by Abel Buel of New Haven.

We list below major varieties, some of considerable rarity:

WITH CLUB RAYS
1787

	V.Good	Fine	V.F.
Club Rays, rounded ends......................	$60.00	$110.00	$225.00
Club Rays, concave ends to rays:			
FUCIO (c instead of G) (Ex. Rare).............	——	——	——
Club Rays, concave ends, FUGIO...............	——	——	——

WITH POINTED RAYS
1787

	V.G.	Fine	V.F.	Ex. F.	Unc.
UNITED above, STATES below (Rare)..	——	——	——	——	——
UNITED STATES at sides of circle.....	$40.00	$65.00	$85.00	$125.00	$200.00

THE FUGIO CENTS

	V.G.	V.F.	Ex. F.	Unc.
STATES UNITED at sides of circle. Cinquefoils (small, five bladed clover design) on label	$35.00	$75.00	$110.00	$190.00
STATES UNITED. 8-pointed stars on label	50.00	100.00	175.00	——
STATES UNITED. Label with raised rims (simply two concentric circles). Large letters in WE ARE ONE	60.00	175.00	——	——

Note: The preceding types with pointed rays have regular obverses punctuated with four cinquefoils.

Obv. no cinquefoils. Cross after date.

	V.G.	V.F.	Ex. F.	Unc.
Rev. UNITED STATES	85.00	200.00	——	——
Same Obv., Rev. STATES UNITED	100.00	225.00	——	——
Same Obv., Rev. label with raised rims				(Ex. Rare)

American Congress   New Haven Restrike

	Ex. F.	Unc.
Copper Pattern. Same Obv.; Reverse with rays and AMERICAN CONGRESS. (Ex. Rare)	——	——
New Haven Restrikes. Narrow rings on reverse.		
Gold (2 known)	——	——
Silver	——	225.00
Copper	——	85.00
Brass	——	80.00

New Haven Restrikes were struck from dies discovered by the fourteen-year-old C. Wyllys Betts in 1858 on the site of the Broome & Platt Store in New Haven, Conn., where the originals were made. Three pairs of dies were found and are still extant.

BIBLIOGRAPHY

Crosby, S. S. *The Early Coins of America*. Boston 1875 (reprinted 1945, 1965).
Dickeson, M. W. *The American Numismatic Manual*. Philadelphia 1859.
Maris, Edward. *A Historic Sketch of the Coins of New Jersey*. Philadelphia 1881 (reprinted 1925).
Miller, Henry C. and Hillyer, Ryder. *The State Coinages of New England*. New York 1920.
Nelson, Philip. *The Coinage of William Wood 1722-1733*. London 1903 (reprinted 1959).
Newman, Eric P. *The Secret of the Good Samaritan Shilling*. New York 1959.
Noe, Sydney P. *The New England and Willow Tree Coinage of Massachusetts*. New York 1943.
Wurtzbach, Carl. *Massachusetts Colonial Silver Money*. 1937.

FIRST UNITED STATES MINT ISSUES

Many members of the House favored a representation of the president's head on the obverse of each coin. Others considered the idea a monarchical practice. Washington is believed to have expressed disapproval of the use of his portrait on our coins.

The majority considered a figure emblematic of Liberty more appropriate and the Senate finally concurred in this opinion. Robert Birch was an engraver employed at designing proposed devices for our coins. He engraved the dies for the disme and half-disme. He has also been associated with a large copper cent of unusual design, which is known as the Birch Cent.

DISME

	Good	Fine	Unc.
1792 Silver (3 Known)....	—	—	—
1792 Copper.....	—	—	—

HALF DISME

	Good	Fine	V. Fine
1792 Silver.....	$650	$1,100	$2,000
1792 Copper (Unique)			

1792 SILVER CENTER CENT

	Fine	Ex. Fine
1792 Silver Center Cent.	—	—
1792 Cent, No Silver Center.....	—	—

1792 BIRCH CENT (Very Rare)

Copper...................... ———

G.W. PT Below Wreath
White Metal (Unique)

1792 PATTERN QUARTER DOLLAR

Copper.......(2 Known)
White Metal...(Unique)

MINTS AND MINT MARKS

Coins struck at Philadelphia (except 1942 to 1945 five-cent pieces) do not carry a mint mark. The mint mark is found only on coins struck at the branch mints. It is a small letter, usually found on the reverse side. The Lincoln cent is one exception to the rule. All coins minted after 1967 have the mint mark on the obverse. The letters that signify the various mints are as follows:

C — Charlotte, North Carolina   D — Denver, Colorado
    (on gold coins only).   (from 1906 to date).
CC — Carson City, Nevada.   O — New Orleans, Louisiana.
D — Dahlonega, Georgia   P — Philadelphia, Pennsylvania.
    (gold coins only, 1838 to 1861).   S — San Francisco, California.

All dies for United States coins are made at the Philadelphia Mint. Dies for use at branch mints are hand stamped with the appropriate mint mark before they are shipped from Philadelphia. Because of this hand operation, the exact positioning and size of the mint mark may vary slightly, depending on where and how deeply the punch was impressed. This also accounts for double-punched and superimposed mint marks such as the 1938 D over D, and D over S Buffalo nickels. Polishing of dies may also alter the apparent size of fine details. Occasionally the mint mark is inadvertently left off a die sent to a branch mint, as was the case with some of the 1968 and 1970 proof dimes, and the 1971 proof nickel.

Prior to 1900, punches for mint marks varied greatly in size. This is particularly noticeable in the 1850 to 1880 period in which the letters range from very small to very large. An attempt to standardize sizes started in 1892 with the Barber series, but exceptions are seen in the 1892 O half dollar and 1905 O dime, both of which have normal and "microscopic" mint marks. A more or less standard size small mint mark was used on all minor coins starting in 1909, and on all dimes, quarters and halves after the Barber series was replaced in 1916. Slight variations in mint mark size occur through 1940 with notable differences in 1928, when both small and large size S mint marks were used.

In recent years a single D or S punch has been used to mark all branch mint dies. The change to the larger D for Denver coins occurred in 1933. Dimes and half dollars of 1934 exist with either the old, smaller size mint mark or the new, larger size D. All other denominations of 1934 and after are standard. The San Francisco mint mark was changed to its present larger size during 1941 and, with the exception of the half dollar, all 1941 S coins are known with either small or large size mint mark. Halves were not changed until 1942, and the 1942 S pieces exist both ways. The 1945 S dime with "microscopic" S is an unexplained abnormality.

PROOF COINS

A "proof" is a specimen striking of coinage for presentation, souvenir, exhibition, or numismatic purposes. Pre-1968 proofs were made only at the Philadelphia Mint. Current proofs are made only at San Francisco.

The term "proof" refers to the method of manufacture and not the condition of a coin. Regular production coins in mint state have coruscating, frosty luster, soft details, and minor imperfections. Proof coins can usually be distinguished by their sharpness of detail, high wire edge, and extremely brilliant, mirrorlike surface. All proofs are originally sold by the mint at a premium.

Very few proof coins were made prior to 1855. Because of their rarity and infrequent sales, they are not all listed in this catalog.

Frosted proofs were issued prior to 1936. These have a brilliant mirror-like field with contrasting dull or frosted design and lettering. With modern proofs the first 15-20 coins struck from new proof dies are also frosted, but this feature is lost as soon as the dies are repolished.

Matte proofs have a granular "sandblast" surface instead of the mirror finish. Matte proof cents, nickels, and gold coins were issued from 1908 to 1916; a few 1921 and 1922 silver dollars were also struck this way.

Brilliant proofs have been issued from 1936 to date. These have a uniformly brilliant mirrorlike surface and sharp, high relief details.

"Proof-like" coins are occasionally seen. These are specimens from the first few impressions of regular coinage dies from any mint. They are not true proofs, but may have most of the characteristics of a proof coin and generally command a premium. Collectors should beware of coins that have been buffed to look like proofs; a magnifying glass will reveal myriad hair lines and lack of detail.

How A Proof Coin Is Made . . .

Selected dies are inspected for perfection and are highly polished and cleaned. They are again wiped clean or polished after every 15 to 25 impressions and are replaced frequently to avoid imperfections from worn dies. Coinage blanks are polished and cleaned to assure high quality in striking. They are then hand fed into the coinage press one at a time, each blank receiving two blows from the dies to bring up sharp, high relief details. The coinage operation is done at slow speed with extra pressure. Finished proofs are individually inspected and are handled by gloves or tongs. They also receive a final inspection by packers before being sonically sealed in special plastic cases.

MODERN PROOF COINS

After a lapse of twenty years, proof coins were struck at the Philadelphia Mint from 1936 to 1942 inclusive. In 1942, when the composition of the five-cent piece was changed, there were two types of this denomination available to collectors. The striking of proof coins was temporarily suspended from 1943 to 1949, and again from 1965 to 1967; during the latter period special mint sets were struck. Proof sets were resumed in 1968. They are delivered from the mint only during the year of issue.

RECENT PROOF SETS — Cent — Nickel — Dime — Quarter — Half

Figures in parentheses represent the total number of full sets minted.

1936 (3,837).............$930.00	1960 with lg. date 1¢	
1937 (5,542)............. 385.00	(1,691,602 both kinds)..	$5.50
1938 (8,045)............. 180.00	1960 with sm. date 1¢.......	19.00
1939 (8,795)............. 160.00	1961 (3,028,244)............	4.25
1940 (11,246)............. 130.00	1962 (3,218,019)............	4.25
1941 (15,287)............. 120.00	1963 (3,075,645)............	4.50
1942 with both	1964 (3,950,762)............	5.00
nickels (21,120)........ 145.00	1968S (3,041,509)..........	5.50
1950 (51,386)............. 110.00	1968S 10¢ without mint mark	——
1951 (57,500)............. 85.00	1969S (2,934,631)...........	5.25
1952 (81,980)............. 50.00	1970S (2,632,810).........	9.50
1953 (128,800)............. 35.00	1970S 10¢ without mint mark	
1954 (233,300)............. 18.00	(2,200).............	475.00
1955 (378,200)............. 24.00	1971S (3,224,138).........	6.00
1956 (669,384)............. 9.00	1971S 5¢ without mint mark	
1957 (1,247,952)............ 6.50	(1,655)..............	500.00
1958 (875,652)............ 11.25	1972S (3,267,667)..........	6.00
1959 (1,149,291)............ 6.25	1973S (includes dollar)......	8.00

SPECIAL MINT SETS

1965 (2,360,000)..$3.25   1966 (2,261,583)..$3.50   1967 (1,863,344)..$5.00

UNITED STATES REGULAR ISSUES
HALF CENTS — 1793-1857

From the standpoint of face value the half cent is the smallest coin struck by the United States. All half cents are scarce, but the series has never enjoyed the popularity of some of the other series, hence the more common dates and varieties are reasonably priced.

There were various intermissions in coinage, and during most of the period 1836 to 1849 the coinage was very small, causing a very noticeable lapse in the series for the average collector. While 1796 is the rarest date, the originals and restrikes of 1831, 1836 and 1840 through 1849, and rare varieties are a'l difficult to obtain.

The half cent was authorized to be coined April 2, 1792. Originally the weight was to have been 132 grains, but this was changed to 104 grains by the Act of January 14, 1793, before coinage commenced. The weight was again changed to 84 grains January 26, 1796 by presidential proclamation in conformity with the Act of March 3, 1795. Coinage was discontinued by the Act of February 21, 1857. All were coined at the Philadelphia Mint.

LIBERTY CAP TYPE 1793-1797

FAIR—*Clear enough to identify.*
GOOD—*Outline of bust clear, no details. Date readable. Reverse lettering incomplete.*
VERY GOOD—*Some hair details. Reverse lettering complete.*
FINE—*Most of hair detail shows.*
VERY FINE—*Hair near ear and forehead worn, other areas distinct.*

Head Facing Left 1793

Designer Joseph Wright; weight 6.74 grams; composition: copper; approx. diameter 22 mm; edge: TWO HUNDRED FOR A DOLLAR.

	Quan. Minted	Fair	Good	V. Good	Fine	V. Fine
1793	35,334	$135.00	$250.00	$375.00	$675.00	$1,150

Head Facing Right 1794-1797

1794 — Designer Robert Scot; weight 6.74 grams; composition: copper; approx. diameter 23.5 mm; edge: TWO HUNDRED FOR A DOLLAR.

1795 — Designer John Smith Gardner; weight 6.74 grams; composition: copper; approx. diameter 23.5 mm; edge: TWO HUNDRED FOR A DOLLAR.

1795-1797 (thin planchet) — Weight 5.44 grams; composition: copper; approx. diameter 23.5 mm; edge: plain (some 1797 experimentally lettered).

	Quan. Minted	Fair	Good	V. Good	Fine	V. Fine
1794	81,600	45.00	75.00	100.00	175.00	320.00

HALF CENTS

Pole to Cap	Punctuated Date	No Pole to Cap

	Quan. Minted	Fair	Good	V. Good	Fine	V. Fine
1795 Lettered Edge, with Pole.......	25,600	$40.00	$65.00	$90.00	$165.00	$285.00
1795 Let. Edge, Punctuated Date....		40.00	65.00	90.00	165.00	285.00
1795 Plain Edge, Punct. Date....	109,000	40.00	65.00	90.00	165.00	285.00
1795 Pl. Edge, no Pole		40.00	65.00	90.00	165.00	285.00
1796 with Pole*.........5,090		525.00	1,050	1,750	2,750	4,500
1796 no Pole............1,390		700.00	1,600	2,350	3,400	5,750

*The deceptive "Dr. Edwards" struck copy of this coin has a different head and larger letters.

1797 Plain Edge	1797 1 Above 1, Plain Edge

1797 All Kinds........119,214					
1797 Lettered Edge...........	115.00	230.00	360.00	575.00	1,050
1797 Plain Edge.............	35.00	55.00	80.00	150.00	280.00
1797 1 above 1, Plain Edge....	30.00	50.00	75.00	130.00	250.00

DRAPED BUST TYPE 1800-1808

FAIR—*Clear enough to identify.*
GOOD—*Bust outline clear, no details, date readable. Reverse lettering worn and incomplete.*
VERY GOOD—*Some drapery shows. Date and legends complete.*
FINE—*Shoulder drapery and hair over brow worn smooth.*
VERY FINE—*Only slight wear in above areas. Slight wear on reverse.*

Designer Robert Scot: weight 5.44 grams; composition: copper; approx. diameter 23.5 mm; plain edge.

1800................211,530	5.25	10.00	15.00	25.00	40.00

HALF CENTS

	Quan. Minted	Fair	Good	V. Good	Fine	V. Fine
1802, 2 over 0, rev. of 1800	⎫ 14,366	$250.00	$500.00	$750.00	$1,000	$1,500
1802, 2 over 0, new rev.	⎭	50.00	100.00	150.00	250.00	425.00
1803	97,900	5.25	10.00	15.00	25.00	42.50

Plain 4	Crosslet 4	Stemless Wreath	Stems to Wreath

	Quan. Minted	Fair	Good	V. Good	Fine	V. Fine
1804 Plain 4, Stems	⎫	11.00	19.00	30.00	40.00	80.00
1804 Pl. 4, Stemless		5.75	10.00	15.00	25.00	42.50
1804 Cr. 4, Stems	1,055,312	5.75	10.00	16.00	27.50	45.00
1804 Cr. 4, Stemless		6.00	11.00	16.00	27.50	45.00
1804 "Spiked Chin"	⎭	8.00	13.00	18.00	30.00	50.00

1804 "Spiked Chin" Variety	Small 5	Large 5

	Quan. Minted	Fair	Good	V. Good	Fine	V. Fine
1805 Sm. 5, Stemless	⎫	5.25	9.00	13.00	22.00	40.00
1805 Small 5, Stems	814,464	30.00	52.50	85.00	225.00	375.00
1805 Large 5, Stems	⎭	5.25	9.00	13.00	22.00	40.00

Small 6	Large 6	1808, 8 over 7	Normal Date

	Quan. Minted	Fair	Good	V. Good	Fine	V. Fine
1806 Small 6, Stems	⎫	14.00	32.00	52.50	90.00	140.00
1806 Sm. 6, Stemless	356,000	6.00	10.00	13.00	20.00	35.00
1806 Large 6, Stems	⎭	6.00	10.00	13.00	20.00	35.00
1807	476,000	6.00	10.00	14.00	25.00	42.50
1808, 8 over 7	⎫ 400,000	25.00	40.00	60.00	100.00	200.00
1808 Normal Date	⎭	6.00	11.00	15.00	27.50	45.00

CLASSIC HEAD TYPE 1809-1836

Designer John Reich. Standards same as previous issue.

FAIR—Worn, but clear enough to identify.
GOOD—LIBERTY only partly visible on hair band. Lettering, date, stars, worn but visible.
VERY GOOD—LIBERTY entirely visible on hair band. Lower curls worn.
FINE—Only part wear on LIBERTY and hair at top worn in spots.
VERY FINE—Lettering clear-cut. Hair only slightly worn.

HALF CENTS

1809 Circle Inside O   **1809 Normal Date**

	Quan. Minted	Good	V. Good	Fine	V. Fine	Unc.
1809 Circle inside 0..	⎫	$11.00	$16.00	$25.00	$42.50	$180.00
1809, 9 over 6......	⎬1,154,572	11.00	16.00	25.00	42.50	180.00
1809 Normal Date..	⎭	10.00	13.00	20.00	30.00	150.00
1810................215,000		14.00	22.00	35.00	55.00	350.00
1811...................63,140		40.00	55.00	90.00	160.00	750.00
1811 Restrike, Rev. of 1802...			Extremely Rare			
1825..................63,000		9.00	13.00	18.00	27.50	120.00
1826................234,000		8.75	12.50	17.50	26.00	115.00

13 Stars   **12 Stars**

1828 13 Stars........	⎫606,000	8.50	12.00	17.00	24.00	100.00
1828 12 Stars........	⎬	11.00	17.00	25.00	45.00	250.00
1829................487,000		8.50	12.00	17.00	24.00	110.00

Beginning in 1831 new coinage equipment and modified dies produced a raised rim on each side of these coins.

Original
Large
Berries   Restrike
Small
Berries

	Quan. Minted	Unc.	Proof
1831 Original (Beware of altered date).............2,200		——	$1,250
1831 Restrike Large Berries (Rev. of 1836).............			1,000
1831 Restrike Small Berries (Rev. of 1852).............			——

	Quan. Minted	V. Good	Fine	V. Fine	Unc.	Proof
1832................154,000*		$11.00	$16.00	$22.50	$100.00	$700.00
1833................120,000*		11.00	16.00	22.50	100.00	500.00
1834................141,000*		11.00	16.00	22.50	100.00	525.00
1835................398,000*		11.00	16.00	22.50	100.00	550.00
1836 Original................						925.00
1836 Restrike (Rev. of 1852)..						——

*The figures given here are thought to be correct, although official mint records give the same quantities for 1833-36 rather than 1832-35.

HALF CENTS

No half cents were struck in 1837. Because of the great need for small change, however, a large number of tokens similar in size to current half cents and large cents were issued privately by businessmen who needed them in commerce. One of the most popular pieces is listed and illustrated below.

	Good	V. Good	Fine	V. Fine
1837 Token (not a coin)............	$15.00	$25.00	$37.50	$80.00

BRAIDED HAIR TYPE 1840-1857

Designer Christian Gobrecht; weight 5.44 grams; composition: copper; diameter 23 mm; plain edge.

	Proof		Proof
1840 Original..............	$750.00	1845 Original..............	$825.00
1840 Restrike..............	650.00	1845 Restrike..............	725.00
1841 Original..............	740.00	1846 Original..............	725.00
1841 Restrike..............	900.00	1846 Restrike..............	685.00
1842 Original..............	775.00	1847 Original..............	700.00
1842 Restrike..............	600.00	1847 Restrike..............	650.00
1843 Original..............	750.00	1848 Original..............	800.00
1843 Restrike..............	625.00	1848 Restrike..............	650.00
1844 Original..............	750.00	1849 Original - Small Date...	1,000
1844 Restrike..............	725.00	1849 Restrike - Small Date..	700.00

Brilliant or Red Uncirculated Half Cents Are Worth More Than Prices Shown.

GOOD—Some of LIBERTY shows and beads partly distinct.

VERY GOOD—Beads uniformly distinct. Hairlines show in spots.

FINE—Hairlines above ear worn. Beads sharp.

VERY FINE—Lowest curl shows wear, hair otherwise distinct.

 Small Date

 Large Date

	Quan. Minted	V. Good	Fine	V. Fine	Unc.	Proof
1849 Large Date........	39,864	$16.00	$22.00	$40.00	$150.00	
1850.................	39,812	15.00	21.00	32.50	110.00	——
1851.................	147,672	13.00	18.00	25.00	90.00	——
1852 Original...............						
1852 Restrike...............						$700.00
1853.................	129,694	13.00	19.00	25.00	90.00	
1854.................	55,358	13.00	19.00	25.00	100.00	475.00
1855.................	56,500	13.00	19.00	25.00	100.00	450.00
1856.................	40,430	14.00	21.00	30.00	120.00	475.00
1857.................	35,180	20.00	30.00	45.00	150.00	550.00

BIBLIOGRAPHY

Cohen, Roger S., Jr. *American Half Cents—The "Little Half Sisters"*. 1971.
Crosby, S. S. *United States Coinage of 1793 — Cents and Half Cents*. Boston, 1897.
Frossard, Edward. *United States Cents and Half Cents 1793-1857*. Irvington, New York, 1879.
Gilbert, Ebenezer. *United States Half Cents*. New York, 1916. Hewitt Reprint, Chicago.

LARGE CENTS — 1793-1857

Cents and half cents were the first coins struck under the authority of the United States Government. Coinage began in 1793 with laws specifying that the cent should weigh exactly twice as much as the half cent. Large cents were coined every year from 1793 to 1857 with the exception of 1815, when a lack of copper prevented production. All were coined at the Philadelphia Mint. Mintage records in some cases may be inaccurate, as many of the early pieces were struck later than the dates shown on the coins. Varieties listed are those most significant to collectors, but numerous minor variations may be found because each of the early dies was individually made. Values of variations not listed in this guide depend on collector interest and demand. Proof large cents were first made in 1817; all proofs are rare, as they were not made available to the general public until the 1850's.

FLOWING HAIR, CHAIN TYPE REVERSE 1793

Weight 13.48 grams; composition: copper; approx. diameter 26-27 mm; edge: bars and slender vine with leaves.

FAIR—Date and devices clear enough to identify.
GOOD—Lettering worn but readable. Bust has no detail.
VERY GOOD—Date and lettering distinct, some details of head visible.
FINE—About half of hair, etc. details show.
VERY FINE—Ear visible. Most of details can be seen.

Obverse

AMERI. Reverse

AMERICA Reverse

	Quan. Minted	Fair	Good	V. Good	Fine	V. Fine
1793 AMERI. in legend..	36,103	$235.00	$400.00	$650.00	$1,225	$2,350
1793 AMERICA*........		185.00	335.00	550.00	1,000	2,150

*Varieties with or without periods after date and legend.

FLOWING HAIR, WREATH TYPE REVERSE 1793

The reverse of this type bears a "single-bow" wreath, as distinguished from the wreath tied with a double bow on the following type. A three-leaf sprig appears above the date on the obverse, and both sides have borders of small beads. Introduction of this reverse answered criticism of the chain design, but the stronger modeling of the face and hair still failed to gain acceptance as representative of Liberty. After three months' production the design was abandoned in favor of the Liberty Cap type.

Instead of the normal sprig above the date, the rare "strawberry leaf" variety has a spray of trefoil leaves and a small blossom. It is not clear why this variety was created, and all known specimens are too badly worn for positive identification of the leaves.

LARGE CENTS

Weight 13.48 grams; composition: copper; approx. diameter 26-27 mm; edge: bars and vine, or lettered ONE HUNDRED FOR A DOLLAR followed by either a single or double leaf.

Wreath Type   **Strawberry Leaf Var.**

	Quan. Minted	Fair	Good	V. Good	Fine	V. Fine
1793 vine & bars edge..		$135.00	$250.00	$415.00	$675.00	$1,300
1793 lettered edge.....	63,353	150.00	260.00	425.00	775.00	1,300
1793 strawberry leaf...			Ex. Rare			

LIBERTY CAP TYPE 1793-1796

Another major change was made in 1793 to satisfy continuing objections to the obverse portrait. This version appears to have been more successful, as it was continued into 1796. The 1793 pieces had beaded borders, but a border of denticles or "teeth" was adopted in 1794. A famous 1794 variety is the possibly experimental "starred" reverse, with a border of 94 tiny stars.

Portrait variations listed below for 1794 are the result of several changes of die engravers; but the so-called "Jefferson head" of 1795 is now thought to be a sample for a proposed coinage contract by a private manufacturer.

Planchets became too thin for edge lettering after the weight reduction ordered late in 1795. The variety with reeded edge was probably an experimental substitute, rejected in favor of a plain edge.

1793-1795 (thick planchet) — Weight 13.48 grams; composition: copper; approx. diameter 29 mm; edge: ONE HUNDRED FOR A DOLLAR followed by a single leaf.

1795-1796 (thin planchet) — Designer John Smith Gardner; weight 10.89 grams; composition: copper; approx. diameter 29 mm; plain edge.

First head style   **Beaded border**   **Second head style**
1793-1794   **1793 only**   **1794 only**
"Head of 1793"   **"Head of 1794"**

LARGE CENTS

1794 starred
reverse

Third head style
1794-1796
"Head of 1795"

"Jefferson Head"

	Quan. Minted	Fair	Good	V. Good	Fine	V. Fine
1793.................	11,056	$300.00	$475.00	$725.00	$1,500	$2,600
1794, "head of 1793"..		35.00	60.00	90.00	200.00	350.00
1794, "head of 1794"..	918,521	20.00	35.00	60.00	110.00	225.00
1794, starred rev.		150.00	350.00	600.00	1,000	——
1794, "head of 1795"..		25.00	47.50	75.00	150.00	250.00
1795 lettered edge......	82,000	27.50	50.00	75.00	150.00	250.00
1795 plain edge........	456,000	20.00	35.00	60.00	110.00	165.00
1795 Jeff. hd. (not reg. issue)..			300.00	400.00	600.00	1,000
1795 reeded edge.............				Ex. Rare		
1796.................	109,825	30.00	55.00	80.00	125.00	240.00

DRAPED BUST TYPE 1796-1807

Designer Robert Scot; weight 10.89 grams; composition: copper; approx. diameter 29 mm;
plain edge.

FAIR—*Clear enough to identify.*
GOOD—*Lettering worn, but clear; date clear. Bust lacks details.*
VERY GOOD—*Drapery partly visible. Less wear in date and lettering.*
FINE—*Hair over brow is smooth, some detail showing elsewhere.*
VERY FINE—*Hairlines slightly worn. Hair over brow better defined.*

Obverse
1796-1807

This head was modified
slightly in 1798. See following page for details.

First reverse style
1794-1796
"Reverse of 1794"

Note double leaf at top
right; 14-16 leaves left,
16-18 leaves right.

Second reverse style
1795-1798
"Reverse of 1796"

Note single leaf at top
right; 17-21 leaves left,
16-19 leaves right.

LARGE CENTS

Note double leaf at top right; 16 leaves left, 19 leaves right.

Third reverse style
1796-1807
"Reverse of 1797"

LIHERTY Error

	Quan. Minted	Fair	Good	V. Good	Fine	V. Fine
1796, 1st reverse......		$23.00	$45.00	$72.50	$120.00	$240.00
1796, 2nd reverse.....	363,375	27.50	47.50	80.00	130.00	260.00
1796, 3rd reverse.....		30.00	55.00	85.00	145.00	275.00
1796 LIHERTY error....		35.00	65.00	100.00	170.00	350.00

Gripped or
Milled Edge

Stems

Stemless

1797 gripped edge, 2nd reverse......		17.50	30.00	47.50	85.00	160.00
1797 pl. edge, 2nd rev.	897,510	20.00	32.50	55.00	100.00	175.00
1797, 3rd rev, stems...		12.50	19.00	30.00	47.50	95.00
1797, 3rd rev, stemless		27.50	52.00	90.00	150.00	275.00

1798, 8 over 7
(style 1 hair)

Style 1 hair appears on all 1796-97, most 1798 varieties and 1800 over 1798. Style 2 hair, used 1798-1807, is most easily recognized by the extra curl near the shoulder (see arrow).

Style 2 hair
1798-1807

1798, 8 over 7, 3rd rev		20.00	35.00	60.00	115.00	230.00
1798, 2nd reverse.....	979,700	19.00	33.00	55.00	105.00	220.00
1798, 3rd rev, 1st hair		8.50	15.00	22.50	40.00	82.50
1798, 3rd rev, 2nd hair		8.50	15.00	22.50	40.00	82.50

1799, 9 over 8

Normal date

1800, 80 over 79

1799, 9 over 8........	904,585		425.00	700.00	1,400	2,600
1799 normal date.....			400.00	675.00	1,350	2,350
1800 over 1798, style 1 hair....		9.50	16.50	25.00	47.50	95.00
1800, 80 over 79, style 2 hair ...	2,822,175	8.00	15.00	23.00	42.50	85.00
1800 normal date ...		7.50	14.00	21.00	37.50	75.00

LARGE CENTS

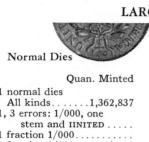 

Normal Dies

→
1801
Reverse
3 Errors

	Quan. Minted	Fair	Good	V. Good	Fine	V. Fine
1801 normal dies						
All kinds.......1,362,837		$8.50	$13.50	$22.50	$42.50	$75.00
1801, 3 errors: 1/000, one						
stem and IINITED		20.00	37.50	65.00	130.00	240.00
1801 fraction 1/000...........		10.00	20.00	35.00	70.00	130.00
1801 fraction 1/100 over 1/000.		13.00	27.50	40.00	72.50	145.00
1802 normal dies....		6.00	10.00	15.00	25.00	60.00
1802 stemless wreath }3,435,100		7.00	13.00	20.00	36.00	70.00
1802 fraction 1/000..)		7.50	15.00	25.00	47.50	95.00

1803 Sm. Date, blunt 1   Small Fraction   Large Fraction

1803 sm. date, sm. fraction					
All kinds.......2,471,353	6.50	11.00	16.00	27.50	70.00
1803 sm. date, lg. fraction.....	6.50	11.00	16.00	27.50	70.00
1803 lg. date, sm. fraction.....	80.00	120.00	190.00	340.00	575.00
1803 lg. date, lg. fraction......	42.50	70.00	125.00	210.00	370.00
1803 stemless wreath.........	11.00	17.00	32.00	55.00	95.00
1803, 1/100 over 1/000........	11.00	21.00	37.50	72.50	130.00

1804 with
broken dies
(see arrows)

All genuine 1804 Cents have
a crosslet 4 in the date and
a large fraction. The 0 in the
date is in line with the O in
OF on the reverse of the coin.

 ←

1804.................756,838   145.00   250.00   350.00   625.00   975.00

RESTRIKE OF 1804 CENT

A fake 1804 was manufactured
from discarded mint dies. An
altered 1803 die was used for the
obverse and a die of the 1820
cent used for the reverse. They
were struck about the year 1860
to satisfy the demand for this
rare date. Known as the "restrike," it was a patchwork job
and is easily distinguished from a genuine 1804 cent.

1804 restrike of 1860....................................Unc. $150.00

LARGE CENTS

	Quan. Minted	Fair	Good	V. Good	Fine	V. Fine
1805................	941,116	$7.00	$13.00	$19.00	$30.00	$65.00
1806................	348,000	13.00	25.00	40.00	75.00	150.00

1807, large
7 over 6

"Comet" Variety

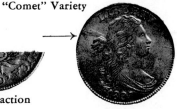

Small Fraction   Large Fraction

1807 large 7 over 6					
All kinds........727,221	8.00	14.00	22.00	35.00	75.00
1807 small 7 over 6, blunt 1 ...	50.00	80.00	120.00	220.00	350.00
1807 small fraction..........	7.00	12.00	20.00	35.00	65.00
1807 large fraction..........	7.00	12.00	20.00	35.00	65.00
1807 "Comet" variety					
(die break behind head)..	11.00	20.00	32.00	60.00	135.00

CLASSIC HEAD TYPE 1808-1814

1808 to 1814 — This group does not compare in sharpness and quality to those struck before (1793-1807), nor to those struck after (1816 on). The copper used was "softer," having less alloy. This impaired the wearing quality of the series. For this reason collectors find greater difficulty in obtaining these dates in choice condition.

Designer John Reich. Standards same as previous issue.

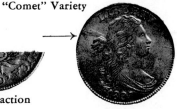

FAIR—Details clear enough to identify.

GOOD—Legends, stars, date worn, but plain.

VERY GOOD—LIBERTY all readable. Ear shows. Details worn but plain.

FINE—Hair on forehead and before ear nearly smooth. Ear and hair under ear sharp.

VERY FINE—All hairlines show some detail. Leaves on rev. show slight wear.

1808................1,109,000	10.50	17.50	35.00	65.00	115.00
1809................222,867	42.50	70.00	125.00	200.00	360.00

1810, 10 over 09   Normal Date   1811, last 1 over 0

1810, 10 over 09.... } 1,458,500	9.50	17.50	28.00	47.50	90.00
1810 normal date ...	9.00	15.00	25.00	40.00	75.00
1811, last 1 over 0.... } 218,025	37.50	55.00	85.00	150.00	265.00
1811 normal date.....	37.50	55.00	85.00	150.00	265.00

LARGE CENTS

	Quan. Minted	Fair	Good	V. Good	Fine	V. Fine
1812	1,075,500	$9.00	$13.50	$22.00	$36.00	$75.00
1813	418,000	14.00	27.50	37.50	77.50	130.00

1814 Plain 4

1814 Crosslet 4

		Fair	Good	V. Good	Fine	V. Fine
1814 plain 4	} 357,830	8.50	14.50	23.00	37.50	70.00
1814 crosslet 4		8.50	14.50	23.00	37.50	70.00

CORONET TYPE 1816-1857

Red to bright red uncirculated large cents (not cleaned) command higher prices. Beware of slightly worn copper coins which have been cleaned and recolored to simulate uncirculated luster.

GOOD—Head details partly visible. Even wear in date and legends.
VERY GOOD—LIBERTY, date, stars, legends clear. Part of hair cord visible.
FINE—All hairlines show. Hair cords show uniformly.
VERY FINE—Hair cords only slightly worn. Hairlines only partly worn, all well defined.

Designer Robert Scot; weight 10.89 grams; composition: copper; approx. diameter 28-29 mm; plain edge.

First head
style
1816-1835

	Quan. Minted	Good	V.G.	Fine	V.F.	Ex. F.	Unc.
1816	2,820,982	$6.50	$10.00	$14.50	$27.50	$55.00	$175.00
1817	} 3,948,400	6.00	9.00	12.50	22.50	45.00	165.00
1817, 15 stars		9.50	15.00	27.50	45.00	100.00	500.00
1818	3,167,000	6.00	9.00	12.50	22.50	45.00	165.00

1819, 9 over 8

1819 Large Date

1819 Small Date

		Good	V.G.	Fine	V.F.	Ex. F.	Unc.
1819, 9 over 8	} 2,671,000	8.00	11.00	17.50	27.50	60.00	275.00
1819 large date		7.00	10.00	15.00	23.00	47.50	165.00
1819 small date		7.00	10.00	15.00	23.00	47.50	165.00

LARGE CENTS

1820, 20 over 19

1820 Small Date

1820 Large Date

	Quan. Minted	Good	V.G.	Fine	V.F.	Ex. F.	Unc.
1820, 20 over 19....		$7.50	$11.00	$15.00	$25.00	$50.00	$200.00
1820 small date.....	4,407,550	6.00	9.00	12.00	20.00	45.00	165.00
1820 large date.....		6.00	9.00	12.00	20.00	45.00	165.00
1821................389,000		15.00	25.00	40.00	75.00	190.00	800.00
1822...............2,072,339		6.00	10.00	15.00	27.50	60.00	275.00

1823, 3 over 2

1823 Normal Date

		Good	V.G.	Fine	V.F.	Ex. F.	Unc.
1823, 3 over 2........	855,730	24.00	37.50	65.00	125.00	400.00	1,800
1823 normal date.....		32.50	45.00	80.00	160.00	700.00	2,400
1823 restrike, from broken obverse die...........................							150.00

1824, 4 over 2

1824 Wide Date

1824 Close Date

		Good	V.G.	Fine	V.F.	Ex. F.	Unc.
1824, 4 over 2......		14.00	22.50	36.00	67.50	170.00	600.00
1824 wide date.....	1,262,000	7.50	10.00	17.00	35.00	70.00	400.00
1824 close date.....		7.50	10.00	17.00	35.00	70.00	400.00

LARGE CENTS

1825 Small A's

1825 Large A's

1826 Close Date

	Quan. Minted	Good	V.G.	Fine	V.F.	Ex. F.	Unc.
1825 small A's......	} 1,461,100	$6.50	$9.00	$15.00	$29.00	$60.00	$275.00
1825 large A's......		6.50	9.00	15.00	29.00	60.00	275.00
1826 wide date.....	} 1,517,425	6.50	9.00	15.00	28.00	55.00	200.00
1826 close date.....		6.50	9.00	15.00	28.00	55.00	200.00
1827...............	2,357,732	5.50	7.50	12.00	19.00	37.50	175.00

1828
Small
Wide Date

1828
Large
Narrow
Date

1828 sm. wide date..	} 2,260,624	10.00	15.00	22.50	37.50	80.00	300.00
1828 lg. nar. date...		5.50	8.50	12.50	25.00	55.00	200.00

Medium Letters

Large Letters

1829 med. letters...	} 1,414,500	7.00	11.00	15.00	30.00	60.00	200.00
1829 large letters...		6.00	9.00	12.00	24.00	50.00	200.00
1830 med. letters...	} 1,711,500	12.00	22.00	40.00	77.50	150.00	300.00
1830 large letters...		6.00	8.00	11.00	19.00	37.50	200.00
1831 med. letters...	} 3,359,260	5.00	7.00	9.50	14.50	30.00	200.00
1831 large letters...		5.00	7.00	9.50	14.50	30.00	200.00
1832 med. letters...	} 2,362,000	5.50	7.50	11.00	17.50	37.50	200.00
1832 large letters...		5.50	7.50	11.00	17.50	37.50	200.00
1833...............	2,739,000	5.50	7.50	11.00	17.50	37.50	200.00

LARGE CENTS

	Large 8 & Stars	Small 8, Large Stars	Large 8, Small Stars

	Quan. Minted	Good	V.G.	Fine	V.F.	Ex. F.	Unc.
1834 lg. 8, stars & rev. letters....	⎫	$8.00	$13.00	$22.00	$37.50	$70.00	$200.00
1834 lg. 8 & stars, med. letters...	⎬1,855,100	10.00	17.50	30.00	60.00	85.00	200.00
1834 lg. 8, sm. stars, med. letters...		6.00	8.50	15.00	22.50	45.00	200.00
1834 sm. 8, lg. stars, med. letters...	⎭	6.00	8.50	15.00	22.50	45.00	200.00

Large 8 & stars, first head	Small 8 & stars, first head	Second head style 1835-1837 "Head of 1836"

		Good	V.G.	Fine	V.F.	Ex. F.	Unc.
1835 lg. 8 & stars...	⎫	7.00	11.00	17.00	30.00	50.00	200.00
1835 sm. 8 & stars..	⎬3,878,400	7.00	11.00	17.00	30.00	50.00	200.00
1835, "head of 1836"	⎭	5.50	7.50	12.50	17.50	35.00	200.00

GOOD—*Considerably worn. LIBERTY readable.*
VERY GOOD—*Hairlines smooth but visible, outline of ear clearly defined.*
FINE—*Hairlines at top of head and behind ear worn but visible. Braid over brow plain, ear clear.*
VERY FINE—*All details more sharp. Hair over brow shows only slight wear.*
Weight 10.89 grams; composition: copper; diameter 27.5 mm; plain edge.

Second head
style
1835-1837

Note plain
hair cord

Third head
style
1837-1839

Note beaded
cord, no
curl in
front of
forehead

"Beaded hair cord"

		Good	V.G.	Fine	V.F.	Ex. F.	Unc.
1836............2,111,000		5.50	7.50	12.50	17.50	35.00	200.00

LARGE CENTS

	Quan. Minted	Good	V.G.	Fine	V.F.	Ex. F.	Unc.
1837, 2nd hd, sm. let		$6.50	$9.50	$16.00	$27.00	$45.00	$200.00
1837, 2nd hd, med. let	5,558,300	5.50	7.00	11.00	17.50	30.00	165.00
1837, 3rd head		5.50	7.00	11.00	17.50	30.00	165.00
1838	6,370,200	5.50	7.00	11.00	17.50	30.00	165.00

1839,
9 over 6

Fourth head
style
"silly head"
1839 only

Note hair
curl in front
of forehead

	Good	V.G.	Fine	V.F.	Ex. F.	Unc.
1839 All kinds 3,128,661						
1839, 9 over 6, 2nd head	100.00	145.00	225.00	375.00	——	——
1839, 3rd head or "beaded cord"	9.00	13.00	22.50	36.00	55.00	200.00
1839, 4th or "silly head"	11.00	15.00	25.00	37.50	60.00	250.00

Fifth head
style
"booby head"
1839 only

Note back
tip of
shoulder is
visible

Sixth head
style
"braided
hair"
1839-1843

Note tip of
bust above 8

The 5th and 6th heads use a modified reverse which omits the line under CENT (see illustration at 1843).

	Good	V.G.	Fine	V.F.	Ex. F.	Unc.
1839, 5th or "booby head"	8.00	12.00	19.00	30.00	70.00	300.00
1839, 6th head "braided hair" .	9.00	13.00	25.00	34.00	60.00	250.00

1840
Small Date

1840
Large Date

	Good	V.G.	Fine	V.F.	Ex. F.	Unc.
1840 small date	2,462,700	6.00	8.00	11.00	16.00	35.00	165.00
1840 large date		6.00	8.00	11.00	16.00	35.00	165.00
1841 small date 1,597,367		6.00	8.00	13.00	19.00	37.50	165.00

LARGE CENTS

1842
Small Date

1842
Large Date

	Quan. Minted	Good	V.G.	Fine	V.F.	Ex. F.	Unc.
1842 small date.....	} 2,383,390	$5.00	$7.50	$10.00	$16.00	$25.00	$150.00
1842 large date.....		5.00	7.50	10.00	16.00	25.00	150.00

Small letters
1839-1843
"Reverse of 1842"

Seventh head
1843-1857
"Obverse of 1844"
Note tip of bust above 1

Large letters
1843-1857
"Reverse of 1844"

		Good	V.G.	Fine	V.F.	Ex. F.	Unc.
1843, 6th hd, sm. let	} 2,428,320	5.50	8.00	11.50	18.00	30.00	150.00
1843, 6th hd, lg. let.		20.00	32.50	57.50	85.00	175.00	625.00
1843, 7th hd, lg. let.		6.50	10.00	15.00	25.00	40.00	200.00

1846 Small Date

1846 Tall Date

1847, 7 over "small" 7

		Good	V.G.	Fine	V.F.	Ex. F.	Unc.
1844 normal date...	} 2,398,752	5.00	6.50	9.50	16.00	25.00	165.00
1844 over 81 (error).		7.00	10.00	13.50	35.00	60.00	250.00
1845...............	3,894,804	4.50	6.00	8.00	12.00	25.00	125.00
1846 small date.....	} 4,120,800	4.00	5.00	6.00	10.00	17.50	125.00
1846 medium date..		4.00	5.00	6.00	10.00	17.50	125.00
1846 tall date......		5.00	6.00	9.00	16.00	30.00	165.00
1847..............	} 6,183,669	4.00	5.00	6.00	10.00	17.50	125.00
1847, 7 over "sm." 7		8.00	10.00	15.00	30.00	50.00	200.00
1848...............	6,415,799	4.00	5.00	6.00	10.00	17.50	125.00
1849...............	4,178,500	4.00	5.00	6.00	10.00	17.50	125.00
1850...............	4,426,844	4.00	5.00	6.00	10.00	17.50	125.00

LARGE CENTS

Both of these errors actually have their final two digits punched over an inverted 18.

1844, 44 over 81   1851, 51 over 81

	Quan. Minted	Good	V.G.	Fine	V.F.	Ex. F.	Unc.
1851 normal date....	9,889,707	$3.50	$4.50	$5.50	$9.00	$17.50	$100.00
1851 over 81 (error).		7.50	11.00	15.00	37.50	75.00	200.00
1852...............5,063,094		3.50	4.50	5.50	9.00	17.50	100.00
1853...............6,641,131		3.50	4.50	5.50	9.00	17.50	100.00
1854...............4,236,156		3.50	4.50	5.50	9.00	17.50	100.00

1855
Upright 5's

1855
Slanting 5's

Original sketches of engraver James B. Longacre's work reveal that slanting 5's were a peculiarity of his work. The upright 5's were probably the work of an apprentice.

1855 upright 5's							
All kinds.......1,574,829		4.50	5.50	8.00	12.00	17.50	100.00
1855 slanting 5's.............		4.50	5.50	8.00	12.00	17.50	100.00
1855 slanting 5's, knob on ear..		8.00	10.00	13.00	30.00	45.00	200.00
1856 upright 5......	2,690,463	4.50	5.50	8.00	12.00	17.50	100.00
1856 slanting 5.....		4.50	5.50	8.00	12.00	17.50	100.00

1857
Small Date

1857
Large Date

1857 small date......	333,456	29.00	37.00	45.00	60.00	80.00	200.00
1857 large date.......		23.50	29.00	37.00	47.00	70.00	200.00

BIBLIOGRAPHY

Sheldon, Wm. H. *Penny Whimsy (1793-1814)*. New York, 1958.
Newcomb, H. R. *United States Copper Cents 1816-1857*. New York, 1944.

SMALL CENTS
FLYING EAGLE TYPE 1856-1858

The Act of February 21, 1857 provided for the coinage of the small cent, and made uncurrent the coins of other countries, particularly the Spanish and Mexican dollars. The new cents weighed 72 grains. Composition, 88% copper, 12% nickel.

The 1856 Eagle Cent was not an authorized mint issue, as the law governing the new size coin was enacted after the date of issue. It is believed that about 1,000 of these pieces were struck. They are properly referred to as patterns.

Collectors are advised to inspect any 1856 Flying Eagle cent carefully.

A few tests will aid in establishing genuineness of this cent, as follows: If the lower half is thick, it is probably an altered 1858. A magnifying glass will often reveal poor workmanship.

The figure 5 slants slightly to the right on a genuine 1856. The vertical bar points to the center of the ball just beneath. On the 1858, this bar points *outside* the ball.

The 1858 cent is found in two major varieties. The A and M in the word AMERICA are joined in the large letter variety, and separated in the small letter variety. The reverse design of the eagle cents is dominated by a wreath of corn, wheat, cotton and tobacco.

GOOD—*All details worn, but readable.*
VERY GOOD—*Feather details and eye of eagle are evident, but worn.*
FINE—*Eagle head details and feather tips sharp.*
EXTRA FINE—*Slight wear, all details sharp.*

Designer James B. Longacre; weight 4.67 grams; composition: .880 copper, .120 nickel; diameter 19 mm; plain edge. All coined at Philadelphia Mint.

| 1858, 8 over 7 | 1858 Large letters | 1858 Small letters |

Quan. Minted

1856 . . . . *est. 1,000*
1857 17,450,000
1858 lg. letters . . . . *(80)* ⎫
1858 sm. letters . . . . *(200)* ⎬ 24,600,000
⎭

	Good	V.G.	Fine	V.F.	E.F.	Unc.	Proof
1856	$650.00	$825.00	$1,000	$1,200	$1,400	$2,100	$2,600
1857	5.00	6.25	9.00	15.00	27.50	200.00	2,300
1858 lg. let . .	5.50	7.00	10.00	17.50	32.50	200.00	2,300
1858, 8 over 7, lg. let .				250.00	500.00	1,000	
1858 sm. let .	5.50	7.00	10.00	17.50	32.50	200.00	2,300

SMALL CENTS
INDIAN HEAD TYPE 1859-1909

The small cent was redesigned in 1859, and a representation of an Indian girl was adopted as the obverse device. The 1859 reverse was also changed to represent a laurel wreath. In 1860 the reverse only was modified to display an oak wreath with a small shield at the top. The weight and composition of the coin was not changed.

Designer James B. Longacre; weight 4.67 grams; composition: .880 copper, .120 nickel; diameter 19 mm; plain edge. All coined at Philadelphia Mint.

GOOD—*No LIBERTY visible.*

VERY GOOD—*At least half of LIBERTY readable.*

FINE—*LIBERTY completely visible.*

VERY FINE—*Slight but even wear on LIBERTY.*

EXTRA FINE—*LIBERTY sharp. All other details sharp. Only slight wear on ribbon end.*

Without shield at top of wreath 1859 only

With shield on reverse 1860 to 1909

Variety 1 — Copper-nickel, laurel wreath reverse 1859

	Quan. Minted	Good	V.G.	Fine	V.F.	E.F.	Unc.	Proof
1859	36,400,000	$3.00	$4.25	$8.25	$14.00	$28.00	$175.00	$650.00

Variety 2 — Copper-nickel, oak wreath with shield 1860-1864

1860 *(1,000)*	20,566,000	2.50	3.50	6.50	10.00	20.00	65.00	460.00
1861 *(1,000)*	10,100,000	6.50	8.50	13.00	17.00	25.00	85.00	525.00
1862 *(550)*	28,075,000	2.00	2.75	4.25	6.00	9.50	35.00	325.00
1863 *(460)*	49,840,000	2.00	2.75	4.25	6.00	9.50	35.00	300.00
1864 *(300)*	13,740,000	4.25	6.00	10.00	14.00	21.00	52.50	600.00

Variety 3 — Bronze 1864-1909

During the year 1864 the alloy of the cent was changed to 95 per cent copper and five per cent tin and zinc. The weight was reduced to 48 grains, resulting in a thinner coin than the "White" Cents. The design remained unchanged. The first 1864 bronze cents did not have the designer's initial L on the bonnet ribbon. Later in the year the letter appeared on only a small quantity. The initial appeared on all dates of Indian Cents thereafter. Consult the illustration details.

Indian Head Cent With "L"

If the coin is turned slightly (so Indian faces observer) the highlighted details of the "L" will appear to better advantage. The point of the bust is pointed on the variety with "L"; rounded without "L." The "L" is the initial of the engraver, Longacre.

SMALL CENTS

Designer James B. Longacre; weight 3.11 grams; composition: .950 copper, .050 tin and zinc; diameter 19 mm; plain edge; mints: Philadelphia, San Francisco.

	Quan. Minted	Good	V.G.	Fine	V.F.	E.F.	Unc.	Proof
1864								
All kinds..39,233,714								
1864 no L........*(150)*		$1.75	$3.25	$6.50	$11.00	$18.00	$52.50	$775.00
1864 L must show..*(20)*		11.00	22.00	40.00	60.00	80.00	225.00	——
1865..*(500)* 35,429,286		1.85	3.00	5.00	8.50	15.00	40.00	325.00
1866..*(725)* 9,826,500		7.50	12.50	22.50	37.50	55.00	125.00	325.00
1867..*(625)* 9,821,000		7.50	12.50	22.50	37.50	55.00	125.00	325.00
1868..*(600)* 10,266,500		7.50	12.50	22.50	37.50	55.00	125.00	325.00

1869, 9 over 8   Closed 3   Open 3

	Good	V.G.	Fine	V.F.	E.F.	Unc.	Proof
*1869 over 8. } 6,420,000	40.00	55.00	80.00	150.00	250.00	700.00	
1869...*(600)*	13.00	22.00	47.50	72.50	105.00	280.00	535.00
1870 *(1,000)* 5,275,000	12.00	20.00	36.00	52.50	70.00	150.00	350.00
1871..*(960)* 3,929,500	15.00	25.00	45.00	60.00	85.00	185.00	410.00
1872..*(950)* 4,042,000	18.00	30.00	52.50	75.00	105.00	250.00	485.00
1873 All kinds 11,676,500							
1873 Closed 3 *(1,100)*..	4.00	7.00	12.50	20.00	35.00	80.00	265.00
1873 Open 3..........	4.00	7.00	12.50	20.00	35.00	80.00	
1874..*(700)* 14,187,500	3.75	6.00	12.50	20.00	32.50	80.00	235.00
1875..*(700)* 13,528,000	3.75	6.00	12.50	20.00	32.50	80.00	235.00
1876 *(1,150)* 7,944,000	6.00	9.00	17.50	27.50	40.00	87.50	200.00
1877..*(510)* 852,500	80.00	115.00	175.00	250.00	400.00	715.00	1,000
1878 *(2,350)* 5,799,850	6.50	9.50	18.50	27.50	40.00	87.50	150.00
1879 *(3,200)* 16,231,200	1.50	2.35	5.00	7.25	12.50	35.00	70.00
1880 *(3,955)* 38,964,955	.90	1.35	3.25	5.00	8.00	28.00	52.50
1881 *(3,575)* 39,211,575	.90	1.35	3.25	5.00	8.00	28.00	52.50
1882 *(3,100)* 38,581,100	.90	1.35	3.25	5.00	8.00	28.00	52.50
1883 *(6,609)* 45,598,109	.80	1.25	3.00	4.50	7.50	25.00	50.00
1884 *(3,942)* 23,261,742	1.50	2.50	4.75	7.50	11.00	35.00	60.00
1885 *(3,790)* 11,765,384	3.25	5.00	9.00	14.00	22.50	50.00	80.00
1886 All kinds (4,290)							
......17,654,290							
1886, 1st head........	1.85	2.85	5.25	9.25	15.00	40.00	67.50

On coins 1859-1886 the last feather of the headdress points between I and C of AMERICA; from mid-1886 it points between C and A.

	Good	V.G.	Fine	V.F.	E.F.	Unc.	Proof
1886, 2nd head........	1.85	2.85	5.25	9.25	15.00	40.00	67.50
1887 *(2,960)* 45,226,483	.45	.80	1.90	3.25	5.75	22.00	47.50

1888, last 8 over 7

	Good	V.G.	Fine	V.F.	E.F.	Unc.	Proof
1888 over 7 } 37,494,414				——	——	——	
1888 (4,582)	.45	.85	2.00	3.35	6.00	22.00	45.00

*Do not confuse with recut variety of 1869.

[81]

SMALL CENTS

	Quan. Minted	Good	V.G.	Fine	V.F.	E.F.	Unc.	Proof
1889 (3,336)	48,869,361	$ .40	$ .80	$2.00	$3.10	$5.75	$22.00	$47.50
1890 (2,740)	57,182,854	.40	.80	1.85	3.00	5.50	21.00	47.50
1891 (2,350)	47,072,350	.40	.80	1.85	3.00	5.50	21.00	47.50
1892 (2,745)	37,649,832	.45	.85	2.00	3.10	5.75	22.00	50.00
1893 (2,195)	46,642,195	.40	.80	1.85	3.00	5.25	22.00	47.50
1894 (2,632)	16,752,132	1.50	3.50	6.25	9.00	14.50	37.00	70.00
1895 (2,062)	38,343,636	.45	.75	1.50	2.65	5.00	21.00	48.50
1896 (1,862)	39,057,293	.45	.75	1.75	2.75	5.00	21.00	50.00
1897 (1,938)	50,466,330	.45	.70	1.50	2.40	4.50	20.00	49.00
1898 (1,795)	49,823,079	.45	.70	1.50	2.40	4.50	20.00	49.00
1899 (2,031)	53,600,031	.45	.65	1.25	2.10	4.00	20.00	49.00
1900 (2,262)	66,833,764	.45	.55	1.00	1.75	4.00	20.00	47.50
1901 (1,985)	79,611,143	.45	.55	1.00	1.75	4.00	17.00	47.50
1902 (2,018)	87,376,722	.45	.55	1.00	1.75	4.00	17.00	47.50
1903 (1,790)	85,094,493	.45	.55	1.00	1.75	4.00	17.00	47.50
1904 (1,817)	61,328,015	.45	.55	1.00	1.75	4.00	17.00	47.50
1905 (2,152)	80,719,163	.45	.55	1.00	1.75	4.00	17.00	47.50
1906 (1,725)	96,022,255	.45	.55	1.00	1.75	4.00	17.00	47.50
1907 (1,475)	108,138,618	.45	.55	1.00	1.75	4.00	17.00	47.50

Location of mint
mark S on reverse
of Indian cent (1908
and 1909 only).

1908 (1,620)	32,327,987	.45	.60	1.10	1.90	4.25	17.00	52.50
1908S	1,115,000	15.00	17.50	22.00	26.00	37.50	95.00	
1909 (2,175)	14,370,645	.75	1.10	1.75	2.60	5.00	20.00	60.00
1909S	309,000	55.00	62.50	75.00	90.00	135.00	235.00	

Select brilliant Unc. and Proof small cents command higher prices.

LINCOLN TYPE, WHEAT EARS REVERSE 1909-1958

Victor D. Brenner designed this cent which was issued to commemorate the
hundredth anniversary of Lincoln's birth. The designer's initials VDB appear
on a limited quantity of cents of 1909. The San Francisco mint produced the
smallest issue before the initials were removed, creating the scarcest though not
the highest priced Lincoln cent. The initials were restored, in 1918, to the
obverse side as illustrated on page 84. This type cent was the first to have
the motto IN GOD WE TRUST.

Designer Victor D. Brenner; weight 3.11 grams; composition: .950 copper, .050 tin and
zinc; diameter 19 mm; plain edge; mints: Philadelphia, Denver, San Francisco.

Location of mint
mark S or D on
obverse of Lin-
coln cent.

SMALL CENTS

GOOD—*Date worn but apparent. Lines in wheat ears missing. Full rims.*

VERY GOOD—*Half of lines show in upper wheat ears.*

FINE—*Wheat lines worn but visible.*

VERY FINE—*Cheek and jaw bones worn but separated. No worn spots on wheat ears.*

EXTRA FINE—*Slight wear. All details sharp.*

Select brilliant uncirculated cents command higher prices.

Cents with well-struck mint marks are also worth more.

Location of
Designer's
initials V. D. B.
on 1909 only

No
V. D. B.
on
Reverse
1909-
1958

Variety 1 — Bronze 1909-1942

	Quan. Minted	Good	V.G.	Fine	V.F.	E.F.	Unc.	Matte Proof
1909 V.D.B.								
(420)	27,995,000	$1.00	$1.25	$1.50	$1.80	$2.25	$6.00	$365.00
1909S, V.D.B.	484,000	87.50	100.00	110.00	120.00	130.00	200.00	
1909 (2,198)	72,702,618	.20	.30	.45	.70	1.35	5.50	80.00
1909S	1,825,000	18.50	21.50	25.00	30.00	40.00	65.00	
1910 (2,405)	146,801,218	.20	.30	.45	.70	1.35	6.50	87.50
1910S	6,045,000	3.25	3.75	4.50	6.50	10.00	40.00	
1911 (1,733)	101,177,787	.20	.30	.45	.85	1.75	7.50	90.00
1911D	12,672,000	1.50	2.00	3.25	6.00	10.00	32.00	
1911S	4,026,000	6.75	8.00	9.25	12.50	18.00	50.00	
1912 (2,145)	68,153,060	.20	.30	.50	1.40	2.50	11.00	97.50
1912D	10,411,000	1.35	2.25	4.00	8.00	15.00	45.00	
1912S	4,431,000	4.00	4.75	6.25	9.50	16.50	45.00	
1913 (2,848)	76,532,352	.15	.25	.45	1.25	2.25	11.00	100.00
1913D	15,804,000	.85	1.25	2.10	5.00	10.00	40.00	
1913S	6,101,000	2.75	3.50	4.50	6.50	11.00	40.00	
1914 (1,365)	75,238,432	.20	.35	.75	2.00	4.50	24.00	190.00
1914D*	1,193,000	30.00	35.00	45.00	75.00	155.00	560.00	
1914S	4,137,000	3.75	4.50	5.50	8.50	15.00	65.00	
1915 (1,150)	29,092,120	.40	.80	3.25	6.75	14.00	60.00	280.00
1915D	22,050,000	.45	.75	1.25	2.50	6.25	23.50	
1915S	4,833,000	3.00	3.60	4.50	7.00	11.00	42.00	
1916 (1,050)	131,833,677	.10	.20	.35	.75	1.50	7.25	300.00
1916D	35,956,000	.20	.35	.70	1.60	3.85	19.00	
1916S	22,510,000	.40	.55	.90	1.75	4.25	24.00	
1917	196,429,785	.10	.20	.30	.70	1.40	6.75	
1917D	55,120,000	.15	.25	.55	1.65	4.50	24.00	
1917S	32,620,000	.20	.30	.55	1.65	4.50	25.00	

*Beware of altered date or mint mark. No VDB on shoulder of genuine 1914D cent.

SMALL CENTS

Designer's
initials
restored
starting 1918

	Quan. Minted	Good	V.G.	Fine	V.F.	E.F.	Unc.	Proof
1918	288,104,634	$ .10	$ .15	$ .30	$ .65	$1.50	$8.25	
1918D	47,830,000	.15	.25	.55	1.60	4.25	26.00	
1918S	34,680,000	.15	.25	.55	1.60	4.40	28.00	
1919	392,021,000	.10	.15	.25	.55	1.40	7.00	
1919D	57,154,000	.10	.20	.40	1.25	3.00	16.50	
1919S	139,760,000	.10	.20	.40	1.10	3.15	17.50	
1920	310,165,000	.10	.15	.25	.55	1.20	6.50	
1920D	49,280,000	.15	.20	.45	1.25	4.25	30.00	
1920S	46,220,000	.15	.20	.45	1.40	4.50	30.00	
1921	39,157,000	.15	.25	.50	1.10	3.80	21.00	
1921S	15,274,000	.55	.90	1.60	4.25	12.00	155.00	
1922D }	7,160,000	2.50	3.00	4.25	7.00	11.25	47.50	
1922 Plain * }		30.00	40.00	67.50	95.00	175.00	850.00	
1923	74,723,000	.10	.15	.30	.70	1.60	7.00	
1923S	8,700,000	.90	1.40	2.10	5.50	12.50	215.00	
1924	75,178,000	.10	.15	.25	.60	1.60	13.00	
1924D	2,520,000	7.75	10.00	13.50	18.75	33.00	180.00	
1924S	11,696,000	.50	.65	1.25	3.50	8.00	90.00	
1925	139,949,000	.10	.15	.25	.50	1.25	5.75	
1925D	22,580,000	.20	.30	.45	1.00	3.00	25.00	
1925S	26,380,000	.20	.30	.50	1.10	3.50	27.50	
1926	157,088,000	.10	.15	.25	.50	1.10	5.50	
1926D	28,020,000	.15	.25	.45	.95	2.50	24.00	
1926S	4,550,000	2.75	3.75	4.75	6.50	12.50	100.00	
1927	144,440,000	.10	.15	.25	.50	1.10	5.25	
1927D	27,170,000	.15	.20	.35	.75	2.25	17.00	
1927S	14,276,000	.30	.40	.85	1.10	3.00	36.00	
1928	134,116,000	.10	.15	.25	.50	1.10	5.00	
1928D	31,170,000	.15	.25	.35	.60	1.40	13.00	
1928S†	17,266,000	.25	.35	.60	1.10	2.40	23.00	
1929	185,262,000	.10	.15	.25	.40	.90	4.00	
1929D	41,730,000	.10	.15	.25	.45	1.00	7.00	
1929S	50,148,000	.10	.15	.25	.45	.90	4.50	
1930	157,415,000	.10	.15	.25	.40	.85	3.00	
1930D	40,100,000	.10	.15	.25	.45	.90	6.00	
1930S	24,286,000	.10	.15	.25	.45	.90	5.25	
1931	19,396,000	.25	.35	.45	.85	1.80	13.50	
1931D	4,480,000	2.50	3.00	3.50	4.50	7.50	40.00	
1931S	866,000	20.00	22.50	25.00	27.50	30.00	45.00	
1932	9,062,000	.65	1.00	1.15	1.60	2.25	10.00	
1932D	10,500,000	.55	.75	1.10	1.60	2.25	10.00	
1933	14,360,000	.50	.60	.70	.80	1.50	14.00	
1933D	6,200,000	2.00	2.25	2.50	3.25	4.00	16.50	
1934	219,080,000		.10	.15	.30	.45	2.25	
1934D	28,446,000	.15	.25	.35	.55	.90	7.50	
1935	245,388,000		.10	.15	.20	.40	1.00	

*The 1922 without D caused by defective die. Beware removed mint mark.
†Large and small mint mark varieties, see page 59.

SMALL CENTS

	Quan. Minted	Good	V.G.	Fine	V.F.	E.F.	Unc.	Proof
1935D	47,000,000		$ .10	$ .15	$ .25	$ .45	$1.60	
1935S	38,702,000		.10	.25	.40	.65	2.50	
1936	(5,569)309,637,569			.10	.15	.30	.90	$57.50
1936D	40,620,000		.10	.20	.30	.45	1.30	
1936S	29,130,000		.10	.25	.40	.55	1.50	
1937	(9,320)309,179,320			.10	.15	.30	.85	30.00
1937D	50,430,000		.10	.15	.25	.35	.90	
1937S	34,500,000		.10	.20	.30	.40	1.00	
1938	(14,734)156,696,734		.10	.15	.20	.30	.90	12.50
1938D	20,010,000	$ .15	.20	.30	.45	.65	1.65	
1938S	15,180,000	.30	.40	.60	.70	.95	2.10	
1939	(13,520)316,479,520			.10	.15	.25	.60	12.50
1939D	15,160,000	.35	.45	.60	.70	1.10	3.00	
1939S	52,070,000	.10	.15	.20	.30	.45	.80	
1940	(15,872)586,825,872				.10	.20	.45	9.00
1940D	81,390,000			.10	.15	.25	.75	
1940S	112,940,000			.10	.15	.25	.50	
1941	(21,100)887,039,100				.10	.20	.50	8.00
1941D	128,700,000				.10	.25	1.00	
1941S*	92,360,000			.10	.15	.30	1.00	
1942	(32,600)657,828,600				.10	.20	.30	7.50
1942D	206,698,000				.10	.20	.35	
1942S	85,590,000	.10	.15	.25	.30	.45	3.00	

*Large and small mint mark varieties, see page 59.

Variety 2 — Zinc-coated steel 1943 only

Owing to a shortage of copper during the critical war year 1943 the Treasury Department resorted to the use of zinc coated steel for our cents. No bronze cents were officially issued in 1943. A few specimens struck on bronze planchets by error are known to exist. Through a similar error, a few of the 1944 cents were struck on steel planchets.

1943 — Weight 2.70 grams; composition: steel, coated with zinc; diameter 19 mm; plain edge.

		V.F.	E.F.	Unc.	Proof
1943	684,628,670	.15	.25	.30	.40
1943D	217,660,000	.15	.25	.30	.60
1943S	191,550,000	.30	.45	.55	.85

Variety 1 resumed 1944-1958

Cartridge cases were salvaged for coinage of 1944 and 1945. Although the color was slightly different for uncirculated specimens, the coins proved satisfactory in every respect. The original alloy of 1864-1942 was resumed in 1946.

1944-1945 — Weight 3.11 grams; composition: .950 copper, .050 zinc; diameter 19 mm; plain edge.

	Quan. Minted	V.F.	E.F.	Unc.	Proof
1944	1,435,400,000	$ .10	$ .20	$ .25	
1944D	430,578,000	.10	.15	.25	
1944S	282,760,000	.10	.20	.30	
1945	1,040,515,000	.10	.15	.25	
1945D	226,268,000	.10	.20	.30	
1945S	181,770,000	.10	.20	.30	
1946	991,655,000	.10	.15	.20	
1946D	315,690,000	.10	.20	.25	
1946S	198,100,000	.10	.20	.30	
1947	190,555,000	.10	.20	.40	

SMALL CENTS

	Quan. Minted	V.F.	E.F.	Unc.	Proof
1947D	194,750,000	$ .10	$ .20	$ .30	
1947S	99,000,000	.15	.25	.60	
1948	317,570,000	.10	.20	.30	
1948D	172,637,500	.10	.20	.30	
1948S	81,735,000	.15	.30	.80	
1949	217,775,000	.10	.20	.40	
1949D	153,132,500	.10	.20	.35	
1949S	64,290,000	.20	.30	1.00	
1950 ....(51,386)	272,686,386	.10	.20	.40	$18.50
1950D	334,950,000	.10	.20	.25	
1950S	118,505,000	.10	.25	.50	
1951 ....(57,500)	284,633,500	.10	.15	.50	9.00
1951D	625,355,000	.10	.15	.30	
1951S	136,010,000	.15	.25	.60	
1952 ....(81,980)	186,856,980	....	.15	.45	6.00
1952D	746,130,000	....	.15	.20	
1952S	137,800,004	....	.20	.45	
1953 ....(128,800)	256,883,800	....	.10	.30	5.50
1953D	700,515,000	....	.10	.20	
1953S	181,835,000	....	.15	.30	
1954 ....(233,300)	71,873,350	.25	.35	.55	4.00
1954D	251,552,500	....	.10	.20	
1954S	96,190,000	....	.20	.35	

1955
doubled die
error

Enlarged detail of
1972 doubled die error

These coins were made from improperly prepared dies that show full doubled outline of date and legend. Do not confuse with less valuable pieces showing only minor traces of doubling.

	Quan. Minted	V.F.	E.F.	Unc.	Proof
1955 Doubled die obv.	} 330,958,200	185.00	235.00	400.00	
1955 ....(378,200)			.10	.20	3.00
1955D	563,257,500	....		.20	
1955S	44,610,000	.35	.45	.55	
1956 ....(669,384)	421,414,384	....		.15	2.00
1956D	1,098,201,100			.10	
1957 ....(1,247,952)	283,787,952	....		.10	1.25
1957D	1,051,342,000	....		.10	
1958 ....(875,652)	253,400,652	....		.15	1.50
1958D	800,953,300	....		.10	

LINCOLN TYPE, MEMORIAL REVERSE 1959 TO DATE

Frank Gasparro designed the Lincoln Memorial reverse which was introduced in 1959 on the 150th anniversary of Lincoln's birth.

1959-1961 — Designer: Obv. V. D. Brenner, Rev. Frank Gasparro; weight 3.11 grams; composition: .950 copper, .050 tin and zinc; diameter 19 mm; plain edge; mints: Philadelphia, Denver, San Francisco. 1962-   Composition changed to: .950 copper, .050 zinc.

SMALL CENTS

	Quan. Minted		Unc.	Proof
1959	.... (1,149,291) 610,864,291		$ .10	$1.35
1959D	.... 1,279,760,000		.10	

Small Date	Large Date	Small Date Numbers aligned at top	Large Date Low 7 in date

			Unc.	Proof
1960 Large date	⎫(1,691,602) 588,096,602		.10	1.00
1960 Sm. date	⎭		3.75	17.00
1960D Large date	........⎫1,580,884,000		.10	
1960D Small date	........⎭		.30	
1961	.... (3,028,244) 756,373,244		.10	1.00
1961D	.... 1,753,266,700		.10	

Starting in 1962 the composition of the cent was changed to 95% copper and 5% zinc. In 1969 the dies were modified to strengthen the design, and Lincoln's head was made slightly smaller. In 1973 dies were further modified and engraver's initials **FG** made larger.

	Unc.	Proof		Unc.	Proof
1962 (3,218,019)			1970 1,898,315,000	$ .05	
...... 609,263,019	$ .10	$1.00	1970D 2,891,438,900	.05	
1962D 1,793,148,400	.10		1970S (2,632,810)		
1963 (3,075,645)			 693,192,814		
...... 757,185,645	.10	1.00	1970S Sm. date	1.25	19.00
1963D 1,774,020,400	.10		1970S Lg. date (low 7)..	.10	.40
1964 (3,950,762)			1971 1,919,490,000	.05	
..... 2,652,525,762	.05	.85	1971D 2,911,045,600	.05	
1964D 3,799,071,500	.05		1971S (3,224,138)		
1965 1,497,224,900	.05		 528,354,192	.05	.40
1966 2,188,147,783	.05		1972 Doubled die obv.*	75.00	
1967 3,048,667,100	.05		1972 2,933,255,000	.05	
1968 1,707,880,970	.05		1972D 2,665,071,400	.05	
1968D 2,886,269,600	.05		1972S (3,267,667)		
1968S (3,041,509)			 380,200,104	.05	.50
...... 261,311,510	.10	.40	1973	.05	
1969 1,136,910,000	.05		1973D	.05	
1969D 4,002,832,200	.05		1973S	.05	.50
1969S (2,934,631)					
...... 547,309,631	.10	.40	*See photo and note on page 86.		

TWO-CENT PIECES
Issued 1864-1873

The Act of April 22, 1864, which changed the weight and composition of the cent, included a provision for the bronze two-cent piece. The weight was specified as 96 grains, the alloy being the same as for the cent.

The two-cent piece is one of the short-lived issues of United States coinage. The motto "In God We Trust" appeared for the first time. Its presence on the new coin was due largely to the increased religious sentiment during the Civil War crisis.

There are two varieties for the first year of issue, 1864: the small motto and

TWO-CENT PIECES

the large motto. The differences are explained in the illustrations below. The small motto variety of 1864 is scarce.

| 1864 Small Motto | 1864 Large Motto |

Details explain the differences in these two well-known varieties. On the obverse the D in God is narrow on the large motto. The stem to the leaf shows plainly on the small motto variety. There is no stem on the large motto coin.

The first T in TRUST touches ribbon crease at left on the small motto variety; there is a $\frac{1}{32}''$ gap on the large motto variety.

It will be noted that the shield device is very similar to the nickel five-cent piece introduced in 1866.

Designer James B. Longacre; weight 6.22 grams; composition: .950 copper, .050 tin and zinc; diameter 23 mm; plain edge. All coined at Philadelphia Mint.

Select uncirculated and proof coins command higher prices.

GOOD—*At least IN GOD visible.*
VERY GOOD—*WE weakly visible.*
FINE—*Complete motto visible. WE weak.*
EXTRA FINE—*WE is bold.*

	Quan. Minted	Good	V.G.	Fine	E.F.	Unc.	Proof
1864 Sm. motto	} 19,847,500	$36.00	$45.00	$62.50	$100.00	$275.00	——
1864 Lg. motto		3.00	4.00	6.00	13.00	57.00	220.00
1865	13,640,000	3.00	4.00	6.00	13.00	57.00	140.00
1866	3,177,000	3.00	4.00	6.50	14.00	60.00	130.00
1867	2,938,750	3.00	4.00	6.50	14.00	60.00	130.00
1868	2,803,750	3.00	4.00	6.50	14.00	60.00	135.00
1869, 9 over 8	} 1,546,500			——		——	
1869		3.75	4.50	9.00	17.00	65.00	135.00
1870	861,250	5.00	6.50	10.00	19.00	68.00	150.00
1871	721,250	6.00	8.00	12.50	27.00	77.50	155.00
1872	65,000	35.00	45.00	57.50	77.50	140.00	250.00
1873 Closed 3. Proofs only (600). (See illustration on page 81)							600.00
1873 Open 3. Restrike (Est. 500)							650.00

THREE-CENT PIECES (NICKEL)
Issued 1865-1889

Designer James B. Longacre; weight 1.94 grams; composition: .750 copper, .250 nickel; diameter 17.9 mm; plain edge. All coined at Philadelphia Mint.

GOOD—*Date and legends complete though worn. III smooth.*
VERY GOOD—*III is half worn. Rims complete.*
FINE—*Hair curls well defined.*
EXTRA FINE—*Slight, even wear.*

THREE-CENT PIECES (NICKEL)

	Quan. Minted	Good	V.G.	Fine	E.F.	Unc.	Proof
1865.	11,382,000	$3.00	$3.50	$4.50	$8.00	$32.50	$500.00
1866.	4,801,000	3.00	3.50	4.50	8.00	32.50	150.00
1867.	3,915,000	3.00	3.50	4.50	8.00	32.50	72.50
1868.	3,252,000	3.00	3.50	4.50	8.00	32.50	75.00
1869.	1,604,000	3.00	3.75	4.75	9.00	35.00	75.00
1870.	1,335,000	3.50	4.00	5.00	9.00	35.00	75.00
1871.	604,000	4.00	5.00	6.00	12.00	37.00	75.00
1872.	862,000	4.00	5.00	6.00	12.00	37.00	75.00
1873 All kinds.	1,173,000						
1873 Closed 3 (1,100).		4.00	5.00	6.00	12.00	35.00	60.00
1873 Open 3.		4.00	5.00	6.00	12.00	35.00	
1874.	790,000	4.00	5.00	6.00	13.00	37.00	75.00
1875.	228,000	6.00	7.50	9.50	18.00	47.00	77.50
1876.	162,000	6.00	7.50	9.50	18.00	47.00	75.00
1877 (Proofs Only).							650.00
1878. . . . . (2,350)	2,350						195.00
1879. . . . . (3,200)	41,200	8.50	10.50	14.00	20.00	52.50	75.00
1880. . . . . (3,955)	24,955	8.50	10.50	14.00	20.00	52.50	75.00
1881. . . . . (3,575)	1,080,575	3.00	3.50	4.50	8.00	32.50	55.00
1882. . . . . (3,100)	25,300	9.50	12.00	15.00	20.00	52.50	60.00
1883. . . . . (6,609)	10,609	11.50	15.00	18.00	21.00	57.50	65.00
1884. . . . . (3,942)	5,642	13.00	17.50	21.50	27.50	70.00	70.00
1885. . . . . (3,790)	4,790	13.00	17.50	21.50	30.00	85.00	85.00
1886. . . . . (4,290)	4,290						90.00
1887, 7 over 6.							215.00
1887 All K(2,960)	7,961	21.00	27.50	35.00	47.50	120.00	200.00
1888. . . . . (4,582)	41,083	9.00	11.50	15.00	20.00	50.00	62.50
1889. . . . . (3,436)	21,561	9.00	11.50	15.00	20.00	50.00	62.50

NICKEL FIVE-CENT PIECES
SHIELD TYPE 1866-1883

The shield type nickel was made possible by the act of May 16, 1866. Its weight was set at 77-16/100 grains with the same composition as the nickel three-cent piece which was authorized in 1865. In 1866 the coin was designed with rays between the stars on the reverse. Some of the pieces minted in 1867 have the same details, but later the rays were eliminated creating two varieties for that year. There was no further change in the type until it was replaced by the Liberty head device in 1883. Proofs only were struck in 1877 and 1878.

Designer James B. Longacre; weight 5 grams; composition: .750 copper, .250 nickel; diameter 20.5 mm; plain edge. All coined at Philadelphia Mint.

GOOD—All letters in motto readable.

VERY GOOD—Motto stands out clearly. Rims worn slightly but even. Part of shield lines visible.

FINE—Half of each olive leaf is smooth.

EXTRA FINE—Leaf tips show slight wear. Cross over shield slightly worn.

Rays Between Stars 1866-1867

		Good	V.G.	Fine	E.F.	Unc.	Proof
1866.	14,742,500	6.50	95.0	16.50	41.50	150.00	1,200
1867 Rays. Both varieties. . . .	30,909,500	8.00	13.50	23.50	57.50	172.50	3,700

NICKEL FIVE-CENT PIECES

Without Rays 1867-1883

	Quan. Minted	Good	V.G.	Fine	E.F.	Unc.	Proof
1867 No rays.............		$3.00	$4.00	$5.50	$12.50	$47.50	$82.50
1868............28,817,000		3.00	4.00	5.50	12.50	47.50	82.50
1869............16,395,000		3.50	4.50	6.50	16.00	50.00	90.00
1870............4,806,000		4.50	6.50	9.00	18.50	52.50	90.00
1871..............561,000		32.50	40.00	50.00	90.00	200.00	300.00
1872............6,036,000		4.50	6.50	9.00	18.50	52.50	85.00
1873 All kinds.....4,550,000							
1873 Closed 3 (1,100).......		4.75	6.75	9.00	19.50	52.50	77.50
1873 Open 3..............		4.75	6.75	9.00	19.50	52.50	
1874............3,538,000		6.50	8.75	12.50	22.00	55.00	95.00
1875............2,097,000		12.00	16.00	22.00	45.00	100.00	152.50
1876............2,530,000		7.25	10.00	13.00	24.00	55.00	80.00
1877 Est. Issued							
......(500)	500						825.00
1878.....(2,350)	2,350						235.00
1879.....(3,200)	29,100	17.00	20.00	26.00	41.00	82.00	100.00
1880.....(3,955)	19,955	20.00	24.00	28.00	44.00	90.00	100.00
1881.....(3,575)	72,375	15.00	16.50	23.50	40.00	75.00	100.00
1882.....(3,100) 11,476,600		3.00	4.00	5.50	12.50	47.50	80.00
1883.....(5,419)		3.50	4.50	6.00	13.50	47.50	80.00
1883, 3 over 2...	1,456,919		24.00	35.00	75.00	185.00	

1883
3 over 2

LIBERTY HEAD TYPE 1883-1913

In 1883 the type was changed to the familiar "Liberty head." This type first appeared without the word CENTS on the coin, merely a large letter "V." These "centless" coins were goldplated and passed for five dollars. Later in that year the word CENTS was added.

Five 1913 Liberty head nickels were originally owned by Col. Green (son of the famous Hetty Green). These have since been dispersed and are now held in the collections of several individuals. These were not a regular issue and were never placed in circulation.

Designer Charles E. Barber; weight 5 grams; composition: .750 copper, .250 nickel; diameter 21.2 mm; plain edge; mints: Philadelphia, Denver, San Francisco.

GOOD—*No details in head. LIBERTY obliterated.*

VERY GOOD—*At least 3 letters in LIBERTY readable.*

FINE—*All letters in LIBERTY show.*

EXTRA FINE—*LIBERTY sharp. Corn grains at bottom of wreath show, on reverse.*

NICKEL FIVE-CENT PIECES

Without CENTS 1883

	Quan. Minted	Good	V.G.	Fine	E.F.	Unc.	Proof
1883 Without CENTS							
.....(5,219)	5,479,519	$1.35	$1.75	$2.75	$5.75	$17.50	$65.00

With CENTS 1883-1913   Location of mint mark

1883 With CENTS

		Good	V.G.	Fine	E.F.	Unc.	Proof
.....(6,783)	16,032,983	4.50	6.00	8.50	15.00	42.50	65.00
1884.....(3,942)	11,273,942	4.50	6.50	10.00	17.50	45.00	65.00
1885.....(3,790)	1,476,490	55.00	70.00	95.00	150.00	250.00	340.00
1886.....(4,290)	3,330,290	27.50	37.50	50.00	75.00	125.00	180.00
1887.....(2,960)	15,263,652	2.75	3.75	6.00	12.00	40.00	62.50
1888.....(4,582)	10,720,483	4.50	7.25	11.00	20.00	40.00	65.00
1889.....(3,336)	15,881,361	2.75	3.75	5.50	11.00	40.00	60.00
1890.....(2,740)	16,259,272	3.75	4.75	7.00	15.00	40.00	60.00
1891.....(2,350)	16,834,350	2.75	3.75	6.00	11.00	40.00	60.00
1892.....(2,745)	11,699,642	3.00	4.00	6.25	12.00	40.00	60.00
1893.....(2,195)	13,370,195	2.50	3.75	5.50	11.00	40.00	60.00
1894.....(2,632)	5,413,132	4.50	6.50	10.00	16.50	50.00	75.00
1895.....(2,062)	9,979,884	1.75	3.00	5.25	10.00	40.00	65.00
1896.....(1,862)	8,842,920	2.25	4.25	8.50	18.50	55.00	115.00
1897.....(1,938)	20,428,735	1.25	2.00	3.50	8.00	35.00	60.00
1898.....(1,795)	12,532,087	1.25	2.00	3.50	8.00	35.00	60.00
1899.....(2,031)	26,029,031	1.00	1.50	2.75	7.25	35.00	60.00
1900.....(2,262)	27,255,995	.60	1.25	2.25	5.75	32.50	60.00
1901.....(1,985)	26,480,213	.50	1.00	2.00	5.00	32.50	60.00
1902.....(2,018)	31,489,579	.50	1.00	2.00	5.00	32.50	60.00
1903.....(1,790)	28,006,725	.50	1.00	2.00	5.00	32.50	60.00
1904.....(1,817)	21,404,984	.50	1.00	2.00	5.00	32.50	60.00
1905.....(2,152)	29,827,276	.50	1.00	2.00	5.00	32.50	60.00
1906.....(1,725)	38,613,725	.50	1.00	2.00	5.00	32.50	60.00
1907.....(1,475)	39,214,800	.50	1.00	2.00	5.00	32.50	75.00
1908.....(1,620)	22,686,177	.50	1.00	2.00	5.00	32.50	60.00
1909.....(4,763)	11,590,526	.75	1.25	2.50	6.00	35.00	60.00
1910.....(2,405)	30,169,353	.50	1.00	2.00	5.00	32.50	60.00
1911.....(1,733)	39,559,372	.50	1.00	2.00	5.00	32.50	60.00
1912.....(2,145)	26,236,714	.50	1.00	2.00	5.00	32.50	65.00
1912D.............8,474,000		1.35	2.25	5.75	45.00	225.00	
1912S..............238,000		25.00	32.50	45.00	100.00	375.00	
1913 Liberty Hd. (5 Known)			1972 Private Sale $100,000				

[91]

NICKEL FIVE-CENT PIECES
INDIAN HEAD or BUFFALO TYPE 1913-1938

These pieces are known as Buffalo, Bison or Indian Head nickels. In the first year of issue, 1913, there were two distinct varieties, the first showing the bison on a mound, and the second with the base redesigned to a thinner straight line.

James E. Fraser designed this nickel employing three different Indians as models. His initial F is beneath the date. The bison was modeled after "Black Diamond" in the New York Zoological Gardens.

Designer James Earle Fraser; weight 5 grams; composition: .750 copper, .250 nickel; diameter 21.2 mm; plain edge; mints: Philadelphia, Denver, San Francisco.

Variety 1
FIVE CENTS
on raised
ground

GOOD—*Legends and date readable. Horn worn off.*

VERY GOOD—*Half horn shows.*

FINE—*Two-thirds horn shows. Obv. rim intact.*

VERY FINE—*Full horn shows. Indian's cheekbone worn.*

EXTRA FINE—*Full horn. Slight wear on Indian's hair ribbon.*

	Quan. Minted	Good	V.G.	Fine	V.F.	E.F.	Unc.	Matte Proof
1913 Var. 1								
(*3,034)	30,993,520	$1.15	$1.50	$2.00	$3.00	$4.50	$16.00	$215.00
1913D Var. 1	5,337,000	3.50	4.65	6.00	8.00	10.00	25.00	
1913S Var. 1	2,105,000	4.75	6.75	8.50	11.00	15.00	37.50	

*Both Varieties.

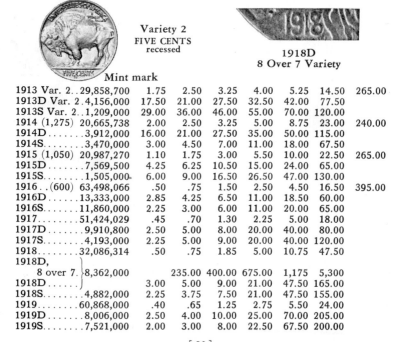

Variety 2
FIVE CENTS
recessed

Mint mark

1918D
8 Over 7 Variety

	Quan. Minted	Good	V.G.	Fine	V.F.	E.F.	Unc.	Matte Proof
1913 Var. 2	29,858,700	1.75	2.50	3.25	4.00	5.25	14.50	265.00
1913D Var. 2	4,156,000	17.50	21.00	27.50	32.50	42.00	77.50	
1913S Var. 2	1,209,000	29.00	36.00	46.00	55.00	70.00	120.00	
1914 (1,275)	20,665,738	2.00	2.50	3.25	5.00	8.75	23.00	240.00
1914D	3,912,000	16.00	21.00	27.50	35.00	50.00	115.00	
1914S	3,470,000	3.00	4.50	7.00	11.00	18.00	67.50	
1915 (1,050)	20,987,270	1.10	1.75	3.00	5.50	10.00	22.50	265.00
1915D	7,569,500	4.25	6.25	10.50	15.00	24.00	65.00	
1915S	1,505,000	6.00	9.00	16.50	26.50	47.00	130.00	
1916 (600)	63,498,066	.50	.75	1.50	2.50	4.50	16.50	395.00
1916D	13,333,000	2.85	4.25	6.50	11.00	18.50	60.00	
1916S	11,860,000	2.25	3.00	6.00	11.00	20.00	65.00	
1917	51,424,029	.45	.70	1.30	2.25	5.00	18.00	
1917D	9,910,800	2.50	5.00	8.00	20.00	40.00	80.00	
1917S	4,193,000	2.25	5.00	9.00	20.00	40.00	120.00	
1918	32,086,314	.50	.75	1.85	5.00	10.75	47.50	
1918D, 8 over 7	8,362,000		235.00	400.00	675.00	1,175	5,300	
1918D		3.00	5.00	9.00	21.00	47.50	165.00	
1918S	4,882,000	2.25	3.75	7.50	21.00	47.50	155.00	
1919	60,868,000	.40	.65	1.25	2.75	5.50	24.00	
1919D	8,006,000	2.50	4.00	10.00	25.00	70.00	205.00	
1919S	7,521,000	2.00	3.00	8.00	22.50	67.50	200.00	

NICKEL FIVE-CENT PIECES

	Quan. Minted	Good	V.G.	Fine	V.F.	E.F.	Unc.
1920	63,093,000	$ .40	$ .55	$1.15	$2.75	$5.75	$22.50
1920D	9,418,000	2.25	3.50	8.50	25.00	50.00	175.00
1920S	9,689,000	1.25	2.50	6.00	22.00	47.50	175.00
1921	10,663,000	.75	1.15	2.60	5.75	11.50	59.00
1921S	1,557,000	7.50	15.00	25.00	60.00	95.00	335.00
1923	35,715,000	.40	.55	1.10	2.50	4.75	21.00
1923S	6,142,000	1.50	2.50	6.00	18.00	42.50	165.00
1924	21,620,000	.40	.60	1.25	2.50	4.80	22.50
1924D	5,258,000	2.00	3.00	8.00	22.00	48.00	175.00
1924S	1,437,000	3.75	6.00	13.50	50.00	110.00	650.00
1925	35,565,100	.40	.60	1.15	2.35	4.75	22.50
1925D	4,450,000	3.00	5.00	9.00	30.00	55.00	200.00
1925S	6,256,000	2.00	4.25	6.25	20.00	45.00	215.00
1926	44,693,000	.35	.55	.95	2.25	4.75	17.50
1926D	5,638,000	1.85	3.50	7.75	24.00	55.00	275.00
1926S	970,000	4.75	7.25	13.00	47.50	125.00	410.00
1927	37,981,000	.35	.50	.85	2.00	4.00	15.00
1927D	5,730,000	.75	1.50	3.00	8.00	17.00	42.50
1927S	3,430,000	1.00	1.75	4.00	13.00	37.50	235.00
1928	23,411,000	.35	.50	.80	1.75	3.75	16.00
1928D	6,436,000	.40	.60	1.40	2.50	4.75	17.50
1928S	6,936,000	.60	1.00	2.00	4.25	8.75	52.50
1929	36,446,000	.35	.45	.75	1.40	2.50	11.75
1929D	8,370,000	.35	.60	.90	1.75	3.50	16.50
1929S	7,754,000	.35	.60	.90	1.75	3.50	16.50
1930	22,849,000	.35	.50	.65	1.10	2.00	14.00
1930S	5,435,000	.60	.85	1.60	3.00	5.50	40.00
1931S	1,200,000	3.25	4.00	5.00	7.00	10.00	52.50
1934	20,213,003	.25	.40	.65	1.10	2.00	11.00
1934D	7,480,000	.30	.45	.70	1.25	2.50	13.50
1935	58,264,000		.20	.35	.60	1.10	5.50
1935D	12,092,000		.25	.50	1.00	2.00	10.50
1935S	10,300,000		.25	.50	1.00	1.90	9.75
1936	119,001,420		.15	.30	.45	.65	4.50
1936 Proof	(4,420)						160.00
1936D	24,814,000		.25	.40	.65	1.15	4.75
1936S	14,930,000		.25	.40	.65	1.20	5.50
1937	79,485,769		.20	.30	.45	.70	4.25
1937 Proof	(5,769)						145.00
1937D ⎱	17,826,000		.25	.40	.60	1.00	5.00
1937D 3-Legged* ⎰		32.50	37.50	42.50	50.00	67.50	250.00
1937S	5,635,000		.25	.50	.75	1.30	6.25
1938D ⎱	7,020,000		.20	.45	.70	1.25	4.75
1938D, D over S ⎰				5.00	7.00	10.00	27.50

*Beware of removed leg.

1937D "3-Legged" Variety

1938D over S Variety

NICKEL FIVE-CENT PIECES
JEFFERSON TYPE 1938 to Date

This nickel was designed by Felix Schlag. He won an award of $1,000 in a competition with some 390 artists. It established the definite public approval of portrait and pictorial rather than symbolic devices on our coinage.

Designer Felix Schlag; weight 5 grams; composition: 1938-1942, 1946-   , .750 copper, .250 nickel; 1942-1945, .560 copper, .350 silver, .090 manganese; diameter 21.2 mm; plain edge; mints: Philadelphia, Denver, San Francisco.

VERY GOOD—Second porch pillar from right nearly gone, other three still visible but weak.

FINE—Cheekbone worn flat. Hairlines and eyebrow faint. Second pillar weak, especially at bottom.

VERY FINE—Second pillar plain and complete on both sides.

EXTRA FINE—Cheekbone, hairlines, eyebrow slightly worn but well defined. Base of triangle above pillars visible but weak.

Mint mark located at right of building

	Quan. Minted	V.G.	Fine	V.F.	E.F.	Unc.	Proof
1938 . . . . . . (19,365)	19,515,365	$ .15	$ .25	$ .40	$ .55	$1.50	$15.00
1938D	5,376,000	1.10	1.35	1.50	2.00	5.00	
1938S	4,105,000	2.00	2.25	2.50	3.00	5.75	
1939 . . . . . . (12,535)	120,627,535	.15	.25	.35	.50	1.10	15.00
1939D	3,514,000	4.00	4.50	5.50	9.00	32.50	
1939S	6,630,000	.70	.90	1.25	2.30	10.00	
1940 . . . . . . (14,158)	176,499,158			.20	.35	.80	20.00
1940D	43,540,000			.25	.40	1.35	
1940S	39,690,000			.30	.60	1.70	
1941 . . . . . . (18,720)	203,283,720			.15	.30	.75	12.50
1941D	53,432,000			.20	.35	1.10	
1941S†	43,445,000			.25	.45	1.10	
1942 . . . . . . (29,600)	49,818,600			.25	.40	1.40	12.50
1942D	13,938,000	.40	.85	1.25	2.00	8.00	

†Large and small mint mark varieties, see page 59.

Wartime Alloy Variety 1942-1945

On October 8, 1942, the wartime five-cent piece composed of copper (56%), silver (35%) and manganese (9%) made its first appearance. The mint mark was made larger and placed above the dome of Monticello. The letter P for the Philadelphia Mint was used for the first time on this piece to indicate the change of alloy. Nickel, a critical war material, was entirely eliminated.

		V.G.	Fine	V.F.	E.F.	Unc.	Proof
1942P . . . . . . (27,600)	57,900,600	.25	.40	.80	1.65	6.50	24.00
1942S	32,900,000	.25	.35	.65	1.00	3.50	
1943P	271,165,000	.25	.35	.50	.65	1.50	
1943D	15,294,000	.75	1.15	1.50	2.00	3.75	
1943S	104,060,000	.30	.40	.50	.65	1.50	
1944P*	119,150,000	.25	.35	.45	.70	2.00	
1944D	32,309,000	.25	.40	.60	.90	3.00	
1944S	21,640,000	.35	.50	.75	.95	3.00	
1945P	119,408,100	.25	.35	.45	.75	2.75	
1945D	37,158,000	.25	.35	.45	.75	1.75	
1945S	58,939,000	.25	.35	.45	.75	1.30	

*1944 nickels without mint marks are counterfeits.

NICKEL FIVE-CENT PIECES
Prewar composition and mint mark style resumed 1946-1964

	Quan. Minted	V.F.	E.F.	Unc.	Proof
1946	161,116,000		$ .20	$ .30	
1946D	45,292,200	$ .20	.30	.80	
1946S	13,560,000	.30	.45	.85	
1947	95,000,000		.20	.35	
1947D	37,822,000		.25	.70	
1947S	24,720,000	.25	.40	.70	
1948	89,348,000		.20	.30	
1948D	44,734,000	.25	.50	1.30	
1948S	11,300,000	.30	.50	1.00	
1949	60,652,000	.15	.25	.65	
1949D	36,498,000	.20	.35	.85	
1949S	9,716,000	.40	.75	1.50	
1950 .... (51,386)	9,847,386	.40	.85	1.60	$21.00
1950D	2,630,030	8.00	9.00	10.00	
1951 .... (57,500)	28,609,500	.20	.30	.60	12.00
1951D	20,460,000	.20	.30	1.25	
1951S	7,776,000	.50	.75	2.75	
1952 .... (81,980)	64,069,980		.20	.35	8.00
1952D	30,638,000	.30	.50	1.60	
1952S	20,572,000	.20	.35	.65	
1953 .... (128,800)	46,772,800		.20	.30	6.50
1953D	59,878,600		.20	.30	
1953S	19,210,900	.20	.30	.55	
1954 .... (233,300)	47,917,350		.15	.25	4.00
1954D	117,183,060		.15	.25	
1954S 1954S, S over D	} 29,384,000	.15 12.00	.20 27.50	.30 60.00	
1955 .... (378,200)	8,266,200	.65	.90	1.30	2.75
1955D 1955D, D over S	} 74,464,100	6.00	.15 12.00	.25 25.00	

1954S, S over D

1955D, D over S

	Quan. Minted	V.F.	E.F.	Unc.	Proof
1956 .... (669,384)	35,885,384		.15	.25	1.25
1956D	67,222,940		.15	.25	
1957 .... (1,247,952)	39,655,952		.15	.25	1.00
1957D	136,828,900		.15	.20	
1958 .... (875,652)	17,963,652	.15	.20	.35	2.00
1958D	168,249,120		.15	.20	
1959 .... (1,149,291)	28,397,291		.15	.30	1.10
1959D	160,738,240			.15	
1960 .... (1,691,602)	57,107,602			.15	1.00
1960D	192,582,180			.15	
1961 .... (3,028,144)	76,668,244			.15	.75
1961D	229,342,760			.15	
1962 .... (3,218,019)	100,602,019			.15	.75
1962D	280,195,720			.15	

NICKEL FIVE-CENT PIECES

	Quan. Minted	Unc.	Proof
1963.........(3,075,645)	178,851,645................	$ .10	$ .75
1963D....................276,829,460................		.10	
1964.........(3,950,762)	1,028,622,762................	.10	.75
1964D....................1,787,297,160................		.10	
1965....................136,131,380................		.10	
1966....................156,208,283................		.10	
1967....................107,325,800................		.10	

The designer's initials **FS** were added below the bust starting in 1966, and dies were further remodeled to strengthen the design in 1971 and again in 1972. Mint mark position was moved to the obverse starting in 1968.

Quan. Minted	Unc.	Proof	Quan. Minted	Unc.	Proof
1968D.....91,227,880	$ .10		1971D....316,144,800	$ .10	
1968S (3,041,509)			1971S Proof only*		
....103,437,510	.10	$ .45	.....(3,224,138)		$3.50
1969D....202,807,500	.10		1972.....202,036,000	.10	
1969S (2,934,631)			1972D......351,694,600	.10	
....123,099,631	.10	.45	1972S Proof only		
1970D....515,485,380	.10		.....(3,267,667)		3.50
1970S (2,632,810)			1973..............		
.....241,464,814	.10	.45	1973D..............		
1971.....106,884,000	.10		1973S Proof only......		3.50

*1971 proof nickels without mint mark were made in error. See pages 59-60.

SILVER THREE-CENT PIECES 1851-1873

This smallest of United States silver coins was authorized by Congress March 3, 1851. The first three-cent silver pieces had no lines bordering the six-pointed star. From 1854 through 1858 there were three lines, while issues of the last fifteen years show only two lines. Issues from 1854 through 1873 have an olive sprig over the III and a bundle of three arrows beneath.

1851-1853 — Designer James B. Longacre; weight .80 gram; composition: .750 silver, .250 copper; diameter 14 mm; plain edge; mints: Philadelphia, New Orleans.

1854-1873 — Weight .75 gram; composition: .900 silver, .100 copper; diameter 14 mm; plain edge. All coined at Philadelphia Mint.

 Variety 1 mint mark o

GOOD—*Star worn smooth. Legend and date readable.*

VERY GOOD—*Outline of shield defined. Legend and date clear.*

FINE—*Only star points worn smooth.*

VERY FINE—*Only partial wear on star ridges.*

	Quan. Minted	Good	V.G.	Fine	V.F.	Unc.	Proof
1851 Variety 1 5,447,400		$5.00	$7.00	$10.00	$19.00	$90.00	
1851O..............720,000		9.00	15.00	25.00	40.00	145.00	
1852............18,663,500		3.75	5.00	8.00	16.00	85.00	
1853............11,400,000		4.00	5.50	8.50	16.00	85.00	

SILVER THREE-CENT PIECES

 Variety 2
Three
Outlines
to Star   Variety 3
Two
Outlines
to Star

	Quan. Minted	Good	V.G.	Fine	V.F.	Unc.	Proof
1854 Variety 2......671,000		$8.00	$10.00	$14.00	$27.50	$275.00	
1855..............139,000		14.00	20.00	32.50	52.50	350.00	$1,200
1856............1,458,000		7.50	9.00	13.50	30.00	275.00	1,200
1857............1,042,000		7.50	9.00	13.50	30.00	275.00	1,100
1858............1,604,000		7.50	9.00	13.50	30.00	275.00	625.00
1859 Variety 3......365,000		10.00	12.00	15.00	27.50	87.50	165.00
1860.....(1,000) 287,000		10.00	12.00	15.00	27.50	87.50	165.00
1861.....(1,000) 498,000		8.00	10.00	14.00	24.00	85.00	155.00
1862, 2 over 1......}343,550		15.00	17.50	25.00	50.00	150.00	
1862.......(550)		9.00	11.00	14.50	25.00	85.00	165.00
1863, 3 over 2.......}21,460		....					——
1863.......(460)		....				230.00	275.00
1864......(470) 12,470		....				280.00	300.00
1865......∴(500) 8,500		....				....	275.00
1866.......(725) 22,725		....				....	210.00
1867.......(625) 4,625		....	Circulated coins			....	200.00
1868.......(600) 4,100		....	1863 to 1872 are			....	190.00
1869.......(600) 5,100		....	rarely encountered.			....	190.00
1870.....(1,000) 4,000		....	They were melted			....	175.00
1871.......(960) 4,360		....	or exported.			....	175.00
1872.......(950) 1,950		....				....	175.00
1873......(600)		600 (Closed 3 Only).................					250.00

HALF DIMES 1794-1873

The half dime types present the same general characteristics as larger United States silver coins. Authorized by the Act of April 2, 1792, they were not coined until February, 1795, although dated 1794. At first the weight was 20.8 grains, and fineness 892.4. By the Act of January 18, 1837 the weight was slightly reduced to 20⅝ grains and the fineness changed to .900. Finally the weight was reduced to 19.2 grains by the Act of February 21, 1853. Both half dimes and dimes offer many varieties in the early dates.

FLOWING HAIR TYPE 1794-1795

Designer Robert Scot; weight 1.35 grams; composition: .8924 silver, .1076 copper; approx. diameter 16.5 mm; reeded edge. All coined at Philadelphia Mint.

FAIR—*Details clear enough to identify.*
GOOD—*Eagle, wreath, bust outlined but lack details.*
VERY GOOD—*Some details remain on face. All lettering readable.*
FINE—*Hair ends show. Hair at top smooth.*
VERY FINE—*Hairlines at top show. Hair about ear defined.*

	Quan. Minted	Fair	Good	V.G.	Fine	V.F.	Unc.
1794........}86,416		$115.00	$210.00	$325.00	$485.00	$750.00	$1900.00
1795........		90.00	170.00	240.00	350.00	600.00	1200.00

HALF DIMES
DRAPED BUST TYPE, SMALL EAGLE REVERSE 1796-1797

1796-1805
FAIR—Details clear enough to identify.
GOOD—Date, stars, LIBERTY readable. Bust outlined but no details.
VERY GOOD—Some details show.
FINE—Hair and drapery lines worn, but visible.
VERY FINE—Only left of drapery indistinct.

	Quan. Minted	Fair	Good	V.G.	Fine	V.F.	Unc.
1796, 6 over 5							
All kinds....10,230		$180.00	$325.00	$500.00	$600.00	$925.00	$2,000
1796 Normal date.......	100.00	185.00	300.00	390.00	550.00	1,600
1796 LIKERTY........		235.00	350.00	475.00	800.00	
1797 15 stars....	95.00	170.00	235.00	335.00	500.00	1,450
1797 16 stars....}44,527	95.00	170.00	235.00	335.00	500.00	1,450
1797 13 stars....	100.00	180.00	260.00	385.00	600.00	1,500

DRAPED BUST TYPE, HERALDIC EAGLE REVERSE 1800-1805

1800 LIBEKTY

	Quan. Minted	Fair	Good	V.G.	Fine	V.F.	Unc.
1800 All kinds....24,000	85.00	140.00	215.00	325.00	450.00	1,250
1800 LIBEKTY........	85.00	140.00	215.00	325.00	450.00	1,350
1801.............33,910	90.00	145.00	225.00	350.00	510.00	1,450
1802.............13,010	700.00	1,400	2,500	3,750	6,000	——
1803.............37,850	80.00	130.00	200.00	300.00	450.00	1,250
1805.............15,600	115.00	215.00	325.00	465.00	800.00	——

CAPPED BUST TYPE 1829-1837
Designer William Kneass; weight 1.35 grams; composition: .8924 silver, .1076 copper; approx. diameter 15.5 mm; reeded edge. All coined at Philadelphia Mint.

GOOD—Bust outlined, no detail. Date and legend readable.
VERY GOOD—Complete legend and date plain. At least 3 letters of LIBERTY show clearly.
FINE—All letters in LIBERTY show.
VERY FINE—Full rim, both sides. Clasp on shoulder and ear well defined.

	Quan. Minted	Good	V.G.	Fine	V.F.	Ex.F.	Unc.
1829.........1,230,000	$9.00	$12.00	$17.50	$30.00	$60.00	$175.00
1830.........1,240,000	8.00	10.00	15.00	27.50	55.00	160.00
1831.........1,242,700	8.00	10.00	15.00	27.50	55.00	160.00
1832...........965,000	8.00	10.00	15.00	27.50	55.00	160.00
1833.........1,370,000	8.00	10.00	15.00	27.50	55.00	160.00
1834.........1,480,000	8.00	10.00	15.00	27.50	55.00	160.00
1835 All kinds..2,760,000						
1835 Lg. date and 5c....	8.00	10.00	15.00	27.50	55.00	160.00
1835 Lg. date, sm. 5c....	8.00	10.00	15.00	27.50	55.00	160.00
1835 Sm. date, lg. 5c....	8.00	10.00	15.00	27.50	55.00	160.00
1835 Sm. date and 5c....	8.00	10.00	15.00	27.50	55.00	160.00
1836 Small 5c.}1,900,000	8.00	10.00	15.00	27.50	55.00	160.00
1836 Large 5c.	8.00	10.00	15.00	27.50	55.00	160.00
1837 Small 5c.}2,276,000	11.00	18.50	30.00	67.50	135.00	275.00
1837 Large 5c.	8.00	10.00	15.00	27.50	55.00	160.00

HALF DIMES
LIBERTY SEATED TYPE 1837-1873
Variety 1 — No stars on obverse 1837-1838

Designer Christian Gobrecht; weight 1.34 grams; composition: .900 silver, .100 copper; diameter 15.5 mm; reeded edge; mints: Philadelphia, New Orleans.

GOOD—*LIBERTY on shield smooth. Date and letters readable.*
VERY GOOD—*At least 3 letters in LIBERTY are visible.*
FINE—*Entire LIBERTY visible, weak spots.*
VERY FINE—*Entire LIBERTY strong and even.*

	Quan. Minted	Good	V.G.	Fine	V.F.	E.F	Unc.
1837 Sm. date	inc. above	$40.00	$55.00	$70.00	$95.00	$150.00	$325.00
1837 Lg. date	inc. above	40.00	55.00	70.00	95.00	150.00	325.00
1838O No stars	70,000	45.00	60.00	90.00	140.00	225.00	550.00

No drapery from elbow 1837-1840

Drapery from elbow starting 1840

Variety 2 — Stars on obverse 1838-1853

	Good	V.G.	Fine	V.F.	E.F	Unc.
1838 No drpy..2,255,000	3.50	4.75	7.50	15.00	30.00	140.00
1839 No drpy..1,069,150	3.50	4.75	7.50	15.00	30.00	140.00
1839O No drapery 1,034,039	5.50	7.00	11.50	20.00	40.00	140.00
1840 No drapery. All kinds..1,344,085	3.50	4.75	7.50	15.00	30.00	140.00
1840O No drapery. All kinds..935,000	6.00	9.00	14.00	30.00	45.00	165.00
1840 Drapery..........	3.00	4.50	7.00	12.00	20.00	100.00
1840O Drapery.........	6.00	9.00	14.00	27.50	40.00	150.00
1841.........1,150,000	3.00	4.00	6.00	11.00	19.00	85.00
1841O.........815,000	4.00	6.00	10.00	17.50	35.00	150.00
1842...........815,000	3.75	4.50	6.00	11.00	19.00	85.00
1842O.........350,000	6.00	11.00	20.00	35.00	60.00	200.00
1843.........1,165,000	3.00	4.00	6.00	11.00	19.00	85.00
1844...........430,000	4.00	6.00	9.00	14.00	25.00	85.00
1844O.........220,000	7.00	12.00	20.00	35.00	60.00	160.00
1845.........1,564,000	3.00	4.00	6.00	11.00	19.00	85.00
1846............27,000	50.00	70.00	95.00	125.00	175.00	325.00
1847.........1,274,000	3.00	4.00	6.00	11.00	19.00	85.00
1848 Med. date .	668,000	3.00	4.00	6.00	11.00	19.00	85.00
1848 Lg. date...	668,000	3.00	4.00	6.00	11.00	19.00	85.00
1848O.........600,000	6.00	8.00	14.00	25.00	40.00	125.00
1849 9 over 6 .	1,309,000	4.00	6.50	9.00	15.00	30.00	100.00
1849 9 over 8 .	1,309,000	4.00	6.50	9.00	15.00	30.00	100.00
1849 Nor. date	1,309,000	3.00	4.00	6.00	11.00	19.00	85.00
1849O.........140,000	25.00	40.00	60.00	90.00	150.00	325.00
1850...........955,000	3.00	4.00	6.00	11.00	19.00	85.00
1850O.........690,000	4.00	6.50	9.00	20.00	35.00	125.00
1851...........781,000	3.00	4.00	6.00	11.00	19.00	85.00
1851O.........860,000	4.00	6.50	9.00	20.00	35.00	125.00
1852.........1,000,500	3.00	4.00	6.00	11.00	19.00	85.00
1852O.........260,000	6.00	9.50	16.00	30.00	50.00	175.00
1853 No arrows..135,000	9.00	14.00	22.00	35.00	60.00	150.00
1853O No arrows 160,000	65.00	90.00	135.00	200.00	300.00	700.00

HALF DIMES

Variety 3 — Arrows at date 1853-1855

Weight 1.24 grams; composition: .900 silver, .100 copper; diameter 15.5 mm; reeded edge; mints: Philadelphia, New Orleans, San Francisco.

As on the dimes, quarters and halves, arrows were placed at the sides of the date for a short period starting in 1853. They were placed there to denote the reduction of weight under the terms of the Act of February 21, 1853.

	Quan. Minted	Good	V.G.	Fine	V.F.	E.F.	Unc.	Proof
1853	13,210,020	$4.00	$6.00	$8.50	$13.00	$25.00	$150.00	
1853O	2,200,000	4.00	6.00	8.50	13.00	25.00	150.00	
1854	5,740,000	3.50	5.00	7.50	12.00	25.00	150.00	
1854O	1,560,000	3.50	5.00	7.50	12.00	25.00	150.00	
1855	1,750,000	3.50	5.00	7.50	12.00	25.00	150.00	$625.00
1855O	600,000	5.00	8.00	12.00	21.00	40.00	185.00	

Variety 2 resumed 1856-1859

	Quan. Minted	Good	V.G.	Fine	V.F.	E.F.	Unc.	Proof
1856	4,880,000	3.00	3.75	4.50	6.50	15.00	85.00	500.00
1856O	1,100,000	3.00	3.75	5.00	10.00	20.00	100.00	
1857	7,280,000	3.00	3.75	4.50	6.50	15.00	85.00	500.00
1857O	1,380,000	3.00	3.75	5.00	10.00	20.00	100.00	

1858 over inverted date

	Quan. Minted	Good	V.G.	Fine	V.F.	E.F.	Unc.	Proof
1858	} 3,500,000	3.00	3.75	4.50	6.50	15.00	85.00	350.00
1858 over inverted date		27.50	33.00	65.00	100.00	175.00	400.00	
1858O	1,660,000	3.00	3.75	5.00	10.00	20.00	100.00	

New die 1859 Philadelphia Mint. Stars hollow in center. Arms slimmer.

	Quan. Minted	Good	V.G.	Fine	V.F.	E.F.	Unc.	Proof
1859	340,000	4.50	6.00	9.00	15.00	30.00	90.00	175.00
1859O	560,000	4.50	6.00	9.00	15.00	30.00	100.00	

In the years 1859 and 1860 interesting half dime patterns were made which do not bear our nation's identity. These are transitional pieces, not made for circulation, but struck at the time the inscription UNITED STATES OF AMERICA was being transferred from the reverse to the obverse.

1859 Obv. of 59, rev. of 60		2000.00
1860 Obv. of 59, rev. of 60		
(With stars)100		1,000.00

Variety 4 — Legend on obverse 1860-1873

	Quan. Minted	Good	V.G.	Fine	V.F.	E.F.	Unc.	Proof
1860 Legend (1,000)	799,000	3.00	3.75	4.50	6.50	15.00	85.00	100.00
1860O	1,060,000	3.50	5.00	7.00	10.00	20.00	100.00	

HALF DIMES

Quan. Minted	Good	V.G.	Fine	V.F.	E.F.	Unc.	Proof
1861 (1,000) 3,361,000	$3.00	$3.75	$4.50	$6.50	$15.00	$85.00	$100.00
1862 (550)..1,492,550	3.00	3.75	4.50	6.50	15.00	85.00	100.00
1863 (460).....18,460	12.50	16.00	21.00	35.00	60.00	150.00	185.00
1863S........100,000	12.50	16.00	21.00	35.00	60.00	150.00	
1864 (470).....48,470						250.00	350.00
1864S.........90,000	12.50	16.00	21.50	40.00	75.00	160.00	
1865 (500).....13,500	12.50	16.00	21.00	35.00	70.00	150.00	240.00
1865S........120,000	8.00	11.00	16.00	27.50	50.00	150.00	
1866 (725).....10,725	8.00	11.00	16.00	27.50	50.00	150.00	180.00
1866S........120,000	8.00	11.00	16.00	27.50	50.00	150.00	
1867 (625)......8,625	8.50	12.00	17.50	27.50	50.00	150.00	180.00
1867S........120,000	8.00	11.00	16.00	27.50	50.00	150.00	
1868 (600)....89,200	4.00	5.50	9.00	15.00	30.00	85.00	115.00
1868S........280,000	4.00	5.50	9.00	15.00	30.00	85.00	
1869 (600)....208,600	4.00	5.50	9.00	15.00	30.00	85.00	115.00
1869S........230,000	4.00	5.50	9.00	15.00	30.00	85.00	
1870 (1,000)..536,600	4.00	5.50	9.00	15.00	30.00	85.00	100.00
1871 (960)..1,873,960	3.00	3.75	4.50	6.50	15.00	85.00	100.00
1871S........161,000	10.00	15.00	21.00	35.00	60.00	150.00	
1872 (950)..2,947,950	3.00	3.75	4.50	6.50	15.00	85.00	100.00

Mint mark
below bow
1860-1869,
1872-1873

Mint mark
above bow
1871-1872

	Good	V.G.	Fine	V.F.	E.F.	Unc.	Proof
1872S Mint mark above bow							
All kinds...837,000	3.50	5.00	7.00	10.00	20.00	100.00	
1872S M. below bow..	3.50	5.00	7.00	10.00	20.00	100.00	
1873 (Closed 3 only)							
(600)....712,600	3.00	3.75	4.50	6.50	15.00	85.00	150.00
1873S (Closed 3 only)							
...........324,000	3.50	5.00	7.00	10.00	20.00	100.00	

BIBLIOGRAPHY

Newlin, H. P. *The Early Half-Dimes of the United States.* Philadelphia, 1883 (reprinted 1933).

Valentine, D. W. *The United States Half Dimes.* New York, 1931.

Breen, Walter. *United States Half Dimes: A Supplement.* New York, 1958.

DIMES — 1796 To Date

The designs of the dimes, first coined in 1796, follow closely those of the half dimes up through the Liberty seated type. The dimes in each instance weigh twice as much as the half dimes. File or adjustment marks as on half dimes.

Bibliography: Kosoff, A. *United States Dimes from 1796.* New York, 1945.

DRAPED BUST TYPE, SMALL EAGLE REVERSE 1796-1797

FAIR—Details clear enough to identify.
GOOD—Date readable. Bust outlined, but no detail.
VERY GOOD—All but deepest drapery folds worn smooth. Hairlines nearly gone and curls lack detail.
FINE—All drapery lines visible. Hair partly worn.
VERY FINE—Only left side of drapery is indistinct.

Designer Robert Scot; weight 2.70 grams; composition: .8924 silver, .1076 copper; approx. diameter 19 mm; reeded edge. All coined at Philadelphia Mint.

DIMES

1797
16 Stars

1797
13 Stars

	Quan. Minted	Fair	Good	V.G.	Fine	V.F.	Unc.
1796	22,135	$210.00	$325.00	$475.00	$750.00	$1,200	$2,850
1797 16 stars	}25,261	150.00	260.00	385.00	625.00	875.00	2,100
1797 13 stars		150.00	260.00	385.00	625.00	875.00	2,100

DRAPED BUST TYPE, HERALDIC EAGLE REVERSE 1798-1807

1798 over 97, 13 stars on rev.						
All kinds..27,550				500.00	1,350	
1798 over 97,						
16 stars on rev. .	82.50	130.00	190.00	300.00	485.00	1,250
1798	82.50	130.00	190.00	300.00	485.00	1,250
1798 Small 8	120.00	200.00	300.00	550.00	900.00	
1800 21,760	80.00	125.00	185.00	250.00	390.00	950.00
1801 34,640	90.00	140.00	200.00	320.00	525.00	950.00
1802 10,975	95.00	160.00	240.00	375.00	625.00	1,100
1803 33,040	90.00	140.00	190.00	300.00	500.00	950.00
1804 13 stars on rev.						
All kinds...8,265	125.00	185.00	245.00	365.00	600.00	1,500
1804 14 stars on rev. .	125.00	185.00	245.00	365.00	600.00	1,500
1805 4 berries	}120,780	62.50	120.00	140.00	180.00	300.00	900.00
1805 5 berries		62.50	120.00	140.00	180.00	300.00	900.00
1807 165,000	55.00	100.00	120.00	150.00	275.00	900.00

CAPPED BUST TYPE 1809-1837
Variety 1 — Large size 1809-1828

FAIR—*Details clear enough to identify.*
GOOD—*Date, letters and stars discernible. Bust outlined, no details.*
VERY GOOD—*Legends and date plain. Minimum of 3 letters in LIBERTY.*
FINE—*Full LIBERTY. Ear and shoulder clasp visible. Part of rim shows both sides.*
VERY FINE—*LIBERTY distinct. Full rim. Ear and clasp plain and distinct.*

Designer John Reich; weight 2.70 grams; composition: .8924 silver, .1076 copper; approx.
diameter 18.5 mm; reeded edge. All coined at Philadelphia Mint.

1809 44,710	40.00	55.00	90.00	115.00	200.00	850.00
1811 over 9 65,180	27.50	40.00	47.50	70.00	120.00	750.00

DIMES

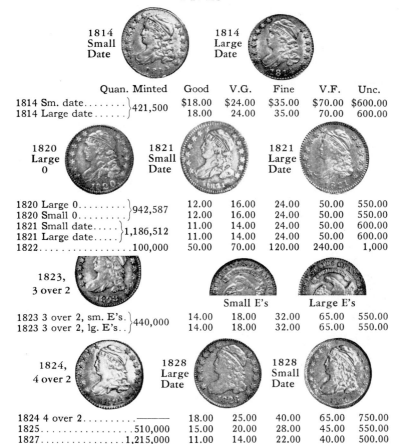

1814
Small
Date

1814
Large
Date

	Quan. Minted	Good	V.G.	Fine	V.F.	Unc.
1814 Sm. date........ }	421,500	$18.00	$24.00	$35.00	$70.00	$600.00
1814 Large date...... }		18.00	24.00	35.00	70.00	600.00

1820
Large
0

1821
Small
Date

1821
Large
Date

1820 Large 0......... }	942,587	12.00	16.00	24.00	50.00	550.00
1820 Small 0......... }		12.00	16.00	24.00	50.00	550.00
1821 Small date..... }	1,186,512	11.00	14.00	24.00	50.00	600.00
1821 Large date..... }		11.00	14.00	24.00	50.00	600.00
1822................100,000		50.00	70.00	120.00	240.00	1,000

1823,
3 over 2

Small E's

Large E's

1823 3 over 2, sm. E's. }	440,000	14.00	18.00	32.00	65.00	550.00
1823 3 over 2, lg. E's.. }		14.00	18.00	32.00	65.00	550.00

1824,
4 over 2

1828
Large
Date

1828
Small
Date

1824 4 over 2.........——		18.00	25.00	40.00	65.00	750.00
1825................510,000		15.00	20.00	28.00	45.00	550.00
1827................1,215,000		11.00	14.00	22.00	40.00	500.00
1828 Large date, curl base 2 ......Both vars. 125,000		25.00	40.00	65.00	110.00	650.00

Variety 2 — Reduced size 1828-1837

New mint equipment was used to make the small date 1828 dimes and subsequent issues. Unlike earlier coinage, these have beaded borders and a uniform diameter. Large date has curl base knob 2; small date has square base knob 2.

1829
Small
10c

Large
10c

1830
30 over 29

DIMES

	Quan. Minted	Good	V.G.	Fine	V.F.	Unc.
1828 Small date, sq. base 2....		$20.00	$25.00	$35.00	$60.00	$600.00
1829 Small 10c.......	⎫	7.50	10.00	18.00	40.00	400.00
1829 Medium 10c.....	⎬770,000	7.50	10.00	18.00	40.00	400.00
1829 Large 10c.......	⎭	12.00	18.00	35.00	50.00	400.00
1830, 30 over 29......			250.00	325.00	450.00	———
1830 Small 10c.......	⎬510,000	7.00	9.00	12.00	20.00	400.00
1830 Large 10c.......		7.00	9.00	12.00	20.00	400.00
1831................771,350		7.00	9.00	12.00	20.00	400.00
1832................522,500		7.00	9.00	12.00	20.00	400.00
1833................	⎬485,000	7.00	9.00	12.00	20.00	400.00
1833 Last 3 high......		7.00	9.00	12.00	20.00	400.00
1834 Small 4.........	⎬635,000	7.00	9.00	12.00	20.00	400.00
1834 Large 4.........		7.00	9.00	12.00	20.00	400.00
1835...............1,410,000		7.00	9.00	12.00	20.00	400.00
1836...............1,190,000		7.00	9.00	12.00	20.00	400.00
1837 All kinds.......1,042,000		7.00	9.00	12.00	20.00	400.00

LIBERTY SEATED TYPE 1837-1891

Variety 1 — No stars on obverse 1837-1838

Designer Christian Gobrecht; weight 2.67 grams; composition: .900 silver, .100 copper; diameter 17.9 mm; reeded edge; mints: Philadelphia, New Orleans.

No Drapery From Elbow
No Stars On Obverse

GOOD—*LIBERTY on shield smooth. Date and letters readable.*

VERY GOOD—*At least 3 letters in LIBERTY are visible.*

FINE—*Entire LIBERTY visible, weak spots.*

VERY FINE—*Entire LIBERTY strong and even.*

Mint marks on Liberty seated dimes are placed on the reverse within, or below, the wreath.

1837 Small date..............	35.00	50.00	80.00	150.00	675.00
1837 Large date..............	35.00	50.00	80.00	150.00	675.00
1838O................406,034	40.00	65.00	115.00	225.00	850.00

Variety 2 — Stars on obverse 1838-1853

 No Drapery From Elbow

1838 Small Stars   1838 Large Stars

1838 Small stars....	⎫	10.00	14.50	22.00	35.00	210.00
1838 Large stars....	⎬1,992,500	6.00	7.00	9.00	15.00	200.00
1838 Partial drapery	⎭	14.00	20.00	30.00	47.50	200.00
1839...............1,053,115		4.00	5.00	8.00	14.00	200.00
1839O.............1,323,000		5.00	8.00	12.00	20.00	200.00
1840 All kinds.......1,358,580		4.00	5.00	8.00	14.00	200.00
1840O.............1,175,000		5.00	8.00	12.00	20.00	200.00
1841........................						———

DIMES

 Drapery From Elbow

	Quan. Minted	Good	V.G.	Fine	V.F.	Unc.	Proof
1840....................		$5.50	$8.50	$12.00	$18.00	$110.00	
1841 All kinds.....1,622,500		3.25	4.25	7.00	15.00	100.00	
1841O...........2,007,500		3.00	4.00	7.00	15.00	100.00	
1842............1,887,500		3.00	4.00	6.00	12.00	100.00	
1842O...........2,020,000		4.00	6.00	8.50	16.00	110.00	
1843............1,370,000		3.00	4.00	6.00	12.00	100.00	
1843O............150,000		17.50	24.00	50.00	125.00	———	
1844...............72,500		25.00	40.00	70.00	135.00	525.00	
1845............1,755,000		3.00	4.00	6.00	12.00	100.00	
1845O............230,000		9.00	14.00	20.00	35.00	———	
1846...............31,300		17.50	20.00	32.50	50.00	275.00	
1847..............245,000		5.00	7.00	10.00	22.00	100.00	
1848..............451,500		4.00	6.00	8.00	16.00	100.00	
1849..............839,000		3.00	4.00	6.00	12.00	100.00	
1849O............300,000		7.00	10.00	18.00	35.00	225.00	
1850............1,931,500		3.00	4.00	6.00	12.00	100.00	
1850O............510,000		6.00	9.00	13.00	25.00	125.00	
1851............1,026,500		3.00	4.00	6.00	12.00	100.00	
1851O............400,000		6.00	9.00	12.00	22.00	150.00	
1852............1,535,500		3.00	4.00	6.00	12.00	100.00	
1852O............430,000		6.00	9.00	13.00	25.00	150.00	
1853 No arrows......95,000		20.00	25.00	35.00	60.00	250.00	

Variety 3 — Arrows at date 1853-1855

Weight 2.49 grams; composition: .900 silver, .100 copper; diameter 17.9 mm; reeded edge; mints: Philadelphia, New Orleans. Also San Francisco and Carson City after 1855.

Arrows At Date   Small Date Arrows Removed

	Good	V.G.	Fine	V.F.	Unc.	Proof
1853 With arrows.12,078,010	3.25	4.50	7.00	16.00	200.00	
1853O...........1,100,000	4.50	6.50	9.00	18.00	215.00	
1854............4,470,000	3.00	4.00	6.00	15.00	200.00	
1854O...........1,770,000	3.25	4.50	7.00	16.00	200.00	
1855............2,075,000	3.00	4.00	6.00	15.00	200.00	$750.00

Variety 2 resumed 1856-1860

	Good	V.G.	Fine	V.F.	Unc.	Proof
1856 Sm. date....⎫5,780,000	3.00	4.00	6.00	12.00	100.00	550.00
1856 Lg. date....⎭	3.00	4.00	6.00	12.00	100.00	
1856O...........1,180,000	3.25	4.50	7.00	15.00	100.00	
1856S...............70,000	27.50	45.00	65.00	115.00	400.00	
1857............5,580,000	2.75	3.75	5.75	9.50	90.00	500.00
1857O...........1,540,000	3.00	4.00	6.00	12.00	100.00	

DIMES

	Quan. Minted	Good	V.G.	Fine	V.F.	Unc.	Proof
1858	1,540,000	$2.75	$3.75	$5.75	$9.50	$100.00	$400.00
1858O	290,000	5.00	7.00	9.00	20.00	100.00	
1858S	60,000	20.00	28.00	50.00	100.00	350.00	
1859	430,000	2.75	3.75	5.75	9.50	100.00	300.00
1859O	480,000	2.75	3.75	5.75	9.50	100.00	
1859S	60,000	18.00	25.00	40.00	70.00	220.00	
1860S	140,000	9.00	14.00	25.00	50.00	220.00	

In 1859 an interesting pattern dime was made which does not bear our nation's identity. It is a "transitional" piece, not made for circulation, but struck at the time the inscription UNITED STATES OF AMERICA was being transferred from the reverse to the obverse.

1859						3,500	

Variety 4 — Legend on obverse 1860-1873

			Good	V.G.	Fine	V.F.	Unc.	Proof
1860	(1,000)	607,000	2.75	3.25	5.50	9.50	90.00	125.00
1860O		40,000	65.00	100.00	150.00	250.00	1,000	
1861	(1,000)	1,884,000	2.75	3.25	5.50	9.50	90.00	125.00
1861S		172,500	14.00	20.00	32.00	60.00	210.00	
1862	(550)	847,550	3.00	4.00	6.00	10.00	90.00	125.00
1862S		180,750	9.00	14.00	25.00	55.00	200.00	
1863	(460)	14,460	20.00	30.00	42.50	65.00	175.00	185.00
1863S		157,500	10.00	15.00	26.00	55.00	200.00	
1864	(470)	11,470	20.00	30.00	42.50	65.00	175.00	185.00
1864S		230,000	9.00	14.00	24.00	45.00	200.00	
1865	(500)	10,500	20.00	30.00	42.50	65.00	175.00	185.00
1865S		175,000	9.00	14.00	24.00	45.00	200.00	
1866	(725)	8,725	20.00	30.00	42.50	65.00	175.00	185.00
1866S		135,000	9.00	14.00	24.00	45.00	200.00	
1867	(625)	6,625	25.00	37.50	52.50	80.00	175.00	185.00
1867S		140,000	9.00	14.00	24.00	45.00	200.00	
1868	(600)	464,600	2.75	3.25	5.50	9.50	90.00	135.00
1868S		260,000	7.00	9.00	13.00	22.00	125.00	
1869	(600)	256,600	2.75	3.25	5.50	9.50	90.00	135.00
1869S		450,000	6.00	8.00	12.50	22.00	125.00	
1870	(1,000)	471,500	2.75	3.25	5.50	9.50	90.00	125.00
1870S		50,000	45.00	60.00	85.00	120.00	375.00	
1871	(960)	907,710	2.75	3.25	5.50	9.50	90.00	125.00
1871CC		20,100	125.00	185.00	275.00	600.00	1,600	
1871S		320,000	9.00	13.00	22.50	42.50	225.00	
1872	(950)	2,396,450	2.75	3.25	5.50	9.50	90.00	125.00
1872CC		24,000	85.00	120.00	175.00	325.00	900.00	
1872S		190,000	10.00	14.00	22.50	35.00	150.00	
1873 All kinds		1,568,600						
1873 Closed 3	(600)		2.75	3.25	5.50	9.50	90.00	125.00
1873 Open 3			4.00	7.00	12.00	16.00	90.00	
1873CC (Unique)		12,400					——	

DIMES

Variety 5 — Arrows at date 1873-1874

Weight 2.50 grams; composition: .900 silver, .100 copper; diameter 17.9 mm; reeded edge; mints: Philadelphia, New Orleans, San Francisco, Carson City.

In 1873 the dime was increased in weight to 38.58 grains. Arrows at date in 1873 and 1874 indicate this change.

	Quan. Minted	Good	V.G.	Fine	V.F.	Unc.	Proof
1873..(800)	2,378,500	$10.00	$14.00	$25.00	$40.00	$300.00	$350.00
1873CC..........18,791		300.00	425.00	600.00	800.00	1,900	
1873S...........455,000		15.00	20.00	30.00	50.00	275.00	
1874..(700)	2,940,700	10.00	14.00	25.00	40.00	250.00	350.00
1874CC..........10,817		85.00	130.00	200.00	400.00	2,000	
1874S...........240,000		17.00	22.00	35.00	60.00	275.00	

Variety 4 resumed 1875-1891

	Quan. Minted	Good	V.G.	Fine	V.F.	Unc.	Proof
1875..(700)	10,350,700	2.25	3.00	4.00	6.50	75.00	110.00
1875CC Below bow							
All kinds....4,645,000		3.50	5.00	7.50	13.00	77.50	
1875CC Above bow.....		2.50	3.50	5.00	10.00	75.00	
1875S Below bow							
All kinds....9,070,000		2.25	3.00	4.00	7.50	75.00	
1875S Above bow.......		2.25	3.00	4.00	7.50	75.00	
1876..(1,150)	11,461,150	2.25	3.00	4.00	7.50	75.00	100.00
1876CC.......8,270,000		2.75	3.75	5.00	10.00	75.00	
1876S........10,420,000		2.25	3.00	4.00	7.50	75.00	
1877..(510)	7,310,510	2.25	3.00	4.00	7.50	75.00	175.00
1877CC.......7,700,000		2.25	3.00	4.00	7.50	75.00	
1877S.........2,340,000		2.25	3.00	4.00	7.50	75.00	
1878..(800)	1,678,800	2.25	3.00	4.00	7.50	75.00	110.00
1878CC.........200,000		14.00	18.00	28.00	40.00	140.00	
1879..(1,100)	15,100	16.00	24.00	32.00	45.00	110.00	110.00
1880..(1,355)	37,355	14.00	18.00	28.00	40.00	110.00	110.00
1881..(975)	24,975	14.00	18.00	28.00	40.00	110.00	110.00
1882..(1,100)	3,911,100	2.25	3.00	4.00	6.50	75.00	90.00
1883..(1,039)	7,675,712	2.25	3.00	4.00	6.50	75.00	90.00
1884..(875)	3,366,380	2.25	3.00	4.00	6.50	75.00	90.00
1884S...........564,969		8.00	12.00	16.00	30.00	110.00	
1885..(930)	2,533,427	2.25	3.00	4.00	6.50	75.00	90.00
1885S............43,690		60.00	80.00	110.00	185.00	500.00	
1886..(886)	6,377,570	2.25	3.00	4.00	6.50	75.00	90.00
1886S...........206,524		9.00	11.00	17.00	28.00	90.00	
1887..(710)	11,283,939	2.25	3.00	4.00	6.50	75.00	90.00
1887S.........4,454,450		2.25	3.00	4.00	6.50	75.00	
1888..(832)	5,496,487	2.25	3.00	4.00	6.50	75.00	90.00
1888S.........1,720,000		3.50	4.50	7.00	10.00	75.00	
1889..(711)	7,380,711	2.25	3.00	4.00	6.50	75.00	90.00
1889S...........972,678		9.00	13.00	19.00	50.00	165.00	
1890..(590)	9,911,541	2.25	3.00	4.00	6.50	75.00	100.00
1890S.........1,423,076		3.50	4.50	7.00	10.00	75.00	
1891..(600)	15,310,600	2.25	3.00	4.00	6.50	75.00	100.00
1891O.........4,540,000		2.75	3.75	5.00	15.00	80.00	
1891S.........3,196,116		2.25	3.00	4.00	6.50	75.00	

DIMES
BARBER or LIBERTY HEAD TYPE 1892-1916

Designed by Charles E. Barber, Chief Engraver of the Mint. He also designed the 25 and 50-cent pieces. His initial B is at the truncation of the neck. Mint mark location is on the reverse below the wreath.

GOOD—Date and letters plain. LIBERTY over brow is obliterated.

VERY GOOD—At least 3 letters visible in LIBERTY.

FINE—All letters in LIBERTY visible, though some are weak.

VERY FINE—All letters of LIBERTY evenly plain.

EXTRA FINE—All letters in LIBERTY are sharp, distinct. Headband edges are distinct.

Designer Charles E. Barber; weight 2.50 grams; composition: .900 silver, .100 copper; diameter 17.9 mm; reeded edge; mints: Philadelphia, Denver, New Orleans, San Francisco.

Quan. Minted	Good	V.G.	Fine	V.F.	E.F.	Unc.	Proof
1892 (1,245) 12,121,245	$1.25	$2.50	$3.75	$6.50	$10.00	$50.00	$110.00
1892O.......3,841,700	2.50	4.50	5.75	9.00	18.00	60.00	
1892S.........990,710	17.00	25.00	35.00	47.50	70.00	125.00	
1893, 3 over 2 ⎫ 3,340,792 1893 (792) ⎭	2.50	4.50	6.50	8.50	13.00	50.00	115.00
1893O.......1,760,000	5.00	7.00	12.00	18.00	30.00	77.50	
1893S........2,491,401	5.00	7.00	12.00	18.00	30.00	75.00	
1894 (972) 1,330,972	5.00	7.00	9.50	14.00	20.00	55.00	115.00
1894O.........720,000	25.00	40.00	67.50	90.00	135.00	325.00	
1894S..............24				1972 Private Sale $50,000			
1895 (880) 690,880	25.00	35.00	52.50	75.00	100.00	200.00	300.00
1895O.........440,000	50.00	80.00	135.00	175.00	285.00	750.00	
1895S.......1,120,000	8.00	12.00	17.50	27.50	52.50	150.00	
1896 (762) 2,000,762	4.00	6.00	8.00	11.00	18.00	50.00	130.00
1896O.........610,000	23.50	35.00	55.00	75.00	110.00	250.00	
1896S.........575,056	27.50	42.50	60.00	85.00	140.00	300.00	
1897 (731) 10,869,264	1.00	2.00	3.50	5.50	10.00	50.00	130.00
1897O.........666,000	20.00	32.50	50.00	65.00	100.00	215.00	
1897S.......1,342,844	6.00	11.00	18.00	27.50	47.50	150.00	
1898 (735) 16,320,735	.75	1.50	2.50	4.00	10.00	50.00	130.00
1898O......2,130,000	3.50	6.00	10.00	25.00	50.00	135.00	
1898S.......1,702,507	3.50	6.00	10.00	25.00	40.00	100.00	
1899 (846) 19,580,846	.65	1.35	2.50	4.50	9.50	50.00	125.00
1899O......2,650,000	3.25	6.00	10.00	22.50	45.00	120.00	
1899S.......1,867,493	4.00	6.25	11.00	25.00	30.00	100.00	
1900 (912) 17,600,912	.80	1.50	2.50	4.75	9.50	50.00	120.00
1900O.......2,010,000	3.50	5.50	11.00	20.00	45.00	140.00	
1900S........5,168,270	1.75	3.50	6.75	10.00	17.50	72.50	
1901 (813) 18,860,478	.75	1.25	2.25	4.50	9.50	50.00	120.00
1901O.......5,620,000	1.65	3.00	7.25	14.00	37.50	125.00	
1901S.........593,022	20.00	45.00	80.00	135.00	185.00	575.00	
1902 (777) 21,380,777	.65	1.25	2.00	4.50	9.00	50.00	120.00
1902O.......4,500,000	1.10	2.25	6.00	11.00	25.00	85.00	
1902S.......2,070,000	3.00	5.00	9.00	18.00	36.00	100.00	
1903 (755) 19,500,755	.65	1.25	2.00	3.50	9.00	50.00	120.00
1903O.......8,180,000	1.00	2.00	5.00	8.00	20.00	70.00	
1903S.........613,300	15.00	22.50	30.00	50.00	75.00	200.00	
1904 (670) 14,601,027	.65	1.25	2.00	3.50	9.00	50.00	125.00
1904S.........800,000	11.00	16.50	23.50	35.00	52.50	155.00	
1905 (727) 14,552,350	.65	1.25	2.00	4.00	9.50	50.00	125.00

DIMES

Quan. Minted	Good	V.G.	Fine	V.F.	E.F.	Unc.	Proof
1905O*......3,400,000	$1.25	$3.00	$6.25	$9.50	$22.50	$85.00	
1905S.......6,855,199	1.00	2.00	4.50	8.00	15.00	55.00	
1906 (675) 19,958,406	.65	1.25	2.00	4.50	9.50	50.00	$125.00
1906D.......4,060,000	1.25	2.50	4.00	6.50	9.50	50.00	
1906O.......2,610,000	1.75	3.50	7.50	11.00	15.00	60.00	
1906S.......3,136,640	1.25	2.75	4.75	6.75	13.50	55.00	
1907 (575) 22,220,575	.65	1.25	2.00	4.50	9.50	50.00	130.00
1907D.......4,080,000	1.10	2.25	5.00	7.00	15.00	55.00	
1907O.......5,058,000	1.00	2.00	4.50	7.00	15.00	55.00	
1907S.......3,178,470	1.25	2.50	5.00	7.00	15.00	55.00	
1908 (545) 10,600,545	.65	1.25	2.00	4.25	9.00	50.00	130.00
1908D.......7,490,000	.65	1.30	2.75	4.50	10.00	50.00	
1908O.......1,789,000	2.50	5.00	7.50	11.00	16.00	65.00	
1908S.......3,220,000	1.25	2.50	4.00	7.00	12.00	60.00	
1909 (650) 10,240,650	.65	1.25	1.75	3.50	7.50	50.00	130.00
1909D........954,000	2.75	5.00	11.00	16.00	27.50	75.00	
1909O.......2,287,000	1.75	3.75	8.00	12.00	25.00	75.00	
1909S.......1,000,000	2.75	5.00	12.00	16.00	30.00	77.50	
1910 (551) 11,520,551	.65	1.00	1.75	3.50	7.50	50.00	130.00
1910D.......3,490,000	1.00	1.75	3.00	4.75	8.50	50.00	
1910S.......1,240,000	2.25	4.00	6.00	8.50	16.00	62.50	
1911 (543) 18,870,543	.65	1.00	1.50	3.00	7.50	50.00	130.00
1911D......11,209,000	.65	1.00	1.75	3.50	8.00	50.00	
1911S.......3,520,000	1.00	1.75	3.00	6.00	13.00	55.00	
1912 (700) 19,350,700	.65	1.00	1.50	3.00	7.50	50.00	135.00
1912D......11,760,000	.65	1.00	1.75	3.50	8.00	50.00	
1912S.......3,420,000	1.10	2.00	4.50	8.00	14.00	57.50	
1913 (622) 19,760,622	.65	1.00	1.50	3.00	7.50	50.00	185.00
1913S........510,000	7.50	12.50	27.50	37.50	80.00	235.00	
1914 (425) 17,360,655	.65	1.00	1.50	3.00	7.50	50.00	275.00
1914D......11,908,000	.65	1.00	1.50	3.00	7.50	50.00	
1914S.......2,100,000	1.35	3.00	4.25	7.50	15.00	60.00	
1915 (450) 5,620,450	.65	1.00	1.50	3.00	7.50	50.00	275.00
1915S........960,000	2.00	3.00	5.00	8.50	15.00	80.00	
1916......18,490,000	.65	1.00	1.50	3.00	7.50	50.00	
1916S.......5,820,000	.65	1.00	1.50	3.00	7.50	50.00	

*Normal and "microscopic" mint mark varieties, see page 59.

WINGED LIBERTY HEAD or "MERCURY" TYPE 1916-1945

Although this coin is commonly called the "Mercury Dime," the main device is in fact a representation of Liberty. The wings crowning her cap are intended to symbolize liberty of thought. The designer's initials AW are to the right of the neck.

GOOD—Letters and dates clear. Lines and bands in fasces are obliterated.
VERY GOOD—One-third of sticks discernible in fasces.
FINE—All sticks in fasces are defined. Diagonal bands worn at center high points only.
EXTRA FINE—Diagonal bands complete, with only slight wear. Hair braids and hair before ear show clearly.

Designer Adolph A. Weinman. Standards same as previous issue; mints: Philadelphia Denver, San Francisco.

1916......22,180,080	.35	.50	1.25	1.75	4.50	15.00
1916D.......264,000	95.00	125.00	200.00	250.00	350.00	800.00

DIMES

Quan. Minted	Good	V.G.	Fine	V.F.	E.F.	Unc.	Proof
1916S.....10,450,000	$1.40	$2.00	$3.65	$4.85	$9.00	$23.00	
1917......55,230,000	.25	.35	.75	1.25	3.50	14.00	
1917D.....9,402,000	1.35	2.25	4.75	8.75	22.00	70.00	
1917S.....27,330,000	.35	.60	1.35	2.75	7.00	27.50	
1918......26,680,000	.40	.65	1.65	3.75	15.00	37.50	
1918D....22,674,800	.40	.70	2.50	4.50	15.00	47.50	
1918S....19,300,000	.50	.90	2.00	3.50	15.00	43.50	
1919......35,740,000	.30	.50	1.25	2.50	8.00	31.00	
1919D.....9,939,000	1.10	2.00	5.00	12.50	35.00	125.00	
1919S......8,850,000	1.10	2.00	5.00	12.50	35.00	135.00	
1920......59,030,000	.25	.35	.65	1.35	4.00	16.00	
1920D....19,171,000	.40	.70	2.00	3.50	12.50	45.00	
1920S.....13,820,000	.40	.70	2.00	3.50	12.50	45.00	
1921.......1,230,000	12.00	20.00	40.00	57.50	150.00	600.00	
1921D.....1,080,000	17.50	26.50	47.50	75.00	175.00	400.00	
1923*.....50,130,000	.25	.50	.90	1.25	3.50	16.50	
1923S......6,440,000	.75	1.25	3.25	6.00	25.00	100.00	
1924......24,010,000	.25	.35	.75	1.25	4.50	27.50	
1924D......6,810,000	.65	1.25	2.25	4.00	16.00	110.00	
1924S......7,120,000	.65	1.25	2.25	4.00	16.00	110.00	
1925......25,610,000	.25	.35	.75	1.25	4.50	27.50	
1925D.....5,117,000	1.50	2.50	4.50	17.50	60.00	250.00	
1925S......5,850,000	.65	1.25	2.25	6.00	20.00	110.00	
1926......32,160,000	.25	.35	.75	1.25	4.00	18.50	
1926D.....6,828,000	.60	.90	1.60	3.50	15.00	60.00	
1926S......1,520,000	5.00	7.00	11.50	19.00	70.00	325.00	
1927......28,080,000	.25	.35	.65	1.00	3.50	14.00	
1927D......4,812,000	.75	1.50	4.00	9.50	35.00	200.00	
1927S......4,770,000	.50	.90	2.25	6.00	20.00	120.00	
1928......19,480,000	.25	.35	.65	1.00	3.50	14.00	
1928D.....4,161,000	.75	1.25	3.50	10.00	30.00	110.00	
1928S†....7,400,000	.40	.75	1.50	3.50	15.00	55.00	
1929......25,970,000	.25	.35	.50	.80	2.75	10.00	
1929D.....5,034,000	.45	.75	1.50	2.50	6.00	15.00	
1929S......4,730,000	.45	.75	1.50	2.50	5.00	20.00	
1930*......6,770,000	.45	.60	1.00	2.00	4.50	16.00	
1930S......1,843,000	2.50	3.50	4.50	8.00	15.00	50.00	
1931.......3,150,000	.75	1.25	2.00	3.00	6.50	35.00	
1931D.....1,260,000	4.50	6.00	8.00	12.50	20.00	60.00	
1931S......1,800,000	2.50	3.50	4.50	8.00	15.00	55.00	
1934......24,080,000	.25	.35	.50	.75	1.50	10.00	
1934D†....6,772,000	.50	.75	1.00	1.50	3.00	27.50	
1935......58,830,000	.20	.30	.40	.60	1.00	4.00	
1935D....10,477,000	.25	.35	.60	1.00	2.75	24.00	
1935S.....15,840,000	.25	.35	.55	.85	1.50	9.00	
1936 (4,130)							
.....87,504,130	.12	.15	.20	.25	.40	3.00	$100.00
1936D....16,132,000	.20	.25	.40	.60	2.00	20.00	
1936S......9,210,000	.20	.25	.50	.75	2.00	10.00	
1937 (5,756)							
.....56,865,756	.12	.15	.20	.25	.40	3.00	50.00

*Dimes dated 1923D and 1930D are counterfeit.

†Large and small mint mark varieties, see page 59.

DIMES

Quan. Minted	Good	V.G.	Fine	V.F.	E.F.	Unc.	Proof
1937D....14,146,000	$ .20	$ .25	$ .40	$ .65	$1.00	$6.50	
1937S......9,740,000	.20	.25	.50	.70	1.15	6.00	
1938 (8,728)							
.....22,198,728	.12	.15	.20	.25	.35	3.75	$32.50
1938D.....5,537,000	.20	.30	.50	.75	1.50	10.00	
1938S......8,090,000	.20	.25	.50	.75	1.50	2.50	
1939 (9,321)							
.....67,749,321	.12	.15	.20	.25	.35	3.00	30.00
1939D....24,394,000	.15	.20	.30	.45	.60	3.00	
1939S.....10,540,000	.20	.25	.50	.90	1.60	12.00	
1940 (11,827)							
.....65,361,827		.15	.20	.25	.35	2.25	25.00
1940D....21,198,000		.15	.20	.25	.50	2.25	
1940S.....21,560,000		.15	.20	.25	.50	2.50	
1941 (16,557)							
....175,106,557		.15	.20	.25	.35	1.50	22.00
1941D....45,634,000		.15	.20	.30	.50	2.25	
1941S*....43,090,000		.15	.20	.25	.50	1.75	

Enlarged detail of Philadelphia 1942 2 over 1 dime. Denver Mint variety is similar but 1 is less prominent.

Quan. Minted	V.G	Fine	V.F.	E.F.	Unc.	Proof
1942, 2 over 1... } 205,432,329	$100.00	$125.00	$150.00	$200.00	$650.00	
1942....(22,329)	....		.20	.35	1.25	$22.00
1942D, 2 over 1.. } 60,740,000	....	150.00	200.00	——	——	
1942D..........	....		.20	.35	1.25	
1942S...........49,300,000	....		.20	.35	2.00	
1943........191,710,000	....		.20	.35	1.25	
1943D..........71,949,000	....		.20	.35	1.25	
1943S..........60,400,000	....		.20	.35	1.50	
1944.........231,410,000	....		.20	.35	1.25	
1944D..........62,224,000	....		.20	.35	1.25	
1944S..........49,490,000	....		.20	.35	1.25	
1945.........159,130,000	....		.20	.35	1.25	
1945D..........40,245,000	....		.20	.35	1.25	
1945S Normal S. } 41,920,000	....		.20	.35	1.25	
1945S Micro S*..	.30	.60	1.25	3.00	8.50	

*Large and small mint mark varieties, see page 59.

ROOSEVELT TYPE 1946 to Date

John R. Sinnock (whose initials JS are at the truncation of the neck) designed this dime showing a portrait of Franklin D. Roosevelt. The design has heavier lettering and a more modernistic character than preceding types.

Mint mark on reverse 1946-1964

Mint mark on obverse starting 1968

DIMES

Designer John R. Sinnock. Standards same as previous issue.

FINE—Flame worn smooth. Horizontal lines on torch do not show. All vertical lines will show.
VERY FINE—Hair above ear slightly worn. All vertical lines on torch plain.
EXTRA FINE—All lines of torch, flame and hair very plain.

	Quan. Minted	Fine	V.F.	E.F.	Unc.	Proof
1946	255,250,000	$ .15	$ .20	$ .30	$ .45	
1946D	61,043,500	.15	.20	.30	.55	
1946S	27,900,000	.15	.25	.40	1.10	
1947	121,520,000	.15	.25	.40	1.00	
1947D	46,835,000	.20	.30	.40	1.10	
1947S	34,840,000	.15	.25	.40	1.00	
1948	74,950,000	.20	.35	.60	1.60	
1948D	52,841,000	.20	.30	.40	1.10	
1948S	35,520,000	.15	.25	.40	1.20	
1949	30,940,000	.30	.50	1.00	7.50	
1949D	26,034,000	.20	.35	.60	2.60	
1949S	13,510,000	.65	1.00	1.75	11.00	
1950 (51,386)	50,181,500	.20	.30	.40	1.60	$15.00
1950D	46,803,000	.20	.30	.50	2.25	
1950S	20,440,000	.40	.70	1.25	6.50	
1951 (57,500)	103,937,602	.15	.25	.35	.90	12.00
1951D	56,529,000	.15	.25	.35	.90	
1951S	31,630,000	.30	.50	1.00	4.50	
1952 (81,980)	99,122,073	.15	.25	.35	.60	6.00
1952D	122,100,000	.15	.20	.30	.65	
1952S	44,419,500	.20	.30	.50	1.80	
1953 (128,800)	53,618,920	.15	.20	.30	.60	5.00
1953D	136,433,000	.15	.20	.30	.45	
1953S	39,180,000	.15	.20	.35	.60	
1954 (233,300)	114,243,503	.15	.20	.25	.35	2.50
1954D	106,397,000	.15	.20	.25	.35	
1954S	22,860,000	.15	.20	.35	.65	
1955 (378,200)	12,828,381	.30	.45	.85	1.25	3.50
1955D	13,959,000	.25	.40	.55	.85	
1955S	18,510,000	.30	.35	.45	.65	
1956 (669,384)	109,309,384				.15	.35	1.10
1956D	108,015,100				.15	.35	
1957 (1,247,952)	161,407,952				.15	.35	1.10
1957D	113,354,330				.20	.60	
1958 (875,652)	32,785,652				.30	.65	2.00
1958D	136,564,600				.15	.35	
1959 (1,149,291)	86,929,291				.15	.35	1.25
1959D	164,919,790				.15	.35	
1960 (1,691,602)	72,081,602				.15	.35	1.00
1960D	200,160,400				.15	.35	
1961 (3,028,244)	96,758,244				.15	.35	.90
1961D	209,146,550				.15	.35	
1962 (3,218,019)	75,668,019				.15	.35	.90
1962D	334,948,380				.15	.35	
1963 (3,075,645)	126,725,645				.15	.25	.90
1963D	421,476,530				.15	.25	
1964 (3,950,762)	933,310,762				.15	.25	.80
1964D	1,357,517,180				.15	.25	

DIMES

Clad Coinage

Weight 2.27 grams; composition: outer layers of copper nickel (.750 copper, .250 nickel) bonded to inner core of pure copper; diameter 17.9 mm; reeded edge.

	Quan. Minted	Unc.	Proof
1965	1,652,140,570	$ .20	
1966	1,382,734,540	.20	
1967	2,244,007,320	.20	
1968	424,470,400	.20	
1968D	480,748,280	.20	
1968S Proof only*	3,041,509		$2.00
1969	145,790,000	.20	
1969D	563,323,870	.20	
1969S Proof only	2,934,631		1.85
1970	345,570,000	.20	
1970D	754,942,100	.20	
1970S Proof only*	2,632,810		$1.85
1971	162,690,000	$ .20	
1971D	377,914,240	.20	
1971S Proof only	(3,244,138)		1.75
1972	431,540,000	.20	
1972D	330,290,000	.20	
1972S Proof only	(3,267,667)		1.75
1973		.20	
1973D		.20	
1973S Proof only			1.50

*Varieties of 1968 and 1970 proof dimes without S mint mark were made in error. See pages 59-60.

TWENTY-CENT PIECES — 1875-1878

This short-lived coin was authorized by the Act of March 3, 1875. Soon after

the appearance of the first twenty-cent pieces, the people complained about the similarity in design and size to the quarter-dollar. The eagle is very similar to that used on the Trade Dollar. The edge of the coin is plain. Most of the 1876CC coins were melted at the mint and never released.

Designer William Barber; weight 5 grams; composition: .900 silver, .100 copper; diameter 22 mm; plain edge; mints: Philadelphia, Carson City, San Francisco.

GOOD—LIBERTY on shield obliterated. Letters and date legible.
VERY GOOD—LIBERTY will not show. Other details will be bold.
FINE—At least 3 letters of LIBERTY show.
VERY FINE—LIBERTY completely readable, but partly weak.
EXTRA FINE—LIBERTY sharp. Only slight wear on high points of coin.

	Quan. Minted	Good	V.G.	Fine	V.F.	E.F.	Unc.	Proof
1875..(1,200)	39,700	$25.00	$30.00	$45.00	$60.00	$100.00	$300.00	$375.00
1875CC	133,290	27.50	35.00	50.00	67.50	110.00	350.00	
1875S	1,155,000	23.00	27.50	43.00	57.50	100.00	300.00	
1876..(1,150)	15,900	30.00	37.50	50.00	70.00	120.00	350.00	400.00
1876CC	10,000	1972 Champa Sale				$24,000.00		
1877..(510)	510							675.00
1878..(600)	600							625.00

QUARTER DOLLARS 1796 To Date

Authorized in 1792, this denomination was not issued until four years later. The first coinage, dated 1796, follows the pattern of the early half-dimes and dimes by the absence of a mark of value. In 1804 the value "25c" was added to the reverse. Figures were used until 1838 when the term "QUAR. DOL." appeared. It was not until 1892 that the value was spelled out entirely.

The first type weighed 104 grains which remained standard until modified to 103⅛ grains by the Act of January 18, 1837. As with the dime and half dime, the weight was reduced and arrows placed at the date in 1853, and rays were placed in the field of the reverse during that year only.

The law of 1873 also affected the quarter, for the weight was slightly increased and arrows again placed at the date.

Proofs of some dates prior to 1855 are known to exist, and all are rare.

BIBLIOGRAPHY

Browning, A. W. *The Early Quarter Dollars of the United States 1796-1838*. New York, 1925.

Haseltine, J. W. *Type Table of United States Dollars, Half Dollars and Quarter Dollars*. Philadelphia, 1881 (reprinted 1927, 1968).

DRAPED BUST TYPE, SMALL EAGLE REVERSE 1796

Designer Robert Scot; weight 6.74 grams; composition: .8924 silver, .1076 copper; approx. diameter 27.5 mm; reeded edge. All coined at Philadelphia.

FAIR—Details clear enough to identify.

GOOD—Date readable. Bust outlined, but no detail.

VERY GOOD—All but deepest drapery folds worn smooth. Hairlines nearly gone and curls lack detail.

FINE—All drapery lines visible. Hair partly worn.

VERY FINE—Only left side of drapery is indistinct.

	Quan. Minted	Fair	Good	V.G.	Fine	V.F.	Unc.
1796	6,146	$550.00	$800.00	$1,300	$2,250	$3,100	$8,000

DRAPED BUST TYPE, HERALDIC EAGLE REVERSE 1804-1807

1804	6,738	95.00	175.00	235.00	400.00	750.00	25,000
1805	121,394	60.00	85.00	100.00	175.00	350.00	1,500
1806 6 over 5	206,124	50.00	75.00	100.00	175.00	350.00	1,600
1806 Normal date	206,124	45.00	70.00	95.00	160.00	300.00	1,400
1807	220,643	45.00	70.00	95.00	160.00	300.00	1,400

QUARTER DOLLARS

CAPPED BUST TYPE 1815-1838
Variety 1 — Large size 1815-1828

FAIR—Details clear enough to identify.
GOOD—Date, letters and stars readable. Hair under headband smooth. Cap lines worn smooth.
VERY GOOD—Rim well defined. Main details visible. Full LIBERTY on cap. Hair above eye nearly smooth.
FINE—All hairlines show but drapery has only part details. Shoulder clasp distinct.
VERY FINE—All details show, but some wear. Clasp and ear sharp.
EXTRA FINE—All details show distinctly. Hair well outlined.

Designer John Reich; weight 6.74 grams; composition: .8924 silver, .1076 copper; approx. diameter 27 mm; reeded edge. All coined at Philadelphia.

1818
8 over 5

Quan. Minted	Fair	Good	V.G.	Fine	V.F.	E.F.	Unc.
1815.........89,235	$18.00	$24.00	$40.00	$65.00	$175.00	$350.00	$1,150
1818 8 over 5	18.00	24.00	40.00	65.00	175.00	350.00	1,100
1818 Normal date... }361,174	17.00	22.50	37.50	60.00	140.00	275.00	1,000
1819 Small 9 }144,000	17.00	22.50	37.50	60.00	140.00	275.00	1,000
1819 Large 9	17.00	22.50	37.50	60.00	140.00	275.00	1,000

1820 Small 0   1820 Large 0   1822, 25 Over 50c

	Fair	Good	V.G.	Fine	V.F.	E.F.	Unc.
1820 Small 0 }127,444	17.00	22.50	37.50	60.00	140.00	250.00	1,000
1820 Large 0	17.00	22.50	37.50	60.00	140.00	250.00	1,000
1821.......216,851	17.00	22.50	37.50	60.00	140.00	250.00	1,000
1822 All kinds.64,080	17.00	22.50	37.50	60.00	140.00	300.00	1,100
1822 25 over 50c....	140.00	185.00	250.00	385.00	700.00	1,000	2,500
1823, 3 over 2 .17,800	500.00	800.00	1,100	1,500	2,500		
1824, 4 over 2...——	28.00	40.00	50.00	85.00	140.00	275.00	1,200

1825 Over 22 (wide date)   1825 Over 23 (close date)

	Fair	Good	V.G.	Fine	V.F.	E.F.	Unc.
1825 over 22 }168,000	18.00	25.00	35.00	55.00	110.00	225.00	1,100
1825 over 23	18.00	25.00	35.00	55.00	110.00	225.00	1,000
1825 over 24	18.00	25.00	35.00	55.00	110.00	225.00	1,100
1827 Original (Curled base 2 in 25c) 4,000 Minted...........(6 or 7 known)							
1827 Restrike (Square base 2 in 25c)...............1972 Delp Sale $10,500							
1828 All kds .102,000	18.00	25.00	35.00	55.00	110.00	225.00	1,000
1828, 25 over 50c....	50.00	75.00	100.00	150.00	275.00	450.00	1,400

QUARTER DOLLARS
Variety 2 — Reduced size, no motto on reverse 1831-1838

GOOD—*Bust is well defined. Hair under headband is smooth. Date, letters, stars readable. Scant rims.*
VERY GOOD—*Details apparent but worn on high spots. Rims strong. Full LIBERTY.*
FINE—*All hairlines visible. Drapery partly worn. Shoulder clasp distinct.*
VERY FINE—*Only top spots worn. Clasp sharp. Ear distinct.*

Designer William Kneass; weight 6.74 grams; composition: .8924 silver, .1076 copper; diameter 24.3 mm; reeded edge. All coined at Philadelphia.

1831 Small Letters Large Letters

	Quan. Minted	Good	V.G.	Fine	V.F.	E.F.	Unc.
1831 Small letters... } 398,000		$16.00	$25.00	$40.00	$80.00	$150.00	$850.00
1831 Large letters...		16.00	25.00	40.00	80.00	150.00	850.00
1832	320,000	16.00	25.00	40.00	80.00	150.00	850.00
1833	156,000	20.00	40.00	60.00	100.00	200.00	1,200
1834	286,000	16.00	25.00	40.00	80.00	150.00	850.00
1835	1,952,000	16.00	25.00	40.00	80.00	150.00	850.00
1836	472,000	16.00	25.00	40.00	80.00	150.00	850.00
1837	252,400	16.00	25.00	40.00	80.00	150.00	850.00
1838	Both types 832,000	16.00	25.00	40.00	80.00	150.00	850.00

QUARTER DOLLARS
LIBERTY SEATED TYPE 1838-1891
Variety 1 — No motto above eagle 1838-1853

GOOD—*Scant rim. LIBERTY on shield worn off. Date and letters readable.*
VERY GOOD—*Rim fairly defined, at least 3 letters in LIBERTY evident.*
FINE—*LIBERTY complete, but partly weak.*
VERY FINE—*LIBERTY strong.*

Designer Christian Gobrecht; weight 6.68 grams; composition: .900 silver, .100 copper; diameter 24.3 mm; reeded edge; mints: Philadelphia, New Orleans.

Mint mark location is on the reverse below the eagle.

No Drapery From Elbow

Drapery From Elbow

1838 No drapery		9.00	15.00	22.50	40.00	85.00	600.00
1839 No drapery	491,146	9.00	15.00	22.50	40.00	85.00	600.00
1840O No drapery							
All kinds	425,200	9.00	15.00	22 50	40.00	85.00	600.00
1840 Drapery	188,127	5.50	10.00	14.00	40.00	65.00	250.00
1840O Drapery		5.50	9.00	13.00	40.00	65.00	250.00
1841	120,000	13.00	17.50	24.00	45.00	65.00	250.00
1841O	452,000	5.00	7.50	11.00	35.00	55.00	250.00

QUARTER DOLLARS

Small Date  Large Date

	Quan. Minted	Good	V.G.	Fine	V.F.	E.F.	Unc.
1842 Small date ..... 1842 Large date	} 88,000				┌Proofs Only ──		
		$5.00	$7.50	$10.00	$20.00	$35.00	$200.00
1842O Small date ... 1842O Large date ...	} 769,000	13.00	18.00	22.50	45.00	70.00	260.00
		5.50	8.50	12.00	24.00	35.00	200.00
1843	645,600	4.00	6.00	9.00	20.00	35.00	200.00
1843O	968,000	4.00	6.00	9.00	20.00	35.00	200.00
1844	421,200	4.00	6.00	9.00	20.00	35.00	200.00
1844O	740,000	4.00	6.00	9.00	20.00	35.00	200.00
1845	922,000	4.00	6.00	9 00	20.00	35.00	200.00
1846	510,000	4.00	6.00	9.00	20.00	35.00	200.00
1847	734,000	4.00	6.00	9.00	20.00	35.00	200.00
1847O	368,000	4.50	6.50	10.00	20.00	35.00	200.00
1848	146,000	5.00	7.50	11.00	20.00	35.00	200.00
1849	340,000	4.00	6.00	9.00	20.00	35.00	200.00
1849O	──	65.00	100.00	150.00	250.00	350.00	650.00
1850	190,800	5.00	7.50	11.00	20.00	35.00	200.00
1850O	412,000	4.00	6.00	9.00	20.00	35.00	200.00
1851	160,000	4.00	6.00	9.00	20.00	35.00	200.00
1851O	88,000	4.50	7.50	12.00	40.00	65.00	240.00
1852	177,060	4.25	6.50	10.00	20.00	35.00	200.00
1852O	96,000	7.00	10.00	15.00	40.00	65.00	250.00
1853* Recut date, no arrows or rays	44,200	50.00	70.00	110.00	160.00	240.00	800.00

*Beware of altered 1858.

Variety 2 —
Arrows at date,
rays around eagle
1853 only

Weight 6.22 grams; composition: .900 silver, .100 copper; diameter 24.3 mm; reeded edge; mints: Philadelphia, New Orleans, San Francisco, Carson City.

The reduction in weight is indicated by the arrows at the date. Rays were added on the reverse side in the field around the eagle. The arrows were retained until 1856, but the rays were omitted after 1853.

1853	15,210,020	7.00	10.00	16.00	35.00	90.00	600.00
1853O	1,332,000	10.00	15.00	20.00	50.00	125.00	650.00

Variety 3 — Arrows at date, no rays 1854-1855

1854	12,380,000	5.00	7.00	11.00	25.00	50.00	350.00
1854O	1,484,000	6.00	8.00	12.00	28.00	55.00	350.00
1855	2,857,000	6.00	8.00	12.00	28.00	55.00	350.00
1855O	176,000	40.00	55.00	80.00	140.00	250.00	600.00
1855S	396,400	40.00	55.00	80.00	140.00	250.00	600.00

QUARTER DOLLARS
Variety 1 resumed 1856-1865

	Quan. Minted	Good	V.G.	Fine	V.F.	Unc.	Proof
1856	7,264,000	$3.75	$4.75	$7.00	$10.00	$165.00	$700.00
1856O	968,000	4.00	5.00	8.00	12.00	175.00	
1856S	286,000	18.00	27.50	40.00	80.00	300.00	
1857	9,644,000	3.75	4.75	7.00	10.00	165.00	700.00
1857O	1,180,000	4.00	5.00	8.00	12.00	175.00	
1857S	82,000	20.00	35.00	50.00	90.00	300.00	
1858	7,368,000	3.75	4.75	7.00	10.00	165.00	500.00
1858O	520,000	4.50	6.50	8.00	12.00	175.00	
1858S	121,000	25.00	30.00	40.00	75.00	300.00	
1859	1,344,000	4.00	5.00	8.00	12.00	165.00	250.00
1859O	260,000	4.50	6.50	8.00	12.00	175.00	
1859S	80,000	25.00	30.00	40.00	80.00	300.00	
1860......(1,000)	805,400	3.75	4.75	7.00	10.00	165.00	215.00
1860O	388,000	5.00	7.00	9.00	13.00	175.00	
1860S	56,000	20.00	25.00	35.00	75.00	325.00	
1861......(1,000)	4,854,600	3.75	4.75	7.00	10.00	165.00	215.00
1861S	96,000	16.50	20.00	30.00	60.00	275.00	
1862.......(550)	932,550	3.75	4.75	7.00	10.00	165.00	215.00
1862S	67,000	18.00	22.50	35.00	70.00	300.00	
1863.......(460)	192,060	6.50	9.00	12.00	20.00	175.00	215.00
1864.......(470)	94,070	8.00	10.00	14.00	25.00	200.00	225.00
1864S	20,000	35.00	55.00	85.00	150.00	550.00	
1865.......(500)	59,300	9.00	12.00	18.00	30.00	200.00	225.00
1865S	41,000	12.00	16.00	25.00	60.00	350.00	
1866 Transitional pattern....(unique)							——

Variety 4 — Motto above eagle 1866-1873

The motto **IN GOD WE TRUST** was added to the reverse side in 1866. As on the half dollar and silver dollar the motto has been retained since that time.

		Good	V.G.	Fine	V.F.	Unc.	Proof
1866.......(725)	17,525	20.00	27.50	35.00	50.00	200.00	225.00
1866S	28,000	15.00	20.00	27.50	60.00	375.00	
1867.......(625)	20,625	7.00	12.00	20.00	30.00	200.00	200.00
1867S	48,000	13.00	17.50	24.00	50.00	265.00	
1868.......(600)	30,000	6.00	9.00	14.00	23.00	200.00	225.00
1868S	96,000	12.00	15.00	20.00	50.00	250.00	
1869.......(600)	16,600	12.00	16.00	24.00	35.00	185.00	240.00
1869S	76,000	12.00	15.00	20.00	50.00	225.00	
1870......(1,000)	87,400	4.50	5.50	8.00	12.00	165.00	200.00
1870CC	8,340	125.00	150.00	200.00	425.00	1,250	
1871.......(960)	119,160	4.00	5.00	6.00	12.00	175.00	215.00
1871CC	10,890	110.00	130.00	165.00	285.00	1,250	
1871S	30,900	10.00	15.00	25.00	50.00	225.00	

QUARTER DOLLARS

	Quan. Minted	Good	V.G.	Fine	V.F.	Unc.	Proof
1872.......(950)	182,950	$4.00	$5.00	$6.00	$12.00	$175.00	$210.00
1872CC..............9,100		165.00	200.00	275.00	500.00	1,500	
1872S...............83,000		15.00	20.00	30.00	50.00	225.00	
1873 Closed 3 (600). ⎰ 212,600		7.50	11.00	16.00	20.00	200.00	215.00
1873 Open 3....... ⎱		7.50	11.00	16.00	20.00	200.00	
1873CC..............4,000			550.00	700.00	1,400	——	

Variety 5 — Arrows at date 1873-1874

Weight 6.25 grams; composition: .900 silver, .100 copper; diameter 24.3 mm; reeded edge; mints: Philadelphia, San Francisco, Carson City.

Arrows were placed at the date in the years 1873 and 1874 to denote the change of weight from 96 to 96.45 grains.

1873.......(540)	1,271,700	20.00	25.00	35.00	75.00	325.00	425.00
1873CC.............12,462		350.00	475.00	700.00	950.00	2,000	
1873S..............156,000		25.00	30.00	40.00	85.00	325.00	
1874.......(700)	471,900	20.00	25.00	35.00	65.00	300.00	400.00
1874S..............392,000		25.00	30.00	40.00	70.00	300.00	

Variety 4 resumed 1875-1891

1875.......(700)	4,293,500	3.75	4.50	6.00	10.00	165.00	175.00
1875CC............140,000		10.00	13.00	20.00	37.50	240.00	
1875S..............680,000		10.00	13.00	20.00	37.50	175.00	
1876......(1,150)	17,817,150	3.75	4.50	6.00	10.00	165.00	175.00
1876CC...........4,944,000		4.00	5.00	7.00	10.00	165.00	
1876S............8,596,000		3.75	4.50	6.00	10.00	165.00	
1877.......(510)	10,911,710	3.75	4.50	6.00	10.00	165.00	200.00
1877CC...........4,192,000		4.00	5.00	7.00	10.00	165.00	
1877S All kinds....8,996,000		3.75	4.50	6.00	10.00	165.00	
1877S over horizontal S.....				95.00	125.00	350.00	
1878.......(800)	2,260,800	3.75	4.50	6.00	10.00	165.00	185.00
1878CC............996,000		7.00	9.00	12.00	20.00	175.00	
1878S..............140,000		150.00	200.00	275.00	400.00	1,000	
1879.......(250)	14,700	20.00	22.50	27.50	35.00	185.00	200.00
1880......(1,355)	14,955	20.00	22.50	27.50	35.00	185.00	200.00

QUARTER DOLLARS

	Quan.	Minted	Good	V.G.	Fine	V.F.	Unc.	Proof
1881.......(975)		12,975	$20.00	$22.50	$27.50	$35.00	$185.00	$200.00
1882......(1,100)		16,300	20.00	22.50	27.50	35.00	185.00	200.00
1883......(1,039)		15,439	20.00	22.50	27.50	35.00	185.00	200.00
1884.......(875)		8,875	25.00	27.50	30.00	37.50	225.00	225.00
1885.......(930)		14,530	20.00	22.50	27.50	35.00	185.00	215.00
1886.......(886)		5,886	30.00	35.00	40.00	60.00	250.00	250.00
1887.......(710)		10,710	22.50	25.00	32.50	40.00	185.00	225.00
1888.......(832)		10,833	22.50	25.00	32.50	40.00	185.00	225.00
1888S.............1,216,000			3.75	4.50	6.00	10.00	165.00	
1889.......(711)		12,711	20.00	22.50	27.50	35.00	185.00	225.00
1890.......(590)		80,590	6.00	8.00	12.00	15.00	165.00	210.00
1891.......(600)	3,920,600		3.75	4.50	6.00	9.00	165.00	210.00
1891O.............68,000			80.00	95.00	125.00	200.00	650.00	
1891S.............2,216,000			3.75	4.50	6.00	10.00	165.00	

BARBER or LIBERTY HEAD TYPE 1892-1916

Like other silver coins of this type the quarter dollars minted from 1892 to 1916 were designed by Charles E. Barber. His initial B is found at the truncation of the neck of Liberty. Mint mark location is on reverse below eagle.

Designer Charles E. Barber; weight 6.25 grams; composition: .900 silver, .100 copper; diameter 24.3 mm; reeded edge; mints: Philadelphia, Denver, New Orleans, San Francisco.

GOOD—Date and legends readable. LIBERTY worn off headband.

VERY GOOD—Minimum of 3 letters in LIBERTY readable.

FINE—LIBERTY completely readable but not sharp.

VERY FINE—All letters in LIBERTY evenly plain.

EXTRA FINE—LIBERTY bold, and its ribbon distinct.

	Quan. Minted	Good	V.G.	Fine	V.F.	E.F.	Unc.	Proof
1892 (1,245)	8,237,245	$1.35	$2.75	$5.00	$11.00	$22.50	$115.00	$175.00
1892O.......2,640,000		3.50	4.75	8.25	14.50	25.00	120.00	
1892S........964,079		10.00	16.00	24.00	37.50	65.00	185.00	
1893 (792)	5,444,815	1.35	2.75	5.00	11.00	22.50	115.00	175.00
1893O.......3,396,000		2.00	3.75	8.00	14.00	25.00	120.00	
1893S.......1,454,535		4.50	6.50	10.00	16.50	27.50	130.00	
1894 (972)	3,432,972	1.75	3.00	6.00	11.00	22.50	115.00	175.00
1894O.......2,852,000		2.00	4.25	8.00	12.00	27.50	125.00	
1894S.......2,648,821		2.25	4.50	8.50	14.00	27.50	125.00	
1895 (880)	4,440,880	1.25	2.25	5.00	10.00	21.00	115.00	160.00
1895O.......2,816,000		2.25	4.00	7.50	16.00	35.00	125.00	
1895S.......1,764,681		3.50	5.50	9.00	16.00	30.00	125.00	
1896 (762)	3,874,762	1.50	2.50	5.00	9.00	20.00	115.00	160.00
1896O.......1,484,000		5.00	9.00	16.00	27.50	65.00	250.00	
1896S........188,039		85.00	145.00	200.00	290.00	500.00	1,400	
1897 (731)	8,140,731	1.35	2.75	5.00	10.00	22.50	115.00	160.00
1897O.......1,414,800		7.50	11.00	17.00	28.00	57.50	175.00	
1897S........542,229		10.00	13.00	21.00	32.50	62.50	225.00	
1898 (735)	11,100,735	1.35	2.75	5.00	10.00	22.50	115.00	160.00
1898O.......1,868,000		2.25	4.25	9.00	16.00	35.00	150.00	
1898S.......1,020,592		3.50	5.00	10.00	17.00	35.00	160.00	

QUARTER DOLLARS

	Quan. Minted	Good	V.G.	Fine	V.F.	E.F.	Unc.	Proof
1899 (846)	12,624,846	$1.35	$2.75	$5.00	$10.00	$22.50	$115.00	$160.00
1899O	2,644,000	2.75	4.00	8.00	16.00	30.00	140.00	
1899S	708,000	7.50	11.00	14.00	20.00	35.00	145.00	
1900 (912)	10,016,912	1.25	2.00	5.00	10.00	21.00	115.00	160.00
1900O	3,416,000	3.00	5.00	9.50	16.00	30.00	140.00	
1900S	1,858,585	1.75	4.00	9.00	15.00	35.00	145.00	
1901 (813)	8,892,813	1.25	2.00	5.00	10.00	21.00	115.00	160.00
1901O	1,612,000	9.00	15.00	30.00	50.00	125.00	375.00	
1901S	72,664	225.00	300.00	400.00	565.00	800.00	2,000	
1902 (777)	12,197,744	1.25	2.00	5.00	10.00	21.00	115.00	160.00
1902O	4,748,000	2.00	4.00	8.00	16.00	30.00	135.00	
1902S	1,524,612	4.00	6.00	13.00	21.00	37.50	150.00	
1903 (755)	9,670,064	1.25	2.00	5.00	10.00	21.00	115.00	160.00
1903O	3,500,000	2.50	4.50	10.00	22.50	60.00	200.00	
1903S	1,036,000	4.25	6.50	13.50	27.50	60.00	215.00	
1904 (670)	9,588,813	1.25	2.00	5.00	10.00	21.00	115.00	175.00
1904O	2,456,000	5.00	8.50	16.00	32.50	65.00	290.00	
1905 (727)	4,968,250	1.25	2.00	5.00	10.00	21.00	115.00	175.00
1905O	1,230,000	5.00	8.50	16.00	32.50	65.00	200.00	
1905S	1,884,000	3.50	6.00	10.00	18.00	40.00	150.00	
1906 (675)	3,656,435	1.25	2.00	5.00	10.00	21.00	115.00	175.00
1906D	3,280,000	1.50	2.25	5.25	10.00	21.00	115.00	
1906O	2,056,000	2.00	2.75	5.50	10.00	25.00	120.00	
1907 (575)	7,192,575	1.25	2.00	4.00	8.00	20.00	115.00	180.00
1907D	2,484,000	1.75	3.00	5.50	8.00	20.00	115.00	
1907O	4,560,000	1.25	2.00	4.00	8.00	20.00	115.00	
1907S	1,360,000	2.50	5.00	8.00	12.50	27.50	130.00	
1908 (545)	4,232,545	1.25	2.00	4.00	8.00	20.00	115.00	180 00
1908D	5,788,000	1.25	2.00	4.00	8.00	20.00	115.00	
1908O	6,244,000	1.25	2.00	4.00	8.00	20.00	115.00	
1908S	784,000	5.00	7.50	15.00	21.00	35.00	145.00	
1909 (650)	9,268,650	1.25	2.00	4.00	7.50	20.00	115.00	180.00
1909D	5,114,000	1.25	2.00	4.00	7.50	20.00	115.00	
1909O	712,000	11.00	16.00	32.00	50.00	100.00	365.00	
1909S	1,348,000	2.25	3.75	6.50	10.00	25.00	125.00	
1910 (551)	2,244,551	1.35	2.75	4.50	8.00	22.00	115.00	175.00
1910D	1,500,000	2.25	3.75	5.50	8.00	22.00	125.00	
1911 (543)	3,720,543	1.25	2.00	4.00	7.50	20.00	115.00	175.00
1911D	933,600	2.50	3.50	7.50	11.50	22.00	130.00	
1911S	988,000	2.25	3.25	7.00	11.00	24.00	130.00	
1912 (700)	4,400,700	1.25	2.00	4.00	7.50	20.00	115.00	175.00
1912S	708,000	4.00	7.50	13.00	24.00	50.00	170.00	
1913 (613)	484,613	5.00	8.50	13.00	22.00	45.00	210.00	210.00
1913D	1,450,800	2.25	4.00	6.00	9.00	25.00	130.00	
1913S	40,000	100.00	145.00	200.00	275.00	575.00	1,300	
1914 (380)	6,244,610	1.25	2.00	4.00	7.50	20.00	115.00	325.00
1914D	3,046,000	1.25	2.00	4.00	7.50	20.00	115.00	
1914S	264,000	10.00	15.00	21.00	45.00	125.00	350.00	
1915 (450)	3,480,450	1.25	2.00	4.00	7.50	20.00	115.00	325.00
1915D	3,694,000	1.25	2.00	4.00	7.50	20.00	115.00	
1915S	704,000	3.00	5.00	8.00	14.00	25.00	125.00	
1916	1,788,000	1.25	2.00	4.00	7.50	20.00	115.00	
1916D	6,540,800	1.25	2.00	4.00	7.50	20.00	115.00	

QUARTER DOLLARS
STANDING LIBERTY TYPE 1916-1930

This type quarter was designed by Hermon A. MacNeil. The left arm of Liberty is upraised bearing a shield in the attitude of protection, from which the cover is being drawn. The right hand bears the olive branch of peace. The designer's initial M is located above and to the right of the date.

There was a modification in 1917. The reverse has a new arrangement of the stars and the eagle is higher.

In 1925 a depression was made in the pedestal on which Liberty stands and which bears the date. On the first issues the dates wore off easily because they were too high and were not protected by other features of the coin. The new "recessed" dates proved more durable as a result of this change.

GOOD—Date and lettering readable. Top of date worn. Liberty's right leg and toes worn off. Left leg and drapery lines show much wear.
VERY GOOD—Distinct date. Toes show faintly. Drapery lines visible above her left leg.
FINE—High curve of right leg flat from thigh to ankle. Left leg shows only slight wear. Drapery lines over right thigh seen only at sides of leg.
VERY FINE—Garment line across right leg will be worn but show at sides.
EXTRA FINE—Flattened only at high spots. Her toes are sharp. Drapery lines across right leg are evident.
(Some modifications must be made for grading variety 2.)

Variety 1

Designer Hermon A. MacNeil. Standards same as previous issue; mints: Philadelphia, Denver, San Francisco.

Uncirculated pieces with fully struck head of Liberty are worth more than prices listed below.

	Quan. Minted	Good	V.G.	Fine	V.F.	E.F.	Unc.
1916	52,000	$250.00	$325.00	$410.00	$490.00	$600.00	$950.00
1917 Variety 1	8,792,000	4.00	5.25	7.75	11.75	20.00	85.00
1917D Variety 1	1,509,200	5.75	7.75	11.00	16.00	24.00	85.00
1917S Variety 1	1,952,000	5.75	7.75	11.00	16.00	24.00	90.00

1918S 8 over 7

Variety 2

Mint mark position is on obverse at left of date

	Quan. Minted	Good	V.G.	Fine	V.F.	E.F.	Unc.
1917 Variety 2	13,880,000	4.00	5.50	7.75	11.50	18.50	50.00
1917D Variety 2	6,224,400	8.00	12.00	16.50	21.00	30.00	85.00
1917S Variety 2	5,552,000	10.00	14.00	18.00	25.00	35.00	95.00
1918	14,240,000	4.00	6.00	10.00	15.00	25.00	70.00
1918D	7,380,000	7.50	10.50	15.00	22.50	30.00	85.00
1918S Norm. date	11,072,000	4.50	6.00	10.00	15.00	25.00	75.00
1918S 8 over 7			300.00	475.00	625.00	900.00	3,250
1919	11,324,000	5.00	6.75	10.00	15.00	25.00	67.50
1919D	1,944,000	25.00	32.50	47.50	65.00	115.00	300.00
1919S	1,836,000	27.50	37.50	50.00	70.00	125.00	350.00

QUARTER DOLLARS

	Quan. Minted	Good	V.G.	Fine	V.F.	E.F.	Unc.
1920	27,860,000	$3.50	$4.50	$6.00	$8.50	$12.00	$45.00
1920D	3,586,400	10.00	15.00	22.50	30.00	55.00	130.00
1920S	6,380,000	7.00	9.50	13.00	18.50	28.00	90.00
1921	1,916,000	22.50	30.00	45.00	62.50	90.00	300.00
1923	9,716,000	2.50	4.00	6.00	8.50	12.00	47.50
1923S	1,360,000	37.50	50.00	65.00	85.00	110.00	300.00
1924	10,920,000	2.50	4.00	6.00	8.50	12.00	50.00
1924D	3,112,000	8.50	12.00	14.00	19.00	25.00	60.00
1924S	2,860,000	9.50	12.50	18.00	25.00	35.00	115.00

Recessed Date Style 1925-1930

	Quan. Minted	Good	V.G.	Fine	V.F.	E.F.	Unc.
1925	12,280,000	.90	1.25	2.75	4.75	9.50	40.00
1926	11,316,000	.90	1.25	2.75	4.75	9.50	40.00
1926D	1,716,000	1.00	1.75	3.50	6.00	10.00	45.00
1926S	2,700,000	1.25	2.50	4.50	18.50	45.00	160.00
1927	11,912,000	.90	1.25	2.75	4.75	9.50	42.50
1927D	976,400	2.25	3.50	6.00	9.50	17.50	80.00
1927S	396,000	5.00	7.50	15.00	75.00	140.00	700.00
1928	6,336,000	.90	1.35	2.75	4.75	9.50	42.50
1928D	1,627,600	.90	1.35	2.75	4.75	10.00	42.50
1928S*	2,644,000	.90	1.35	2.75	4.75	10.00	42.50
1929	11,140,000	.90	1.35	2.75	4.75	10.00	42.50
1929D	1,358,000	.90	1.35	2.75	4.75	10.00	50.00
1929S	1,764,000	.90	1.35	2.75	4.75	10.00	50.00
1930	5,632,000	.90	1.35	2.75	4.75	10.00	42.50
1930S	1,556,000	.90	1.35	2.75	4.75	10.00	45.00

*Large and small mint mark varieties, see page 59.

WASHINGTON TYPE 1932 to Date

GOOD—Letters and date flat, but separated from rim. No hairlines near face.
VERY GOOD—Wing tips outlined. Rims are fine and even. Tops of letters at rim are flattened.
FINE—Hairlines about ear are visible. Tiny feathers on eagle's breast are faintly visible.
EXTRA FINE—Hairlines sharp. Wear spots confined to top of eagle's legs and center of breast.

This type was intended to be a commemorative issue marking the two-hundredth anniversary of Washington's birth. John Flanagan, a New York sculptor, was the designer. The initials JF are found at the base of the neck. Mint mark position is on the reverse below wreath, 1932 to 1964.

	Quan. Minted	Good	V.G.	Fine	E.F.	Unc.	Proof
1932	5,404,000	$ .75	$1.10	$1.55	$3.50	$27.50	
1932D	436,800	32.50	40.00	48.00	75.00	250.00	
1932S	408,000	32.50	37.50	45.00	60.00	115.00	
1934 Light motto	31,912,052	.40	.75	2.00	5.00	18.00	
1934 Hvy. motto		.40	.60	1.25	3.00	10.00	
1934D	3,527,200	1.25	1.75	4.00	13.00	67.50	
1935	32,484,000	.40	.50	1.00	2.75	7.50	
1935D	5,780,000	.50	1.00	2.00	9.50	67.50	
1935S	5,660,000	.50	.90	1.75	8.50	30.00	
1936 (3,837)	41,303,837	.40	.45	.75	1.50	7.00	$335.00
1936D	5,374,000	1.00	1.50	4.00	35.00	225.00	
1936S	3,828,000	.75	1.00	1.50	7.00	30.00	

QUARTER DOLLARS

	Quan. Minted	Good	V.G.	Fine	E.F.	Unc.	Proof
1937......(5,542)	19,701,542	$ .40	$ .50	$ .75	$2.00	$7.50	$70.00
1937D............	7,189,600	.40	.85	1.25	4.00	10.00	
1937S............	1,652,000	5.00	6.00	8.00	20.00	60.00	
1938......(8,045)	9,480,045	.50	1.00	1.75	12.00	40.00	50.00
1938S............	2,832,000	1.75	2.10	3.00	9.00	27.50	
1939......(8,795)	33,548,795	.40	.75	1.00	2.50	6.50	30.00
1939D............	7,092,000	.40	.75	1.00	2.75	8.00	
1939S............	2,628,000	2.00	2.50	3.00	8.50	30.00	
1940.....(11,246)	35,715,246	.40	.75	1.00	2.50	7.50	25.00
1940D............	2,797,600	1.50	1.85	2.85	10.00	40.00	
1940S............	8,244,000	.40	.80	1.00	2.00	6.50	
1941.....(15,287)	79,047,287		.40	.75	1.25	1.75	22.50
1941D............	16,714,800		.40	.90	1.60	6.50	
1941S*...........	16,080,000		.40	.50	1.50	6.50	
1942.....(21,123)	102,117,123		.40	.50	1.10	2.00	22.50
1942D............	17,487,200		.40	.50	1.15	3.50	
1942S............	19,384,000		.40	.60	2.00	27.50	
1943.............	99,700,000		.40	.50	1.10	2.50	
1943D............	16,095,600		.40	.50	1.10	3.25	
1943S............	21,700,000		.40	.50	1.50	5.50	
1944.............	104,956,000		.40	.50	.90	1.25	
1944D............	14,600,800		.40	.50	1.10	3.00	
1944S............	12,560,000		.40	.50	1.25	2.50	
1945.............	74,372,000		.40	.50	.90	1.25	
1945D............	12,341,600		.40	.50	1.10	3.00	
1945S	17,004,001		.40	.50	1.00	2.25	
1946.............	53,436,000		.40	.50	.75	1.25	
1946D............	9,072,800		.40	.50	1.10	3.00	
1946S............	4,204,000		.40	.50	1.75	4.00	
1947.............	22,556,000		.40	.50	.75	1.60	
1947D............	15,338,400		.40	.50	.75	1.60	
1947S............	5,532,000		.40	.50	1.50	3.50	
1948.............	35,196,000			.50	.75	1.10	
1948D............	16,766,800			.75	1.00	2.50	
1948S............	15,960,000			.50	.75	1.75	
1949.............	9,312,000			.75	2.25	9.00	
1949D............	10,068,400			.80	1.10	4.25	
1950.....(51,386)	24,971,512			.55	.85	1.50	15.00
1950D............	21,075,600			.60	.90	1.75	
1950S............	10,284,004			.75	1.10	3.00	
1951.....(57,500)	43,505,602			.50	.60	1.00	15.00
1951D............	35,354,800			.50	.75	1.00	
1951S............	8,948,000			.90	1.50	6.50	
1952.....(81,980)	38,862,073			.50	.60	1.00	7.50
1952D............	49,795,200			.50	.60	1.00	
1952S............	13,707,800			.75	1.00	2.75	
1953....(128,800)	18,664,920			.50	.75	2.00	6.00
1953D............	56,112,400			.40	.60	.85	
1953S............	14,016,000			.40	.60	1.75	
1954....(233,300)	54,645,503			.40	.50	.75	2.75
1954D............	46,305,500			.40	.50	.75	
1954S............	11,834,722			.40	.60	1.25	
1955....(378,200)	18,558,381			.40	.60	2.00	3.50

*Large and small mint mark varieties, see page 59.

QUARTER DOLLARS

	Quan. Minted	Fine	E.F.	Unc.	Proof
1955D................3,182,400	$2.00	$2.50	$3.25	
1956...........(669,384) 44,813,384.......			.85	$1.35
1956D................32,334,500.......			.85	
1957..........(1,247,952) 47,779,952.......			.85	1.15
1957D................77,924,160.......			.85	
1958...........(875,652) 7,235,652.......		.90	1.75	2.50
1958D................78,124,900.............			.75	
1959..........(1,149,291) 25,533,291.............			.75	1.50
1959D................62,054,232.............			.70	
1960..........(1,691,602) 30,855,602.............			.70	1.25
1960D................63,000,324.............			.70	
1961..........(3,028,244) 40,064,244.............			.70	1.10
1961D................83,656,928.............			.70	
1962..........(3,218,019) 39,374,019.............			.70	1.10
1962D...............127,554,756.............			.70	
1963..........(3,075,645) 77,391,645.............			.70	1.10
1963D...............135,288,184.............			.70	
1964..........(3,950,762) 564,341,347.............			.70	1.00
1964D...............704,135,528.............			.70	

Clad Coinage

Starting in 1968 mint mark position is on the obverse at right of ribbon.

Weight 5.67 grams; composition: outer layers of copper nickel (.750 copper, .250 nickel) bonded to inner core of pure copper; diameter 24.3 mm; reeded edge.

Quan. Minted	Unc.	Proof		Quan. Minted	Unc.	Proof
1965.....1,819,717,540	$ .50			1970S Proof..2,632,810		$1.50
1966......821,101,500	.50			1971.....109,284,000	$ .50	
1967.....1,524,031,848	.50			1971D.....258,634,428	.50	
1968......220,731,500	.50			1971S Proof..3,224,138		1.00
1968D.....101,534,000	.50			1972......215,048,000	.50	
1968S Proof..3,041,509		$2.00		1972D.....311,067,732	.50	
1969......176,212,000	.50			1972S Proof..3,267,667		1.00
1969D....114,372,000	.50			1973.................	.50	
1969S Proof..2,934,631		1.50		1973D................	.50	
1970......136,420,000	.50			1973S Proof..........		1.00
1970D.....417,341,364	.50					

HALF DOLLARS 1794 to Date

The half dollar, authorized by the Act of April 2, 1792, was not minted until December, 1794. The early types of this series have been extensively collected by die varieties, of which many exist for most dates. Valuations given below are in each case for the most common variety, and scarcer ones as listed by Beistle and Overton (see page 143, Bibliography) generally command higher prices.

The weight of the half-dollar was 208 grains and its fineness .8924 when first issued. This standard was not changed until 1837 when the law of January 18, 1837 specified 206¼ grains, .900 fine.

Arrows at the date in 1853 indicate the reduction of weight to 192 grains, in conformity with the Act of February 21, 1853. During that year only, rays were added to the field on the reverse side. Arrows remained in 1854 and 1855.

In 1873 the weight was raised by law to 192.9 grains and arrows were again placed at the date, to be removed in 1875.

HALF DOLLARS

FLOWING HAIR TYPE 1794-1795

FAIR—Clear enough to identify.
GOOD—Date and letters sufficient to be readable. Main devices outlined, but lack details.
VERY GOOD—Major details discernible. Letters well formed but worn.
FINE—Hair ends distinguishable. Top hairlines show, but otherwise worn smooth.
VERY FINE—Hair in center shows some detail. Other details more bold.

Designer Robert Scot; weight 13.48 grams; composition: .8924 silver, .1076 copper; approx. diameter 32.5 mm; edge: FIFTY CENTS OR HALF A DOLLAR with decorations between words.

1794

→ 3 Leaves
Under Wings

	Quan. Minted	Fair	Good	V.G.	Fine	V.F.
1794	5,300	$165.00	$275.00	$400.00	$600.00	$1,125
1795 All kinds	317,844	100.00	130.00	180.00	285.00	535.00
1795 Recut date		150.00	235.00	365.00	525.00	775.00
1795 3 leaves under each wing		180.00	350.00	550.00	800.00	1,200

Varieties of 1795 are known with final S in STATES over D, with A in STATES over E, and with Y in LIBERTY over a star.

DRAPED BUST TYPE, SMALL EAGLE REVERSE 1796-1797

Grading same as above for Fair to Fine.

VERY FINE—Right side of drapery slightly worn. Left side to curls is smooth.

1796, 15 Stars

1796, 16 Stars

1796 15 stars (Quantity included in 1797 report)		850.00	1,500	2,500	3,800	5,000
1796 16 stars		900.00	1,700	2,700	4,100	5,200
1797 15 stars	3,918	900.00	1,700	2,700	4,100	5,200

HALF DOLLARS

DRAPED BUST TYPE, HERALDIC EAGLE REVERSE 1801-1807

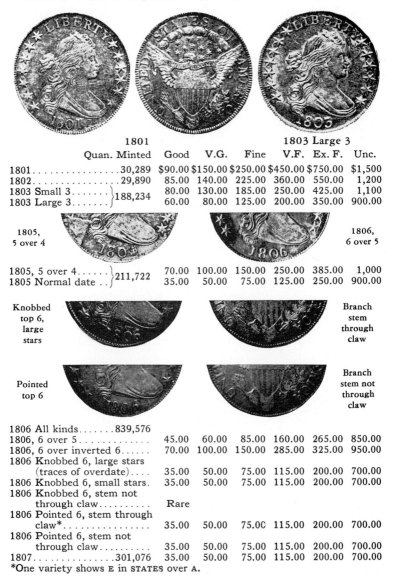

1801

1803 Large 3

	Quan. Minted	Good	V.G.	Fine	V.F.	Ex. F.	Unc.
1801................	30,289	$90.00	$150.00	$250.00	$450.00	$750.00	$1,500
1802................	29,890	85.00	140.00	225.00	360.00	550.00	1,200
1803 Small 3.......	}188,234	80.00	130.00	185.00	250.00	425.00	1,100
1803 Large 3.......		60.00	80.00	125.00	200.00	350.00	900.00

1805, 5 over 4

1806, 6 over 5

		Good	V.G.	Fine	V.F.	Ex. F.	Unc.
1805, 5 over 4......	}211,722	70.00	100.00	150.00	250.00	385.00	1,000
1805 Normal date ..		35.00	50.00	75.00	125.00	250.00	900.00

Knobbed top 6, large stars

Branch stem through claw

Pointed top 6

Branch stem not through claw

		Good	V.G.	Fine	V.F.	Ex. F.	Unc.
1806 All kinds.......	839,576						
1806, 6 over 5.............		45.00	60.00	85.00	160.00	265.00	850.00
1806, 6 over inverted 6......		70.00	100.00	150.00	285.00	325.00	950.00
1806 Knobbed 6, large stars (traces of overdate)....		35.00	50.00	75.00	115.00	200.00	700.00
1806 Knobbed 6, small stars.		35.00	50.00	75.00	115.00	200.00	700.00
1806 Knobbed 6, stem not through claw..........		Rare					
1806 Pointed 6, stem through claw*................		35.00	50.00	75.0C	115.00	200.00	700.00
1806 Pointed 6, stem not through claw..........		35.00	50.00	75.00	115.00	200.00	700.00
1807.............301,076		35.00	50.00	75.00	115.00	200.00	700.00

*One variety shows E in STATES over A.

HALF DOLLARS

CAPPED BUST TYPE, Lettered edge 1807-1836

John Reich designed the first Turban Head concept of Liberty. The head of Liberty facing left was used on all U.S. coin denominations for the next thirty years. Reich was the first artist to consistently include the denomination on our gold and silver coins. He was from Germany and a bondman freed from servitude by a mint official.

GOOD—Date and letters readable. Bust worn smooth with outline distinct.
VERY GOOD—LIBERTY visible but faint. Legends distinguishable. Clasp at shoulder visible. Curl above it nearly smooth.
FINE—Clasp and adjacent curl clearly outlined with slight details.
VERY FINE—Clasp at shoulder clear. Curl has wear only on highest point. Hair over brow distinguishable.
EXTRA FINE—Clasp and adjacent curl fairly sharp. Brow and hair above distinct. Curls well defined.

Designer John Reich; weight 13.48 grams; composition: .8924 silver, .1076 copper; approx. diameter 32.5 mm; edge varieties, 1807-1814: FIFTY CENTS OR HALF A DOLLAR; 1814-1831: star added between DOLLAR and FIFTY; 1832-1836: vertical lines added between words.

First style 1807-1808

1807 Small Stars   1807 Large Stars   1807, 50 over 20

	Quan. Minted	Good	V.G.	Fine	V.F.	Ex. F.	Unc.
1807 Small stars		$25.00	$35.00	$47.50	$95.00	$190.00	$650.00
1807 Large stars	750,500	22.50	30.00	42.50	80.00	125.00	485.00
1807 same, 50 over 20		22.50	30.00	42.50	80.00	125.00	525.00
1808, 8 over 7	1,368,600	20.00	27.50	40.00	60.00	95.00	300.00
1808.............		16.00	22.00	30.00	40.00	60.00	300.00

Remodeled Portrait and Eagle 1809-1834

1809 experimental edge, xxxx between words

1809 experimental edge, IIIII between words

HALF DOLLARS

	Quan. Minted	Good	V.G.	Fine	V.F.	E.F.	Unc.
1809 normal......⎫		$15.00	$20.00	$25.00	$32.50	$50.00	$225.00
1809 xxxx edge ..⎬1,405,810		20.00	30.00	40.00	55.00	80.00	275.00
1809 iiiiiii edge...⎭		17.50	25.00	35.00	45.00	75.00	275.00
1810.............1,276,276		15.00	20.00	25.00	32.50	50.00	225.00

"Punctuated" date 18.11   1811 Small 8   1811 Large 8

	Quan. Minted	Good	V.G.	Fine	V.F.	E.F.	Unc.
1811 (18.11)⎫							
11 over 10...⎬1,203,644		17.50	27.50	50.00	85.00	110.00	300.00
1811 small 8......		12.00	15.00	20.00	28.00	40.00	200.00
1811 large 8......⎭		13.00	16.00	22.00	30.00	50.00	225.00
1812, 2 over 1⎫							
small 8.....		17.50	30.00	60.00	90.00	125.00	300.00
1812, 2 over 1⎬1,628,059							
large 8......		19.00	32.50	65.00	95.00	130.00	335.00
1812............⎭		12.00	15.00	20.00	30.00	45.00	225.00

1812, 2 over 1 small 8   1812, 2 over 1 large 8   1813, 50 C. over UNI

	Quan. Minted	Good	V.G.	Fine	V.F.	E.F.	Unc.
1813............⎫		12.00	15.00	20.00	30.00	45.00	225.00
1813, 50C. over⎬1,241,903							
UNI.......		20.00	30.00	55.00	90.00	120.00	400.00
1814, 4 over 3....⎫		16.00	28.00	35.00	60.00	90.00	275.00
1814 E over A in⎬1,039,075							
STATES....		13.00	15.00	20.00	30.00	60.00	260.00
1814 normal......⎭		14.00	16.00	20.00	30.00	60.00	225.00

1814,
4 over 3

1814
E over A
in STATES

HALF DOLLARS

1817, 7 over 3　　　　1817, 7 over 4　　　1817 Punctuated Date

	Quan. Minted	Good	V.G.	Fine	V.F.	E.F.	Unc.
1815, 5 over 2	47,150	$100.00	$145.00	$225.00	$300.00	$500.00	$1,600
1817, 7 over 3	⎫	18.00	30.00	45.00	65.00	95.00	350.00
1817, 7 over 4	⎬ 1,215,567				5,500	——	
1817 dated 181.7		18.00	30.00	45.00	65.00	95.00	300.00
1817 normal	⎭	13.00	16.00	20.00	30.00	40.00	200.00

1818, 1st 8 small, 2nd 8 over 7　　1818, 1st 8 large, 2nd 8 over 7

1819 Small 9 over 8　　　1819 Large 9 over 8

		Good	V.G.	Fine	V.F.	E.F.	Unc.
1818, 8 over 7 small 8	⎫	12.50	16.00	22.50	30.00	45.00	230.00
1818, 8 over 7 large 8	⎬ 1,960,322	12.50	16.00	22.50	30.00	45.00	225.00
1818 normal	⎭	12.50	16.00	22.50	30.00	45.00	225.00
1819 sm. 9 over 8	⎫	13.50	17.50	24.00	32.50	50.00	240.00
1819 lg. 9 over 8	⎬ 2,208,000	13.50	17.50	24.00	32.50	50.00	230.00
1819 normal	⎭	13.50	17.70	24.00	32.50	50.00	225.00

1820, 20 over 19　　　1820, 20 over 19　　Curl base no knob 2,
Square Base 2　　　　Curl Base 2　　　　　small date

Square base knob 2,　　Square base no knob　　1822, 2 over 1
large date　　　　　　2, large date

HALF DOLLARS

	Quan. Minted	Good	V.G.	Fine	V.F.	E.F.	Unc.
1820, 20 over 19 square 2......		$17.00	$24.00	$35.00	$45.00	$75.00	$225.00
1820, 20 over 19 curl 2........		17.00	24.00	35.00	45.00	75.00	225.00
1820 curl base 2, small date.....	751,122	17.00	24.00	35.00	45.00	75.00	240.00
1820 sq. base knob 2, large date.....		17.00	24.00	35.00	45.00	75.00	225.00
1820 sq. base no knob 2, lg. date		17.00	24.00	35.00	45.00	75.00	225.00
1821.............1,305,797		14.00	17.50	21.00	26.00	40.00	200.00
1822, 2 over 1....	1,559,573	40.00	55.00	80.00	100.00	150.00	400.00
1822.............		14.00	17.50	21.00	26.00	40.00	200.00

1823 Broken 3   1823 Patched 3   1823 Ugly 3

	Quan. Minted	Good	V.G.	Fine	V.F.	E.F.	Unc.
1823 broken 3....		30.00	45.00	65.00	80.00	90.00	275.00
1823 patched 3...	1,694,200	30.00	45.00	65.00	80.00	90.00	275.00
1823 ugly 3.......		15.00	18.00	27.50	40.00	50.00	225.00
1823 normal......		12.50	15.00	20.00	28.00	45.00	200.00

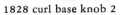

"Various dates"   1824, 4 over 1   1824, 4 over 4   1824, 4 over 4
(probably 4 over 2 over 0)

	Quan. Minted	Good	V.G.	Fine	V.F.	E.F.	Unc.
1824 over various dates......		15.00	18.00	24.00	35.00	48.00	225.00
1824, 4 over 1....	3,504,954	15.00	18.00	24.00	35.00	48.00	235.00
1824, 4 over 4 (2 var.).....		15.00	18.00	24.00	35.00	48.00	225.00
1824 normal......		12.00	15.00	18.00	25.00	37.50	200.00
1825.............2,943,166		12.00	15.00	18.00	25.00	37.50	200.00
1826.............4,004,180		12.00	15.00	18.00	25.00	37.50	200.00
1827, 7 over 6....		16.00	22.00	28.00	42.50	65.00	275.00
1827 curl base 2..	5,493,400	16.00	22.00	28.00	42.50	65.00	275.00
1827 sq. base 2....		12.50	15.00	20.00	27.50	42.50	200.00

1828 curl base knob 2   1828 square base 2, large 8's   1828 square base 2, small 8's

HALF DOLLARS

1828 large letters   1828 small letters

	Quan. Minted	Good	V.G.	Fine	V.F.	E.F.	Unc.
1828 All kinds	3,075,200						
1828 curl base no knob 2		$12.50	$15.00	$20.00	$27.50	$42.50	$200.00
1828 curl base knob 2		35.00	45.00	60.00	85.00	100.00	400.00
1828 sq. base 2, lg. 8's		15.00	20.00	25.00	35.00	60.00	225.00
1828 sq. base 2, sm. 8's, lg. let.		12.50	15.00	20.00	27.50	42.50	200.00
1828 sq. base 2, sm. 8's & let.		20.00	35.00	40.00	75.00	125.00	250.00
1829, 9 over 7	3,712,156	12.50	15.00	20.00	27.50	42.50	225.00
1829		12.50	15.00	20.00	27.50	42.50	200.00

Raised segment lines to right, 1830

Raised segment lines to left, 1830-1831

1832 large letters rev.

Adopted edge 1830-1836

1830 large 0	4,764,800	12.50	15.00	20.00	27.50	42.50	200.00
1830 small 0		12.50	15.00	20.00	27.50	42.50	200.00
1831	5,873,660	12.50	15.00	20.00	27.50	42.50	200.00
1832 normal	4,797,000	12.50	15.00	20.00	27.50	42.50	200.00
1832 large letters		12.50	15.00	20.00	27.50	42.50	225.00
1833	5,206,000	12.50	15.00	20.00	27.50	42.50	200.00

1830 small 0   1834 large date   1834 small date

1834 lg. letters rev.   1834 sm. letters rev.   1836, 50 C. over 00

Portrait Modified Slightly 1834-1836

1834 small date, stars, letters	6,412,004	12.50	15.00	20.00	27.50	42.50	200.00
1834 large date, small letters		12.50	15.00	20.00	27.50	42.50	215.00
1834 lg. date & let.		12.50	15.00	20.00	27.50	42.50	215.00
1835	5,352,006	12.50	15.00	20.00	27.50	42.50	200.00
1836	6,546,200	12.50	15.00	20.00	27.50	42.50	200.00
1836, 50 C. over 00		30.00	40.00	50.00	70.00	95.00	350.00

HALF DOLLARS

Variety 2 — Reeded edge, reverse "50 CENTS" 1836-1837

Designer Christian Gobrecht; weight 13.36 grams; composition: .900 silver, .100 copper; diameter 30 mm; reeded edge; mints: Philadelphia, New Orleans.

GOOD—*LIBERTY discernible on headband.*

VERY GOOD—*Minimum of 3 letters in LIBERTY must be clear.*

FINE—*LIBERTY complete.*

VERY FINE—*LIBERTY is sharp. Shoulder clasp is clear.*

EXTRA FINE—*LIBERTY sharp and strong. Hair details show.*

	Quan. Minted	Good	V.G.	Fine	V.F.	E.F.	Unc.
1836	1,200	$55.00	$75.00	$100.00	$160.00	$250.00	$800.00
1837	3,629,820	15.00	25.00	40.00	55.00	110.00	350.00

Variety 3 — Reeded edge, reverse "HALF DOL." 1838-1839

1838-O

The 1838O was the first branch mint half dollar, though not mentioned in the Director's report. The New Orleans chief coiner stated that only 20 were struck. In 1838-39 the mint mark appears on the obverse; thereafter it is on the reverse through 1915.

1838	3,546,000	15.00	25.00	40.00	55.00	110.00	350.00
1838O	(20)	Charles Jay Sale 1967					$14,000.00
1839 All kinds	3,334,560	15.00	25.00	40.00	55.00	110.00	350.00
1839O	178,976	55.00	75.00	100.00	125.00	200.00	450.00

LIBERTY SEATED TYPE 1839-1891

Variety 1 — No motto above eagle 1839-1853

Designer Christian Gobrecht; weight 13.36 grams; composition: .900 silver, .100 copper; diameter 30.6 mm; reeded edge; mints: Philadelphia, New Orleans.

GOOD—*Scant rim. LIBERTY on shield worn off. Date and letters readable.*

VERY GOOD—*Rim fairly defined. At least 3 letters in LIBERTY are evident.*

FINE—*LIBERTY complete, but weak.*

VERY FINE—*LIBERTY mostly sharp.*

EXTRA FINE—*LIBERTY entirely sharp. Scroll edges and clasp distinct.*

1839 No drapery from elbow	35.00	50.00	80.00	120.00	225.00	600.00

HALF DOLLARS

Modified obverse, drapery from elbow. Small letters in legend 1839-1841.

Drapery from elbow
starting 1839

Small letters in
legend 1839-41

1840 (only) with
medium letters, large
eagle (style of 1838)

	Quan. Minted	Good	V.G.	Fine	V.F.	E.F.	Unc.
1839......................		$10.00	$13.00	$17.00	$27.50	$60.00	$225.00
1840 Sm. letters ..	} 1,435,008	6.00	8.00	12.00	20.00	50.00	200.00
1840 Med. letters .		25.00	37.50	60.00	100.00	185.00	300.00
1840O..............855,100		6.00	8.00	12.00	20.00	50.00	200.00
1841..............310,000		9.00	13.00	18.00	30.00	60.00	225.00
1841O..............401,000		7.50	9.50	14.00	22.00	55.00	200.00

Modified reverse with large letters in legend 1842-1853

Small Date

Medium Date

Large Letter Reverse

		Good	V.G.	Fine	V.F.	E.F.	Unc.
1842 Sm. date....	} 2,012,764	6.00	8.00	12.00	20.00	50.00	200.00
1842 Med. date...		6.00	8.00	12.00	20.00	50.00	200.00
1842O Small date and letters							
All kinds.....957,000		55.00	75.00	150.00	250.00	500.00	——
1842O Med. date, lg. letters.		6.00	8.00	12.00	20.00	50.00	200.00
1843..............3,844,000		6.00	8.00	12.00	20.00	50.00	200.00
1843O..............2,268,000		6.00	8.00	12.00	20.00	50.00	200.00
1844..............1,766,000		6.00	8.00	12.00	20.00	50.00	200.00
1844O...........	} 2,005,000	6.00	8.00	12.00	20.00	50.00	200.00
1844O Double date		30.00	40.00	75.00	150.00	300.00	500.00
1845..............589,000		6.00	8.00	12.00	20.00	50.00	200.00
1845O...........	} 2,094,000	6.00	8.00	12.00	20.00	50.00	200.00
1845O No drapery		18.00	27.50	40.00	65.00	150.00	350.00

HALF DOLLARS

In 1846 date size was again enlarged. The 1846 medium date is approximately the size of the 1842 medium date shown above. Tall date is similar to 1853.

	Quan. Minted	Good	V.G.	Fine	V.F.	E.F.	Unc.
1846 Med. date All.	2,210,000	$6.00	$8.00	$12.00	$20.00	$50.00	$200.00
1846 Tall date............		6.00	8.00	12.00	20.00	50.00	200.00
1846 over horizontal 6 (error)		40.00	60.00	85.00	135.00	175.00	380.00
1846O Med. date	2,304,000	6.00	8.00	12.00	20.00	50.00	200.00
1846O Tall date...		27.50	40.00	65.00	120.00	150.00	300.00
1847, 7 over 6....	1,156,000						
1847 Normal date.		6.00	8.00	12.00	20.00	50.00	200.00
1847O............	2,584,000	6.00	8.00	12.00	20.00	50.00	200.00
1848...............	580,000	6.00	8.00	12.00	20.00	50.00	200.00
1848O............	3,180,000	6.00	8.00	12.00	20.00	50.00	200.00
1849..............	1,252,000	6.00	8.00	12.00	20.00	50.00	200.00
1849O............	2,310,000	6.00	8.00	12.00	20.00	50.00	200.00
1850..............	227,000	27.50	35.00	50.00	80.00	125.00	300.00
1850O............	2,456,000	6.50	8.50	12.00	20.00	50.00	200.00
1851..............	200,750	27.50	35.00	50.00	80.00	125.00	325.00
1851O............	402,000	6.50	8.50	12.00	20.00	50.00	200.00
1852.............	77,130	30.00	37.50	65.00	140.00	200.00	400.00
1852O............	144,000	22.50	30.00	40.00	75.00	100.00	265.00
1853O..........	(Ex. Rare)						

Variety 2 —
Arrows at date,
rays around eagle
1853 only

Weight 12.44 grams; composition: .900 silver, .100 copper; diameter 30.6 mm; reeded edge; mints: Philadelphia, New Orleans, San Francisco.

1853..............	3,532,708	12.50	20.00	35.00	65.00	200.00	1,000
1853O All kinds....	1,328,000	12.50	20.00	35.00	65.00	200.00	1,100

Variety 3 — Arrows at date, no rays 1854-1855

1854..............	2,982,000	6.00	8.00	12.00	20.00	50.00	310.00
1854O............	5,240,000	6.00	8.00	12.00	20.00	50.00	310.00
1855 over 1854.....	759,500						
1855 Normal date ..		6.00	8.00	12.00	20.00	50.00	325.00
1855O............	3,688,000	6.00	8.00	12.00	20.00	50.00	310.00
1855S..............	129,950	40.00	60.00	110.00	200.00	300.00	800.00

Variety 1 resumed 1856-1866

1856...............	938,000	5.00	7.00	10.00	18.00	35.00	200.00
1856O............	2,658,000	5.00	7.00	10.00	18.00	35.00	200.00
1856S............	211,000	13.00	18.00	27.00	75.00	100.00	310.00
1857..............	1,988,000	5.00	7.00	10.00	18.00	35.00	200.00
1857O............	818,000	5.00	7.00	10.00	18.00	35.00	200.00
1857S.............	158,000	16.00	23.00	35.00	77.50	110.00	325.00

HALF DOLLARS

	Quan. Minted	Good	V.G.	Fine	V.F.	Unc.	Proof
1858	4,226,000	$5.00	$7.00	$10.00	$18.00	$200.00	$650.00
1858O	7,294,000	5.00	7.00	10.00	18.00	200.00	
1858S	476,000	7.00	12.00	20.00	31.00	250.00	
1859	748,000	5.00	7.00	10.00	18.00	200.00	365.00
1859O	2,834,000	5.00	7.00	10.00	18.00	200.00	
1859S	566,000	7.00	12.50	20.00	31.00	225.00	
1860......(1,000)	303,700	5.00	7.00	10.00	18.00	200.00	250.00
1860O	1,290,000	5.00	7.00	10.00	18.00	200.00	
1860S	472,000	6.00	9.00	13.00	22.00	210.00	
1861......(1,000)	2,888,400	5.00	7.00	10.00	18.00	200.00	250.00
1861O	2,532,633	5.00	7.00	10.00	18.00	200.00	

The 1861O quantity includes 330,000 struck under the United States government; 1,240,000 for the State of Louisiana after it seceded from the Union; and 962,633 after Louisiana joined the Confederate States of America. As all these 1861O coins were struck from U.S. dies it is impossible to distinguish one from another. They should not be confused with the very rare Confederate half dollar of 1861 which has a distinctive reverse.

	Quan. Minted	Good	V.G.	Fine	V.F.	Unc.	Proof
1861S	939,500	6.00	8.00	12.00	20.00	210.00	
1862......(550)	253,550	6.00	8.00	12.00	20.00	200.00	260.00
1862S	1,352,000	6.00	8.00	12.00	20.00	200.00	
1863......(460)	503,660	6.00	8.00	12.00	20.00	200.00	260.00
1863S	916,000	6.00	8.00	12.00	20.00	200.00	
1864......(470)	379,570	6.00	8.00	12.00	20.00	200.00	260.00
1864S	658,000	6.00	8.00	12.00	20.00	200.00	
1865......(500)	511,900	6.00	8.00	12.00	20.00	200.00	260.00
1865S	675,000	6.00	8.00	12.00	20.00	200.00	
1866S No motto		40.00	65.00	100.00	200.00	1,000	
1866 Transitional pattern...(unique)							———

Variety 4 —
Motto "In God We Trust"
added above eagle
1866-1873

	Quan. Minted	Good	V.G.	Fine	V.F.	Unc.	Proof
1866......(725)	745,625	6.00	8.00	12.00	20.00	180.00	235.00
1866S All Kinds ...1,054,000		6.00	8.00	12.00	20.00	180.00	
1867......(625)	449,925	6.00	8.00	12.00	20.00	200.00	240.00
1867S	1,196,000	5.00	7.00	10.00	18.00	180.00	
1868......(600)	418,200	6.00	8.00	12.00	20.00	200.00	240.00
1868S	1,160,000	5.00	7.00	10.00	18.00	180.00	
1869......(600)	795,900	6.00	8.00	12.00	20.00	180.00	250.00
1869S	656,000	5.00	7.00	10.00	18.00	180.00	
1870......(1,000)	634,900	5.00	7.00	10.00	18.00	180.00	225.00
1870CC	54,617	50.00	75.00	110.00	225.00	775.00	
1870S	1,004,000	6.00	8.00	12.00	20.00	200.00	
1871......(960)	1,204,560	5.00	7.00	10.00	18.00	180.00	225.00
1871CC	139,950	42.50	65.00	100.00	200.00	675.00	
1871S	2,178,000	5.00	7.00	10.00	18.00	180.00	

HALF DOLLARS

	Quan. Minted	Good	V.G.	Fine	V.F.	Unc.	Proof
1872.......(950)	881,550	$5.00	$7.00	$10.00	$18.00	$180.00	$225.00
1872CC.............	272,000	30.00	50.00	75.00	125.00	550.00	
1872S.............	580,000	6.00	8.00	12.00	20.00	200.00	
1873 Closed 3..(600) }801,800		5.00	7.00	10.00	18.00	180.00	225.00
1873 Open 3.......∫		15.00	25.00	40.00	50.00	400.00	
1873CC............122,500		35.00	60.00	100.00	150.00	1,000	
1873S No arrows......5,000		Unknown in any collection.					

Variety 5 —
Arrows at date
1873-1874

Weight 12.50 grams; composition: .900 silver, .100 copper; diameter 30.6 mm; reeded edge; mints: Philadelphia, Carson City, San Francisco.

1873.......(550)	1,815,700	15.00	25.00	40.00	75.00	385.00	550.00
1873CC............	214,560	25.00	35.00	65.00	100.00	475.00	
1873S.............	228,000	22.50	30.00	50.00	85.00	425.00	
1874.......(700)	2,360,300	15.00	27.50	40.00	75.00	375.00	525.00
1874CC............	59,000	35.00	55.00	110.00	185.00	700.00	
1874S.............	394,000	25.00	35.00	65.00	100.00	425.00	

Variety 4 resumed 1875-1891

1875.......(700)	6,027,500	5.00	7.00	10.00	18.00	180.00	210.00
1875CC...........	1,008,000	7.50	9.00	12.50	30.00	225.00	
1875S............	3,200,000	5.00	7.00	10.00	18.00	180.00	
1876......(1,150)	8,419,150	5.00	7.00	10.00	18.00	180.00	210.00
1876CC...........	1,956,000	5.00	7.00	10.00	18.00	190.00	
1876S............	4,528,000	6.00	8.00	12.00	20.00	200.00	
1877.......(510)	8,304,510	5.00	7.00	10.00	18.00	180.00	240.00
1877CC...........	1,420,000	7.00	9.00	14.00	22.00	200.00	
1877S............	5,356,000	5.00	7.00	10.00	18.00	180.00	
1878.......(800)	1,378,400	6.00	8.00	12.00	20.00	190.00	225.00
1878CC...........	62,000	85.00	110.00	150.00	250.00	1,000	
1878S............	12,000	350.00	475.00	750.00	1,500	3,750	
1879......(1,100)	5,900	45.00	50.00	60.00	65.00	250.00	260.00
1880...,...(1,355)	9,755	40.00	45.00	55.00	60.00	250.00	250.00
1881.......(975)	10,975	40.00	45.00	55.00	60.00	250.00	250.00
1882......(1,100)	5,500	45.00	50.00	60.00	65.00	250.00	250.00
1883......(1,039)	9,039	40.00	45.00	55.00	60.00	250.00	250.00
1884.......(875)	5,275	45.00	50.00	60.00	65.00	250.00	275.00
1885.......(930)	6,130	45.00	50.00	60.00	65.00	250.00	275.00
1886.......(886)	5,886	65.00	70.00	75.00	80.00	260.00	275.00
1887.......(710)	5,710	50.00	60.00	70.00	80.00	260.00	280.00
1888.......(832)	12,833	40.00	45.00	55.00	60.00	250.00	280.00
1889.......(711)	12,711	40.00	45.00	55.00	60.00	250.00	280.00
1890.......(590)	12,590	40.00	45.00	55.00	60.00	250.00	300.00
1891.......(600)	200,600	6.00	8.00	12.00	20.00	200.00	300.00

HALF DOLLARS
BARBER or LIBERTY HEAD TYPE 1892-1915

Like the dime and quarter dollar, this type was designed by Charles E. Barber, whose initial B is at the truncation of the neck.

GOOD—*Date and legends readable. LIBERTY worn off headband.*
VERY GOOD—*Minimum of 3 letters readable in LIBERTY.*
FINE—*LIBERTY completely readable, but not sharp.*
VERY FINE—*All letters in LIBERTY evenly plain.*
EXTRA FINE—*LIBERTY bold, and its ribbon distinct.*

Designer Charles E. Barber; weight 12.50 grams; composition: .900 silver, .100 copper; diameter 30.6 mm; reeded edge; mints: Philadelphia, Denver, New Orleans, San Francisco.

Mint mark
location on
reverse below
eagle
←

Quan. Minted	Good	V.G.	Fine	V.F.	E.F.	Unc.	Proof
1892 (1,245) 935,245	$6.00	$9.00	$13.00	$22.00	$55.00	$225.00	$260.00
1892O*......390,000	45.00	55.00	65.00	80.00	110.00	240.00	
1892S......1,029,028	37.50	50.00	65.00	80.00	110.00	275.00	
1893 (792) 1,826,792	5.00	7.00	13.00	22.00	55.00	230.00	270.00
1893O.....1,389,000	10.00	15.00	22.00	35.00	62.50	250.00	
1893S.......740,000	30.00	45.00	57.50	70.00	85.00	265.00	
1894 (972) 1,148,972	6.00	9.00	14.00	23.00	55.00	235.00	270.00
1894O.....2,138,000	6.00	9.00	16.00	30.00	65.00	250.00	
1894S......4,048,690	4.00	7.00	14.00	30.00	60.00	250.00	
1895 (880) 1,835,218	3.50	5.00	11.00	22.00	55.00	250.00	270.00
1895O.....1,766,000	5.00	7.00	16.00	30.00	65.00	250.00	
1895S......1,108,086	10.00	15.00	25.00	40.00	65.00	250.00	
1896 (762) 950,762	6.00	9.00	16.00	25.00	55.00	240.00	275.00
1896O.......924,000	10.00	15.00	25.00	50.00	100.00	325.00	
1896S......1,140,948	30.00	40.00	60.00	85.00	140.00	425.00	
1897 (731) 2,480,731	3.00	4.00	8.00	22.00	55.00	240.00	275.00
1897O.......632,000	25.00	37.50	55.00	75.00	130.00	375.00	
1897S.......933,900	32.50	47.50	60.00	75.00	130.00	400.00	
1898 (735) 2,956,735	3.00	4.00	8.00	22.00	53.00	240.00	275.00
1898O.......874,000	6.00	10.00	17.00	28.00	60.00	250.00	
1898S......2,358,550	5.00	6.50	11.00	24.00	55.00	250.00	
1899 (846) 5,538,846	3.00	4.00	8.00	23.00	55.00	240.00	275.00
1899O.....1,724,000	4.00	6.00	11.00	24.00	55.00	250.00	
1899S......1,686,411	5.50	7.50	12.00	24.00	60.00	250.00	
1900 (912) 4,762,912	3.00	4.00	8.00	23.00	55.00	240.00	275.00
1900O.....2,744,000	3.00	4.00	9.00	24.00	55.00	250.00	
1900S......2,560,322	3.00	4.00	9.00	24.00	55.00	250.00	
1901 (813) 4,268,813	3.00	4.00	8.00	22.00	55.00	240.00	275.00
1901O.....1,124,000	4.00	8.00	17.00	50.00	130.00	400.00	
1901S.......847,044	10.00	20.00	45.00	100.00	270.00	1,000	
1902 (777) 4,922,777	3.00	4.00	7.00	21.00	55.00	240.00	275.00
1902O.....2,526,000	3.00	4.00	8.00	24.00	60.00	250.00	

*Normal and "microscopic" mint mark varieties, see page 59.

HALF DOLLARS

Quan. Minted	Good	V.G.	Fine	V.F.	E.F.	Unc.	Proof
1902S......1,460,670	$3.00	$5.00	$12.00	$37.50	$95.00	$300.00	
1903 (755) 2,278,755	3.00	4.00	6.50	23.00	55.00	240.00	$275.00
1903O 2,100,000	3.00	4.00	10.00	32.50	70.00	275.00	
1903S......1,920,772	3.00	5.00	11.00	40.00	100.00	480.00	
1904 (670) 2,992,670	3.00	4.00	8.00	22.00	55.00	240.00	280.00
1904O 1,117,600	3.00	6.00	10.00	28.00	62.00	250.00	
1904S.......553,038	9.50	18.00	31.50	57.50	140.00	500.00	
1905 (727) 662,727	5.00	9.00	14.00	28.00	63.00	260.00	285.00
1905O.......505,000	8.00	15.00	25.00	43.00	80.00	300.00	
1905S......2,494,000	3.00	4.00	8.00	23.00	55.00	250.00	
1906 (675) 2,638,675	3.00	4.00	7.00	22.00	55.00	240.00	260.00
1906D.....4,028,000	3.00	4.00	7.00	22.00	55.00	240.00	
1906O 2,446,000	3.00	4.00	7.00	22.00	55.00	240.00	
1906S......1,740,154	3.00	5.00	10.00	23.00	55.00	250.00	
1907 (575) 2,598,575	3.00	4.00	7.00	22.00	55.00	240.00	285.00
1907D.....3,856,000	3.00	4.00	7.00	22.00	55.00	250.00	
1907O 3,946,600	3.00	4.00	7.00	22.00	55.00	250.00	
1907S......1,250,000	3.00	4.00	10.00	23.00	60.00	250.00	
1908 (545) 1,354,545	3.00	4.00	9.00	23.00	55.00	240.00	300.00
1908D.....3,280,000	3.00	4.00	7.00	22.00	55.00	240.00	
1908O 5,360,000	3.00	4.00	7.00	22.00	55.00	240.00	
1908S......1,644,828	3.00	4.00	9.00	23.00	55.00	250.00	
1909 (650) 2,368,650	3.00	4.00	7.00	22.00	55.00	240.00	300.00
1909O.......925,400	4.00	6.00	9.00	24.00	60.00	250.00	
1909S......1,764,000	3.00	4.00	7.00	22.00	55.00	240.00	
1910 (551) 418,551	6.00	9.00	14.00	28.00	65.00	265.00	315.00
1910S......1,948,000	3.00	4.00	7.00	22.00	55.00	250.00	
1911 (543) 1,406,543	3.00	4.00	7.00	22.00	55.00	250.00	315.00
1911D.......695,080	4.00	6.00	10.00	23.00	55.00	250.00	
1911S......1,272,000	3.00	4.00	7.00	22.00	55.00	240.00	
1912 (700) 1,550,700	3.00	4.00	7.00	22.00	55.00	240.00	300.00
1912D.....2,300,800	3.00	4.00	7.00	22.00	55.00	240.00	
1912S......1,370,000	3.00	4.00	7.00	22.00	55.00	240.00	
1913 (627) 188,627	15.00	20.00	30.00	45.00	85.00	300.00	425.00 —
1913D.......534,000	4.00	5.00	10.00	24.00	60.00	260.00	
1913S.......604,000	4.00	5.00	10.00	25.00	65.00	280.00	
1914 (380) 124,610	18.00	28.00	45.00	65.00	110.00	350.00	675.00 —
1914S.......992,000	3.00	5.00	10.00	23.00	55.00	250.00	
1915 (450) 138,450	20.00	25.00	40.00	55.00	100.00	325.00	600.00 —
1915D.....1,170,400	3.00	4.00	7.00	22.00	55.00	240.00	
1915S......1,604,000	3.00	4.00	7.00	22.00	55.00	250.00	

LIBERTY WALKING TYPE 1916-1947

This type was designed by A. A. Weinman. The designer's monogram **AW** appears under the tip of the wing feathers. On the 1916 coins and some of the 1917 coins the mint mark is located on the obverse below the motto.

GOOD—*Rims are defined. Motto IN GOD WE TRUST readable.*
VERY GOOD—*Motto is distinct. About half of skirt lines at left are clear.*
FINE—*All skirt lines evident, but worn in spots. Details in sandal below motto are clear.*
VERY FINE—*Skirt lines sharp including leg area. Little wear on breast and right arm.*
EXTRA FINE—*All skirt lines bold.*

Designer Adolph A. Weinman; weight 12.50 grams; composition: .900 silver, .100 copper; diameter 30.6 mm; reeded edge; mints: Philadelphia, Denver, San Francisco.

HALF DOLLARS

Uncirculated, well struck specimens worth 25-50% above prices listed.

	Quan. Minted	Good	V.G.	Fine	V.F.	E.F.	Unc.	Proof
1916	608,000	$9.00	$11.00	$18.50	$25.00	$40.00	$130.00	
1916D on Obv.	1,014,400	6.00	9.00	14.00	20.00	32.50	110.00	
1916S on Obv.	508,000	20.00	27.50	40.00	52.50	77.50	225.00	
1917	12,292,000	1.25	2.00	2.75	6.00	10.00	37.50	
1917D on Obv.	765,400	6.00	9.00	19.00	28.00	52.50	145.00	
1917D on Rev.	1,940,000	2.50	3.75	9.00	22.50	50.00	190.00	
1917S on Obv.	952,000	6.50	11.00	32.50	65.00	110.00	450.00	
1917S on Rev.	5,554,000	2.00	2.75	5.00	11.00	25.00	135.00	
1918	6,634,000	1.50	2.00	4.75	13.00	29.00	150.00	
1918D	3,853,040	1.75	3.00	5.50	15.00	42.50	175.00	
1918S	10,282,000	1.25	2.25	4.00	12.50	34.00	140.00	
1919	962,000	5.00	6.50	12.00	30.00	60.00	440.00	
1919D	1,165,000	4.00	6.50	12.00	60.00	135.00	600.00	
1919S	1,552,000	4.00	6.50	15.00	60.00	160.00	700.00	
1920	6,372,000	1.25	1.75	4.00	7.00	13.50	110.00	
1920D	1,551,000	3.50	5.50	10.00	27.50	75.00	550.00	
1920S	4,624,000	2.00	3.00	8.00	22.50	70.00	420.00	
1921	246,000	35.00	50.00	65.00	110.00	225.00	950.00	
1921D	208,000	65.00	75.00	100.00	150.00	275.00	1200.00	
1921S	548,000	10.00	15.00	32.00	65.00	300.00	2750.00	
1923S	2,178,000	2.00	3.00	6.00	30.00	85.00	375.00	
1927S	2,392,000	1.75	2.25	3.50	10.00	27.50	225.00	
1928S†	1,940,000	1.75	2.25	3.25	8.00	25.00	215.00	
1929D	1,001,200	2.75	3.50	5.00	9.00	20.00	110.00	
1929S	1,902,000	1.50	2.25	3.25	6.00	19.00	105.00	
1933S	1,786,000	1.50	2.25	3.00	6.00	20.00	125.00	
1934	6,964,000	1.00	1.25	1.50	2.00	3.00	18.00	
1934D†	2,361,400	1.25	1.50	2.00	2.50	6.00	38.00	
1934S	3,652,000	1.00	1.25	1.75	4.00	20.00	80.00	
1935	9,162,000	1.00	1.25	1.50	2.00	3.00	16.00	
1935D	3,003,800	1.00	1.25	1.75	2.75	9.00	50.00	
1935S	3,854,000	1.00	1.25	1.50	2.50	15.00	72.50	
1936 (3,901)	12,617,901		1.00	1.25	1.50	3.00	15.00	$285.00
1936D	4,252,400	1.00	1.25	1.50	2.25	3.50	25.00	
1936S	3,884,000	1.00	1.25	1.50	2.50	7.00	42.50	
1937 (5,728)	9,527,728		1.00	1.25	1.50	3.00	16.00	110.00
1937D	1,760,001	2.50	3.00	4.00	6.00	12.00	75.00	
1937S	2,090,000	1.50	2.00	3.00	4.50	12.00	57.00	
1938 (8,152)	4,118,152	1.00	1.25	1.50	2.25	6.00	36.00	85.00
1938D	491,600	24.00	27.50	30.00	35.00	55.00	200.00	
1939 (8,808)	6,820,808		1.00	1.25	2.00	4.00	15.00	75.00
1939D	4,267,800	1.00	1.25	1.50	2.25	4.50	20.00	

HALF DOLLARS

Quan. Minted	Good	V.G.	Fine	V.F.	E.F.	Unc.	Proof
1939S........2,552,000	$1.25	$1.50	$2.00	$3.00	$9.00	$32.00	
1940 (11,279) 9,167,279		1.00	1.25	1.50	2.50	12.00	$70.00
1940S........4,550,000	1.00	1.25	1.50	2.00	4.00	16.00	
1941 (15,412)24,207,412		1.00	1.25	1.50	2.25	10.00	*65.00
1941D.....11,248,400		1.00	1.25	1.50	2.50	18.00	
1941S........8,098,000		1.00	1.25	1.50	5.00	40.00	
1942 (21,120)47,839,120		1.00	1.25	1.50	2.00	8.00	65.00
1942D......10,973,800		1.00	1.25	1.50	3.00	18.00	
1942S†......12,708,000		1.00	1.25	1.50	4.00	20.00	
1943........53,190,000				1.50	2.50	8.00	
1943D.....11,346,000				1.00	2.50	20.00	
1943S.....13,450,000				1.00	3.00	20.00	
1944........28,206,000				1.00	1.50	8.00	
1944D......9,769,000				1.00	2.00	10.00	
1944S.......8,904,000				1.00	2.00	11.00	
1945........31,502,000				1.00	1.50	8.00	
1945D......9,966,800				1.00	1.75	10.00	
1945S......10,156,000				1.00	1.75	10.00	
1946........12,118,000				1.00	1.75	9.00	
1946D.......2,151,000				2.00	4 00	18.00	
1946S........3,724,000				1.00	2.00	11.00	
1947........4,094,000				1.00	2.00	16.00	
1947D.......3,900,600				1.00	2.00	12.50	

*Proofs struck with or without designer's initials.
†Large and small mint mark varieties, see page 59.

FRANKLIN-LIBERTY BELL TYPE 1948-1963

The designer was John R. Sinnock, and his initials appear under the shoulder.

EXTRA FINE—*Wear spots appear at top of end curls and hair back of ears. On reverse, Liberty Bell will show wear at top.*

Mint mark location

Select, well struck uncirculated halves command higher prices.

Quan. Minted	E.F.	Unc.	Proof
1948.....3,006,814	$4.00	$9.00	
1948D...4,028,600	2.75	6.00	
1949.....5,714,000	4.00	20.00	
1949D...4,120,600	3.25	20.00	
1949S....3,744,000	5.00	21.50	
1950 (51,386)			
.......7,793,509	2.75	13.00	$50.00
1950D...8,031,600	2.25	15.00	

Quan. Minted	E.F.	Unc.	Proof
1951 (57,500)			
......16,859,602	$2.00	$8.50	$50.00
1951D...9,475,200	3.50	15.00	
1951S...13,696,000	2.50	10.00	
1952 (81,980)			
......21,274,073	1.50	3.75	25.00
1952D..25,395,600	1.50	3.00	
1952S....5,526,000	3.00	13.00	

HALF DOLLARS

Quan. Minted	E.F.	Unc.	Proof
1953 (128,800)			
......2,796,920	$5.00	$11.00	$22.50
1953D..20,900,400	1.25	2.50	
1953S....4,148,000	2.25	5.25	
1954 (233,300)			
.....13,421,503	1.25	2.25	9.50
1954D..25,445,580	1.10	1.75	
1954S....4,993,400	1.75	3.00	
1955 (378,200)			
......2,876,381	6.50	8.00	12.50
1956 (669,384)			
......4,701,384	2.00	3.75	5.00
1957 (1,247,952)			
......6,361,952	1.50	2.75	3.00
1957D..19,966,850	1.10	1.75	
1958 (875,652)			
......4,917,652	1.75	3.00	5.00

Quan. Minted	E.F.	Unc.	Proof
1958D..23,962,412	$1.00	$1.50	
1959 (1,149,291)			
......7,349,291	1.35	2.50	$3.00
1959D..13,053,750	1.10	2.00	
1960 (1,691,602)			
......7,715,602	1.25	2.00	3.00
1960D..18,215,812	1.00	1.75	
1961 (3,028,244)			
......11,318,244	1.10	1.75	2.25
1961D..20,276,442	1.00	1.75	
1962 (3,218,019)			
......12,932,019	1.10	1.75	2.25
1962D..35,473,281	1.00	1.60	
1963 (3,075,645)			
......25,239,645	1.00	1.50	2.50
1963D..67,069,292	1.00	1.50	

KENNEDY TYPE 1964 to Date

Gilroy Roberts, former Chief Sculptor of the Mint, designed the obverse of this coin. His stylized initials are on the truncation of the forceful bust of President John F. Kennedy. The reverse, which uses the presidential coat of arms for the motif, is the work of Frank Gasparro.

Designers Gilroy Roberts and Frank Gasparro. 1964: Standards same as previous issue; 1965-1970: weight 11.50 grams; composition: outer layers of .800 silver, .200 copper bonded to inner core of .210 silver, .790 copper; 1971: weight 11.34 grams; composition: outer layers of copper nickel (.750 copper, .250 nickel) bonded to inner core of pure copper; diameter 30.6 mm; reeded edge.

1964

Mint mark location

1968-

Silver Coinage 1964

Quan. Minted	Unc.	Proof
1964 (3,950,762)		
......277,254,766	$1.25	$4.00

Quan. Minted	Unc.	Proof
1964D.....156,205,446	$1.35	

Silver Clad Coinage 1965-1970

	Unc.	Proof
1965.......65,879,366	1.35	
1966......108,984,932	1.00	
1967......295,046,978	1.00	
1968D.....246,951,930	1.00	
1968S Proof..3,041,509		3.50

	Unc.	Proof
1969D.....129,881,800	1.00	
1969S Proof..2,934,631		$3.25
1970D.......2,150,000	16.50	
1970S Proof..2,632,810		7.50

HALF DOLLARS

Copper-Nickel Clad Coinage — Modified Design

Quan. Minted	Unc.	Proof	Quan. Minted	Unc.	Proof
1971......155,164,000	$1.00		1973................	$1.00	
1971D.....302,097,424	1.00		1973D..............	1.00	
1971S Proof..3,224,138		$3.00	1973S Proof.........		$2.50
1972......153,180,000	1.00				
1972D.....141,890,000	1.00				
1972S Proof..3,267,667		3.00			

BIBLIOGRAPHY

Beistle, M. L. *Register of United States Half Dollar Die Varieties and Sub-Varieties.* Shippensburg, Pa., 1929.

Haseltine, J. W. *Type Table of United States Dollars, Half Dollars and Quarter Dollars.* Philadelphia, 1881 (reprinted 1927, 1968).

Overton, Al C. *Early Half Dollar Die Varieties 1794-1836.* Colorado Springs, 1967. Revised edition, 1970.

SILVER DOLLARS

1794 to Date

The silver dollar was authorized by Congress April 2, 1792. Weight and fineness were specified at 416 grains and 892.4 fine. The first issues appeared in 1794 and until 1804 all silver dollars had the value stamped on the edge: HUNDRED CENTS, ONE DOLLAR OR UNIT. After a lapse in coinage of the silver dollar covering the period 1804 to 1840, these coins had reeded edges and the value was placed on the reverse side.

The weight was changed by the law of January 18, 1837 to $412\frac{1}{2}$ grains, fineness .900. The coinage was discontinued by the act of February 12, 1873 and reauthorized by the Act of February 28, 1878. The dollar was again discontinued after 1935 and since then only the copper-nickel pieces first authorized in 1971 have been coined for circulation.

ORIGIN OF THE DOLLAR

The word Dollar evolves from German Taler, the name given to the first large-sized European silver coin. Designed as a substitute for the gold Florin, the coin originated in the Tyrol in 1484. So popular did these large silver coins become during the 16th century that many other countries struck similar pieces, giving them names derived from taler. In the Netherlands the coin was called Rijksdaalder, in Denmark Rigsdaler, in Italy Tallero, in Poland Talar, in France Jocandale, in Russia Jefimok. All these names are abbreviations of "Joachimsthaler." Until the discovery of the great silver deposits in Mexican and South American mines, the mint with the greatest output of large silver coins was that of Joachimsthal in the Bohemian Erzgebirge.

The Spanish Dollar, or piece-of-eight, was widely used and familiar to everyone in the English-American colonies. It was only natural therefore that the word "dollar" was adopted officially as the standard monetary unit of the United States by Congress on July 6, 1785.

FLOWING HAIR TYPE 1794-1795

FAIR—Clear enough to identify.
GOOD—Date and letters readable. Main devices outlined, but lack details.
VERY GOOD—Major details discernible. Letters well formed but worn.
FINE—Hair ends distinguishable. Top hairlines show, but otherwise worn smooth.
VERY FINE—Hair in center shows some detail. Other details more bold.

Designer Robert Scot; weight 26.96 grams; composition: .8924 silver, .1076 copper; approx. diameter 39-40 mm; edge: HUNDRED CENTS ONE DOLLAR OR UNIT with decorations between words.

SILVER DOLLARS

	Quan. Minted	Fair	Good	V.G.	Fine	V.F.	E.F.	Unc.
1794...............1,758		$850	$1,350	$2,250	$3,250	$5,750	$9,500	$16,000

Two Leaves Beneath   1795   Three Leaves Beneath
Each Wing (11 Varieties)   Each Wing

1795 All kinds.......203,033							
1795 Two leaves..........	150	240	300	375	650	1,200	3,000
1795 Three leaves.........	150	240	300	375	650	1,200	3,000

DRAPED BUST TYPE, SMALL EAGLE REVERSE 1795-1798

FAIR—*Clear enough to identify.*
GOOD—*Bust outlined, no detail. Date readable, some leaves evident.*
VERY GOOD—*Drapery worn except deepest folds. Hairlines smooth.*
FINE—*All drapery lines distinguishable. Hairlines near cheek and neck show some detail.*
VERY FINE—*Left side of drapery worn smooth.*

1795 (Two varieties)........	140	200	285	375	575	1,000	2,600

SILVER DOLLARS

Small
Date

Large
Date

Small
Letters

Large
Letters

	Quan. Minted	Fair	Good	V.G.	Fine	V.F.	E.F.	Unc.
1796 Sm. date, sm. let. (3 vars.)								
All kinds........72,920		$130	$180	$275	$360	$500	$1,000	$2,500
1796 Sm. date lg. let.		130	180	275	360	500	1,000	2,500
1796 Lg. date sm. let........		130	180	275	360	500	1,000	2,500
1797 9 stars left, 7 right								
Sm. let. All kinds..7,776		275	375	450	600	1,250	——	——
1797 9 stars l., 7 r., lg. let. ..		140	200	285	375	550	1,000	2,600
1797 10 stars left, 6 right....		140	200	285	375	550	1,000	2,600
1798 All kinds.......327,536		140	200	285	375	550	1,000	2,600

HERALDIC EAGLE REVERSE 1798-1804

GOOD—*Letters and date readable. E PLURIBUS UNUM obliterated.*

VERY GOOD—*Motto partially readable. Only deepest drapery details visible. All other lines smooth.*

FINE—*All drapery lines distinguishable. Hairlines near cheek and neck show some detail.*

VERY FINE—*Left side of drapery worn smooth.*

	Quan. Minted	Good	V.G.	Fine	V.F.	E.F.	Unc.
1798 Large heraldic eagle, knob 9..		$115	$150	$250	$300	$550	$1,325
1798 Lg. eagle, 10 arrows..........		115	150	250	300	550	1,325
1798 Close date..................		115	150	250	300	550	1,325
1798 Wide date, 13 arrows (11 var.)		115	150	250	300	550	1,325

1799
Over
98,
Stars
7 & 6
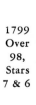
Stars
8 & 5

[145]

SILVER DOLLARS

	Quan. Minted	Good	V.G.	Fine	V.F.	E.F.	Unc.
1799 9 over 8 rev. with 15 stars							
All kinds.............423,515	$125	$160	$275	$350	$600	$1,400
1799 9 over 8 rev. with 13 stars....	125	160	275	350	600	1,400
1799 Irregular date, 15-star rev. ...	125	160	275	350	600	1,400
1799 Irregular date, 13-star rev. ...	125	160	275	350	600	1,400
1799 Normal date................	125	160	275	350	600	1,400
1799 Stars - 8 left, 5 right.........	125	160	275	350	600	1,400
1800 All kinds.............220,920	115	150	250	300	550	1,300
1800 Very wide date, low 8........	115	150	250	300	550	1,300
1800 "Dotted date" from die breaks	115	150	250	300	550	1,300
1800 Only 12 arrows..............	115	150	250	300	550	1,300
1800 Only 10 arrows..............	115	150	250	300	550	1,300
1800 AMERICAI (2 varieties)........	115	150	250	300	550	1,300
1801 (4 vars.)..............54,454	115	150	250	300	550	1,350
1801 Proof restrike (rev. struck							
from first die of 1804 dollar)..					(Proof)	——	

1802 Over 1

		Good	V.G.	Fine	V.F.	E.F.	Unc.
1802 2 over 1, narrow date..		125	160	275	350	600	1,350
1802 2 over 1, wide date....	41,650	125	160	275	350	600	1,350
1802 Narrow norm. date....		125	160	275	350	600	1,350
1802 Wide norm. date......		125	160	275	350	600	1,350
1802 Proof restrike..............						(Proof)	——

Small 3

Large 3

		Good	V.G.	Fine	V.F.	E.F.	Unc.
1803 Large 3 (1 variety)....	85,634	125	160	275	350	600	1,350
1803 Small 3 (5 varieties)...		125	160	275	350	600	1,350
1803 Proof restrike..............						(Proof)	——

THE 1804 DOLLAR

This piece is one of the most publicized rarities in the United States series. There are specimens known as originals (class 1), of which eight are known, and restrikes (class 2), of which seven are known.

Numismatists have found that the 1804 "original" dollars were struck at the mint between 1834 and 1835, for use in presentation proof sets. The first known specimen, a proof, was obtained from a mint officer by Mr. Stickney on May 9, 1843, in exchange for an "Immune Columbia" piece of gold. Later, in 1859, the pieces known as restrikes were made at the mint to supply the needs of collectors who wanted specimens of these dollars.

Evidence that these pieces were struck during the later period is based on the fact that the 1804 dollars differ from issues of 1803 or earlier and conform more closely to those struck after 1836, their edges or borders having beaded segments and raised rim, not elongated denticles such as are found on the earlier dates.

Although the mint records state that 19,570 dollars were coined in 1804, in no place does it mention that they were dated 1804. It was the practice in

SILVER DOLLARS

those days to use old dies as long as they were serviceable with no regard in the annual reports for the dating of the coins. It is probable that the 1804 total for dollars actually covered coins that were dated 1803.

CLASS 1

Note position of words STATES OF with relation to clouds

1804 Class 1, Original (Appleton specimen sold for $77,500.00 in 1970.)

CLASS 2

Compare with Class 1 above

1804 Class 2, Restrike (Idler specimen sold for $80,000.00 in 1972.)

BIBLIOGRAPHY

Bolender, M. H. *The United States Early Silver Dollars from 1794 to 1803*. Freeport, Ill., 1950.
Newman, Eric P. and Bressett, Kenneth E. *The Fantastic 1804 Dollar*. Racine, Wis., 1962.
Haseltine, J. W. *Type Table of United States Dollars, Half Dollars and Quarter Dollars*. Philadelphia, 1881 (reprinted 1927 and 1968).

GOBRECHT PATTERN DOLLARS

Christian Gobrecht was born December 23, 1785. He went to Philadelphia in 1811 and became an engraver of bank notes, seals, calico printers' rolls, bookbinders' dies, etc. He was appointed assistant to Mint Engraver William Kneass in 1836. According to Edgar H. Adams, he prepared a series of dies

SILVER DOLLARS

for pattern dollars, after designs by Sully, exquisite in design and character. The first pattern shows the familiar seated figure of Liberty on the obverse. The name C. Gobrecht F. (F.=Fecit=made it) was placed just under the figure of Liberty and over the date. In the field on the reverse was a large eagle in full flight surrounded by twenty-six stars and the legend UNITED STATES OF AMERICA ONE DOLLAR.

In response to criticism Gobrecht removed his name from the die after a few specimens had been struck, some in silver and some in copper.

Director Patterson ordered the name replaced, this time on the base. Patterns were also made in 1836 with the stars omitted from the reverse.

In 1838 the engraver's name was omitted altogether from the design and thirteen stars were placed around the seated figure of Liberty on the obverse. Stars were omitted from the reverse on one pattern and retained on another. Similar pieces were struck in 1839.

1836 C. GOBRECHT F. in field between base and date. Rev. Eagle   Proof
    flying left amid stars. Plain edge (Rare.) (18)...............   ———
1836 Obv. as above. Rev. Eagle flying in plain field.
    Plain edge (Ex. rare.) (5).................................   ———

1836 C. GOBRECHT on base. Rev. Eagle flying left in field containing stars.
    Plain edge. Although scarce, this is the   V.F.   Ex. F.   Proof
    most common variety. (1,000)................ $1,000 $1,500 $2,150
1836 As above, reeded edge. (Ex. rare.) (3).........   ———

SILVER DOLLARS

Proof

1838 As above, reeded edge. Generally considered to be very rare.
25 Struck. Also unknown quantity of restrikes.............. $4000.00
1838 Obv. as above. Rev. Eagle in plain field. Plain edge.
(Ex. rare.) (3).. ———
1838 Seated Liberty. Obv. Name of designer is left off and stars added
around obverse border. Rev. Eagle flying left surrounded by
stars. Plain edge. (Ex. rare.) (3).......................... ———
1839 Obv. same as 1838. Rev. Eagle in plain field. Plain edge.
(Ex. rare.) (3).. ———
1839 Obv. as above. Rev. Eagle amid stars. Plain edge.
(Ex. rare.) (3).. ———
1839 Obv. as above. Rev. Eagle in plain field. Reeded edge.
Most common 1839 variety. (Rare) (300)................. 4000.00

Quantities shown for the above patterns are probably inaccurate as restrikes of many are known to have been made.

LIBERTY SEATED TYPE — REGULAR ISSUES 1840-1873

When in 1840 silver dollars were again issued for general circulation, the
seated figure of Liberty device was adopted for the obverse. For some mysteri-
ous reason the flying eagle design was rejected, and the more familiar form
with olive branch and arrows was used.

Designer Christian Gobrecht; weight 26.73 grams; composition: .900 silver, .100 copper;
diameter 38.1 mm; reeded edge; mints: Philadelphia, New Orleans, Carson City, San
Francisco.

Mint mark
location
on reverse
below eagle

←

VERY GOOD—Any 3 letters of LIBERTY at least two-thirds complete.
FINE—All 7 letters of LIBERTY visible though weak.
VERY FINE—LIBERTY is strong but its ribbon shows slight wear.

[149]

SILVER DOLLARS

	Quan. Minted	V.G.	Fine	V.F.	Unc.	Proof
1840	61,005	$40.00	$60.00	$70.00	$375.00	$1,250
1841	173,000	35.00	45.00	62.50	325.00	1,150
1842	184,618	35.00	45.00	62.50	325.00	1,150
1843	165,100	35.00	45.00	62.50	325.00	1,150
1844	20,000	55.00	90.00	125.00	375.00	1,200
1845	24,500	55.00	90.00	125.00	375.00	1,200
1846	110,600	30.00	40.00	50.00	310.00	1,000
1846O	59,000	40.00	55.00	70.00	350.00	
1847	140,750	35.00	45.00	62.50	300.00	1,000
1848	15,000	70.00	85.00	120.00	350.00	1,200
1849	62,600	35.00	50.00	65.00	300.00	1,000
1850	7,500	80.00	125.00	200.00	400.00	1,250
1850O	40,000	45.00	55.00	85.00	350.00	
1851 Orig., high date	1,300	500.00	700.00	900.00	2,000	3,250
1851 Restrike, date centered						2,500
1852 Original	1,100				3,250	
1852 Restrike						2,250
1853	46,110	55.00	80.00	120.00	425.00	1,850
1854	33,140	90.00	140.00	200.00	500.00	1,750
1855	26,000	110.00	165.00	225.00	550.00	1,750
1856	63,500	57.50	75.00	115.00	425.00	1,250
1857	94,000	50.00	70.00	110.00	410.00	1,000
1858	Estimated (80)					2,250
1859	256,500	37.50	50.00	70.00	300.00	450.00
1859O	360,000	35.00	45.00	60.00	275.00	
1859S	20,000	60.00	90.00	120.00	450.00	
1860 (1,330)	218,930	35.00	45.00	70.00	275.00	375.00
1860O	515,000	30.00	40.00	50.00	275.00	
1861 (1,000)	78,500	45.00	60.00	85.00	300.00	400.00
1862 (550)	12,090	45.00	65.00	90.00	350.00	450.00
1863 (460)	27,660	45.00	65.00	90.00	350.00	450.00
1864 (470)	31,170	45.00	65.00	90.00	350.00	450.00
1865 (500)	47,000	45.00	65.00	90.00	350.00	450.00
1866 Transitional pattern	(2 known)					——

Motto "In God We Trust" Added To Reverse

1866 (725)	49,625	50.00	70.00	85.00	300.00	450.00
1867 (625)	47,525	50.00	70.00	85.00	300.00	450.00
1868 (600)	162,700	40.00	55.00	75.00	275.00	450.00
1869 (600)	424,300	35.00	45.00	65.00	275.00	450.00

SILVER DOLLARS

	Quan. Minted		V.G.	Fine	V.F.	Unc.	Proof
1870........(1,000)	416,000		$35.00	$45.00	$65.00	$275.00	$425.00
1870CC...............12,462			90.00	130.00	180.00	600.00	
1870S......................						19,000	
1871.........(960)	1,074,760		30.00	40.00	50.00	250.00	425.00
1871CC................1,376			475.00	650.00	950.00	3,000	
1872.........(950)	1,106,450		30.00	40.00	50.00	250.00	425.00
1872CC................3,150			220.00	325.00	425.00	1,500	
1872S..................9,000			70.00	110.00	150.00	550.00	
1873.........(600)	293,600		35.00	45.00	60.00	275.00	425.00
1873CC................2,300			650.00	900.00	1,400	3,000	
1873S...................700...............Unknown in any collection.							

LIBERTY HEAD OR MORGAN TYPE 1878-1921

The mint law of 1873 made no provision for the standard silver dollar. During the lapse in coinage of this piece the gold dollar became the unit coin and the trade dollar was used for our commercial transactions with the Orient.

The legal tender character was restored to the silver dollar by the Act of February 28, 1878 known as the Bland-Allison Act. The weight, 412½ grains and fineness .900 were to conform with the act of January 18, 1837.

George T. Morgan, formerly a pupil of Wyon in the Royal Mint in London, designed the new dollar. His initial M is found at the truncation of the neck, at the last tress. It also appears on the reverse on the left-hand loop of the ribbon. Mint mark location on reverse below wreath.

Coinage of the silver dollar was suspended after 1904 when the bullion supply became exhausted. Under provisions of the Pittman Act of 1918, 270,232,722 silver dollars were melted and later, in 1921, coinage of the silver dollar was resumed. The Morgan design, with some slight refinements, was employed until the new Peace design was adopted later in that year.

VERY FINE—Two-thirds of hairlines from top of forehead to ear must show. Ear well defined. Feathers on eagle's breast worn.

EXTRA FINE—All hairlines strong and ear bold. Eagle's feathers all plain but slight wear on breast and wing tips.

First Reverse — 8 tail feathers, 1878 Philadelphia only

SILVER DOLLARS

Most uncirculated silver dollars have scratches or nicks because of handling of mint bags. Perfect coins without blemishes are generally worth 50% more than listed values.

Beware of early strike Philadelphia mint uncirculated dollars offered as proofs.

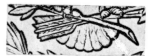

Second Reverse — parallel top arrow feather, concave breast.

Third Reverse — slanted top arrow feather, convex breast.

Designer George T. Morgan. Standards same as previous issue. Additional mint: Denver.

	Quan. Minted	V.F.	Ex. F.	Unc.	Proof
1878, 8 tail feathers....(700)	750,000	$6.00	$8.00	$20.00	$340.00
1878, 7 tail feathers....(300)	9,759,550				
1878, 7 feathers, second reverse........		4.50	5.50	11.00	525.00
1878, 7 feathers, third reverse..........		4.50	6.00	12.00	
1878, 7 feathers over 8 feathers........		10.00	12.00	22.00	
1878CC....................2,212,000		8.00	10.00	30.00	
1878S.......................9,774,000		4.50	5.50	8.00	
1879...............(1,100) 14,807,100		4.50	5.50	7.00	260.00
1879CC.....................756,000		33.00	65.00	425.00	
1879O.....................2,887,000		4.50	5.50	17.00	
1879S second reverse........⎫ 9,110,000		5.00	9.00	22.00	
1879S third reverse..........⎭		4.50	5.50	7.00	
1880, 8 over 7*............⎫ 12,601,355		—	—	—	
1880...............(1,355)⎭		4.50	5.50	8.00	270.00

1880CC, 80 over 79†   1880CC, 8 over high 7*   1880CC, 8 over low 7

	Quan. Minted	V.F.	Ex. F.	Unc.	Proof
1880CC, 80 over 79, 2nd rev.†..⎫		140.00	185.00	425.00	
1880CC second reverse........⎪		35.00	45.00	80.00	
1880CC, 8 over high 7, 3rd rev.*⎬591,000		—	—	140.00	
1880CC, 8 over low 7, 3rd rev. .⎪		—	—	325.00	
1880CC third reverse..........⎭		32.00	40.00	80.00	
1880O, 8 over 7*............⎫ 5,305,000		40.00	60.00	190.00	
1880O....................⎭		4.50	5.50	11.00	
1880S, 8 over 7*............⎫ 8,900,000		—	—	50.00	
1880S....................⎭		4.50	5.50	7.00	
1881...............(975) 9,163,975		4.50	5.50	8.00	270.00
1881CC....................296,000		50.00	60.00	85.00	
1881O....................5,708,000		4.50	5 50	7.00	
1881S....................12,760,000		4.50	5.50	7.00	

*Several die varieties. †7 and 9 show within the 80, no tip below second 8.

SILVER DOLLARS

	Quan. Minted	V.F.	Ex. F.	Unc.	Proof
1882.............(1,100)	11,101,000	$4.50	$5.50	$7.00	$270.00
1882CC..................	1,133,000	15.00	20.00	35.00	
1882O.................. }		4.50	5.50	7.00	
1882O, O over S*......... }	6,090,000	5.00	7.50	16.50	
1882S..................	9,250,000	4.50	5.50	7.00	
1883.............(1,039)	12,291,039	4.50	5.50	7.00	270.00
1883CC..................	1,204,000	15.00	20.00	35.00	
1883O..................	8,725,000	4.50	5.50	7.00	
1883S..................	6,250,000	7.00	12.00	275.00	
1884.............(875)	14,070,875	4.50	5.50	7.00	270.00
1884CC..................	1,136,000	22.50	27.50	35.00	
1884O..................	9,730,000	4.50	5.50	7.00	
1884S..................	3,200,000	7.00	13.50	450.00	
1885.............(930)	17,787,767	4.50	5.50	7.00	270.00
1885CC..................	228,000	48.00	52.50	70.00	
1885O..................	9,185,000	4.50	5.50	7.00	
1885S..................	1,497,000	6.00	8.00	35.00	
1886.............(886)	19,963,886	4.50	5.50	7.00	270.00
1886O..................	10,710,000	4.75	7.00	90.00	
1886S..................	750,000	17.00	24.00	85.00	
1887, 7 over 6........ } (710)	20,290,710	4.50	5.50	7.00	270.00
1887................. }					
1887O, 7 over 6........... }	11,550,000	4.50	5.50	11.00	
1887O.................. }					
1887S..................	1,771,000	7.50	9.50	35.00	
1888.............(832)	19,183,833	4.50	5.50	7.00	270.00
1888O..................	12,150,000	4.50	5.50	9.00	
1888S..................	657,000	23.00	27.00	90.00	
1889.............(811)	21,726,811	4.50	5.50	7.00	270.00
1889CC..................	350,000	115.00	250.00	1,500	
1889O..................	11,875,000	5.00	6.00	23.00	
1889S..................	700,000	23.00	27.00	65.00	
1890.............(590)	16,802,590	4.50	5.50	8.00	300.00
1890CC..................	2,309,041	13.00	18.50	70.00	
1890O..................	10,701,000	4.50	5.50	19.00	
1890S..................	8,230,373	4.50	5.50	24.00	
1891.............(650)	8,694,206	4.50	5.50	30.00	300.00
1891CC..................	1,618,000	13.00	20.00	70.00	
1891O..................	7,954,529	4.50	6.00	25.00	
1891S..................	5,296,000	4.50	6.00	27.50	
1892.............(1,245)	1,037,245	7.00	8.00	70.00	270.00
1892CC..................	1,352,000	30.00	42.50	225.00	
1892O..................	2,744,000	5.25	7.00	45.00	
1892S..................	1,200,000	20.00	95.00	6,000	
1893.............(792)	378,792	20.00	35.00	200.00	300.00
1893CC..................	677,000	45.00	85.00	550.00	
1893O..................	300,000	33.00	70.00	450.00	
1893S..................	100,000	300.00	625.00	9,000	
1894.............(972)	110,972	80.00	100.00	475.00	650.00
1894O..................	1,723,000	8.00	18.00	175.00	
1894S..................	1,260,000	17.00	30.00	200.00	
1895†.............(880)	12,880				6,000

*Several die varieties. †Beware of removed mint mark.

SILVER DOLLARS

	Quan. Minted	V.F.	Ex. F.	Unc.	Proof
1895O..........................450,000		$30.00	$55.00	$1,400	
1895S..........................400,000		60.00	115.00	1,400	
1896..................(762) 9,976,762		4.50	5.50	7.00	$275.00
1896O.......................4,900,000		5.00	9.00	125.00	
1896S.......................5,000,000		21.00	57.50	375.00	
1897..................(731) 2,822,731		4.50	5.50	9.00	275.00
1897O.......................4,004,000		5.00	10.00	100.00	
1897S.......................5,825,000		4.50	6.00	32.00	
1898..................(735) 5,884,735		4.50	5.50	9.00	275.00
1898O.......................4,440,000		4.50	5.50	7.50	
1898S.......................4,102,000		7.00	12.00	85.00	
1899..................(846) 330,846		13.50	17.50	35.00	300.00
1899O......................12,290,000		4.50	5.50	7.00	
1899S.......................2,562,000		9.00	14.00	180.00	
1900..................(912) 8,830,912		4.50	5.50	9.00	275.00
1900O.....................⎫		4.50	5.50	7.00	
1900O, O over CC*.........⎬12,590,000		8.25	13.50	40.00	
1900S.......................3,540,000		8.00	11.00	95.00	
1901..................(813) 6,962,813		12.00	22.50	225.00	300.00
1901O......................13,320,000		4.50	5.50	7.00	
1901S.......................2,284,000		9.00	15.00	90.00	
1902..................(777) 7,994,777		4.50	5.50	35.00	275.00
1902O.......................8,636,000		4.50	5.50	7.00	
1902S.......................1,530,000		40.00	55.00	150.00	
1903..................(755) 4,652,755		4.50	5.50	20.00	275.00
1903O.......................4,450,000		29.00	34.00	42.00	
1903S.......................1,241,000		20.00	57.50	1,400	
1904..................(650) 2,788,650		5.00	6.25	35.00	280.00
1904O.......................3,720,000		4.50	5.50	7.00	
1904S.......................2,304,000		14.00	32.00	400.00	
1921.......................44,690,000		4.25	5.25	7.00	——
1921D......................20,345,000		4.50	5.50	11.00	
1921S......................21,695,000		4.50	5.50	10.00	

*Several die varieties.

BIBLIOGRAPHY

Van Allen, Leroy C. and Mallis, A. George. *Guide to Morgan and Peace Dollars*. 1971.

Most uncirculated silver dollars have scratches or nicks because of handling of mint bags. Perfect coins without blemishes are generally worth 50% more than listed values.

PEACE TYPE 1921-1935

The dollar issued from 1921 to 1935 was a commemorative peace coin, which might easily have been a half dollar. The Peace Dollar, in fact, was issued without congressional sanction, under the terms of the Pittman Act, which referred to the bullion and in no way affected the design.

Anthony De Francisci, a medalist, designed this dollar. His monogram is located in the field of the coin under the neck of Liberty.

The new Peace Dollar was placed in circulation January 3, 1922. 1,006,473 pieces were struck in December, 1921.

SILVER DOLLARS

The high relief of the 1921 design was found impractical for coinage and was slightly modified in 1922. The four known matte proof specimens of 1922 are of the high relief style of 1921.

Legislation dated August 3, 1964 authorized the coinage of 45 million silver dollars, and 316,076 dollars of the Peace design dated 1964 were struck at the Denver mint. Plans for completing this coinage were subsequently abandoned and all of these coins were melted. None were preserved or released for circulation.

VERY FINE—*Hair over eye well worn. Some strands over ear well defined. Some eagle feathers on top and outside edge of right wing will show.*

EXTRA FINE—*Hairlines over brow and ear are strong though slightly worn. Outside wing feathers at right and those at top are visible but faint.*

Designer Anthony De Francisci. Standards same as previous issue. Mints: Philadelphia, Denver, San Francisco.

Mint mark location on reverse below ONE

	Quan. Minted	V. Fine	Ex. Fine	Unc.	Matte Proof
1921	1,006,473	$18.00	$24.00	$75.00	——
1922	51,737,000	4.00	5.00	7.00	——
1922D	15,063,000	4.00	5.00	10.00	
1922S	17,475,000	4.00	5.00	10.00	
1923	30,800,000	4.00	5.00	7.00	
1923D	6,811,000	4.00	5.00	11.00	
1923S	19,020,000	4.00	5.00	10.00	
1924	11,811,000	4.00	5.00	7.00	
1924S	1,728,000	8.00	14.00	70.00	
1925	10,198,000	4.00	5.00	7.00	
1925S	1,610,000	6.00	8.00	40.00	
1926	1,939,000	6.00	7.50	16.50	
1926D	2,348,700	5.00	6.00	17.00	
1926S	6,980,000	4.00	5.00	20.00	
1927	848,000	15.00	19.00	35.00	
1927D	1,268,900	11.00	15.00	75.00	
1927S	866,000	12.00	18.00	100.00	
1928	360,649	75.00	85.00	135.00	
1928S	1,632,000	7.00	10.00	60.00	
1934	954,057	14.00	18.00	45.00	
1934D	1,569,500	9.00	12.00	60.00	
1934S	1,011,000	24.00	70.00	600.00	
1935	1,576,000	9.00	12.00	35.00	
1935S	1,964,000	9.00	18.00	140.00	

SILVER DOLLARS

EISENHOWER DOLLAR 1971—

Intended to honor both the late President Dwight D. Eisenhower and the first landing of man on the moon, this design is the work of mint engraver Frank Gasparro, whose initials are on the truncation and below the eagle. The reverse is an adaptation of the official Apollo 11 insignia. Collectors' coins were struck in 40% silver composition and the circulation issue in copper-nickel. Mint mark location is above the date.

Designer Frank Gasparro. Silver issue: weight 24.59 grams; composition: outer layers of .800 silver, .200 copper bonded to inner core of .210 silver, .790 copper. Copper-nickel issue: weight 22.68 grams; composition: outer layers of .750 copper, .250 nickel bonded to inner core of pure copper. Diameter 38.1 mm; reeded edge.

	Quan. Minted	Unc.	Proof
1971 Copper-nickel clad	47,799,000	$1.50	
1971D Copper-nickel clad	68,587,424	1.50	
1971S Silver clad (4,265,234)	11,133,764	4.50	$12.00
1972 Copper-nickel clad	75,890,000	1.50	
1972D Copper-nickel clad	92,548,511	1.50	
1972S Silver clad (1,811,631)	4,004,687	5.00	13.00
1973 Copper-nickel clad		1.50	
1973D Copper-nickel clad		1.50	
1973S Copper-nickel clad			4.00
1973S Silver-clad		4.00	12.00

Since 1971, dies for the Eisenhower dollar have been modified several times by changing the relief, strengthening the design, and making the world above the eagle round and more clearly defined.

Low relief dies were used for all copper-nickel issues of 1971, all uncirculated silver of 1971, and most copper-nickel coins of 1972.

High relief dies were used for all proofs of 1971, all silver issues of 1972, and the reverse of some exceptional Philadelphia copper-nickel coins of 1972 (identified by round world and weakly defined continents).

Modified high relief reverse dies were used for late 1972 Philadelphia copper-nickel coins and will probably be used for all issues of 1973.

TRADE DOLLARS 1873 - 1885

This coin was issued for circulation in the Orient to compete with dollar-size coins of other countries. It weighed 420 grains compared to 412½ grains, the weight of the regular silver dollar.

At first the coin was legal tender, but in 1876 Congress restricted its use to export demands. After 1878, strikings were specimen proofs only.

The law authorizing Trade Dollars was repealed in February, 1887.

VERY GOOD—*About half of mottoes IN GOD WE TRUST and E PLURIBUS UNUM will show. Rim on both sides well defined.*
FINE—*Mottoes and LIBERTY readable but worn.*
EXTRA FINE—*Mottoes and LIBERTY are sharp. Only slight wear on rims.*

Designer William Barber; weight 27.22 grams; composition: .900 silver, .100 copper; diameter 38.1 mm; reeded edge; mints: Philadelphia, Carson City, San Francisco.

1875S
S over CC

Mint mark
location
on reverse
below eagle

	Quan. Minted	V.G.	Fine	E.F.	Unc.	Proof
1873 . . . . (865)	397,500	$32.50	$40.00	$72.50	$250.00	$475.00
1873CC	124,500	42.50	60.00	130.00	325.00	
1873S	703,000	32.50	50.00	85.00	255.00	
1874 . . . . (700)	987,800	30.00	40.00	67.50	210.00	400.00
1874CC	1,373,200	40.00	55.00	110.00	260.00	
1874S	2,549,000	32.50	40.00	67.50	210.00	
1875 . . . . (700)	218,900	37.50	57.50	100.00	265.00	425.00
1875CC	1,573,700	40.00	55.00	95.00	250.00	
1875S		30.00	40.00	67.50	200.00	
1875S, S over CC . . .	} 4,487,000	—	—	200.00	1,000.00	
1876 . . . . (1,150)	456,150	30.00	40.00	70.00	210.00	400.00
1876CC	509,000	45.00	62.50	100.00	275.00	
1876S	5,227,000	30.00	37.50	65.00	200.00	
1877 . . . . (510)	3,039,710	30.00	37.50	65.00	200.00	485.00
1877CC	534,000	50.00	75.00	145.00	300.00	
1877S	9,519,000	30.00	37.50	65.00	200.00	
1878 . . . . (900)	900					500.00
1878CC	97,000	120.00	190.00	325.00	850.00	
1878S	4,162,000	30.00	37.50	65.00	200.00	
1879 . . . . (1,541)	1,541	. . . .				425.00
1880 . . . . (1,987)	1,987	. . . .				425.00
1881 . . . . (960)	960	. . . .				425.00
1882 . . . . (1,097)	1,097	. . . .				425.00
1883 . . . . (979)	979	. . . .				500.00
1884 . . . . (10)	10	. . . . 1972 Delp Sale				$17,000
1885 . . . . (5)	5	. . . .				—

BIBLIOGRAPHY

Willem, John M. *The United States Trade Dollar*. Second edition Racine, Wis., 1965.

GOLD

Gold has served as money or established the monetary value of currencies longer than any other material. The use of gold coins was widespread in Europe by the fourth century B.C.

The earliest coins circulated in the United States were foreign coins, mostly gold, brought from Europe. The Coinage Act in 1792 established an independent monetary system with the dollar as the basic United States monetary unit containing 24¾ grains of fine gold, based on the world price of $19.39 a troy ounce (480 grains). Congress changed the gold specification in 1834 and again in 1837, when it set the dollar-price of gold at $20.67 an ounce. It remained there for almost a hundred years.

In 1934 residents of the United States were prohibited from holding gold in this country for monetary purposes — a prohibition that was extended in 1961 to include U.S. citizens holding gold abroad. For all practical purposes, gold ceased to exist as a monetary unit in the United States in 1934, when the gold content of the dollar was reduced to $13^5/_7$ grains and the dollar-price of gold was increased to $35 an ounce. Use of gold in international trade was further restricted when the world price of gold again rose, and in 1972 it was officially revalued by the United States government at $38.00 per ounce, and in 1973 again raised to $42.22 per ounce.

GOLD DOLLARS 1849-1889

Coinage of the gold dollar was authorized by the Act of March 3, 1849. The weight was 25.8 grains, fineness .900. The first type, struck until 1854, is known as the Liberty Head or Small-sized type. Its size is the smallest of all U.S. coins.

In 1854 the piece was made larger in diameter and thinner. The design was changed to a feather headdress on a female, generally referred to as the Indian Head or Large-sized type. In 1856 the type was changed slightly by enlarging the size of the head.

The Type 1 dollars after 1849 all have a closed wreath on the reverse.

LIBERTY HEAD TYPE 1849-1854

FINE—Full LIBERTY but knobs over coronet partially worn.
VERY FINE—LIBERTY on headband complete and readable. Knobs on coronet are defined.
EXTRA FINE—Slight wear on Liberty's hair. Knobs on coronet sharp.

Type 1 (closed wreath)
Mint mark on reverse below wreath

Designer James B. Longacre; weight 1.67 grams; composition: .900 gold, .100 copper; diameter 13 mm; reeded edge.

	Quan. Minted	Fine	V. Fine	E. Fine	Unc.
1849 Open wreath - All kinds	688,567	$60.00	$75.00	$95.00	$175.00
1849 Closed wreath (wreath ends closer to Fig. 1)		60.00	75.00	95.00	175.00
1849C Closed wreath	⎱11,634	150.00	200.00	450.00	700.00
1849C Open wreath (3 known)	⎰	1956 A.N.A. Sale $6,000.00			
1849D Open wreath	21,588	125.00	235.00	375.00	550.00
1849O Open wreath	215,000	60.00	75.00	95.00	175.00
1850	481,953	60.00	75.00	95.00	175.00
1850C	6,966	175.00	300.00	475.00	750.00
1850D	8,382	150.00	250.00	375.00	600.00
1850O	14,000	60.00	100.00	135.00	200.00
1851	3,317,671	60.00	75.00	95.00	175.00
1851C	41,267	120.00	175.00	260.00	375.00
1851D	9,882	150.00	240.00	360.00	500.00
1851O	290,000	60.00	75.00	95.00	175.00

GOLD DOLLARS

	Quan. Minted	Fine	V. Fine	E. Fine	Unc.	Proof
1852	2,045,351	$60.00	$75.00	$95.00	$150.00	
1852C	9,434	150.00	240.00	375.00	500.00	
1852D	6,360	150.00	250.00	400.00	550.00	
1852O	140,000	60.00	75.00	95.00	175.00	
1853	4,076,051	60.00	75.00	95.00	175.00	
1853C	11,515	125.00	185.00	275.00	425.00	
1853D	6,583	150.00	250.00	375.00	600.00	
1853O	290,000	60.00	75.00	95.00	175.00	
1854	736,709	60.00	75.00	95.00	175.00	
1854D	2,935	275.00	425.00	575.00	950.00	
1854S	14,632	125.00	165.00	280.00	400.00	

INDIAN HEAD TYPE, Small head 1854-1856

Type 2

FINE—*Feather curl tips partially worn away.*
VERY FINE—*Feather curl tips outlined but details worn.*
EXTRA FINE—*Slight wear on tips of feather curls on headdress.*

Standards same as previous issue. Diameter changed to 15 mm.

1854	902,736	225.00	300.00	600.00	1,500
1855	758,269	225.00	300.00	600.00	1,500
1855C	9,803	325.00	425.00	700.00	2,000
1855D	1,811	1,000	1,700	2,600	4,250
1855O	55,000	225.00	300.00	600.00	1,500
1856S	24,600	225.00	300.00	600.00	1,500

INDIAN HEAD TYPE, Large head 1856-1889

Type 3

FINE—*Full LIBERTY on headband but beads partially worn. Curled feathers flat—no detail.*
VERY FINE—*Curled feathers have slight detail. Details worn smooth at eyebrow, hair below headdress and behind ear and bottom curl.*
EXTRA FINE—*Slight wear above and to right of eye and on top of curled feathers.*

1856 Upright 5	33,660	60.00	75.00	95.00	175.00	
1856 Slant 5	1,729,276	60.00	75.00	95.00	175.00	$1,250
1856D	1,460	1,250	2,000	2,750	4,000	
1857	774,789	60.00	75.00	95.00	175.00	1,250
1857C	13,280	160.00	225.00	375.00	525.00	
1857D	3,533	300.00	500.00	750.00	1,000	
1857S	10,000	100.00	135.00	210.00	300.00	
1858	117,995	65.00	80.00	100.00	190.00	1,100
1858D	3,477	400.00	750.00	1,200	1,750	
1858S	10,000	100.00	150.00	225.00	325.00	
1859	168,244	60.00	75.00	95.00	175.00	950.00
1859C	5,235	175.00	300.00	425.00	650.00	
1859D	4,952	225.00	325.00	475.00	750.00	
1859S	15,000	100.00	160.00	225.00	350.00	
1860 (154)	36,668	60.00	75.00	95.00	175.00	850.00
1860D	1,566	1,350	2,750	3,750	6,000	
1860S	13,000	100.00	160.00	225.00	350.00	
1861 (349)	527,499	60.00	75.00	95.00	175.00	800.00
1861D		3,000	4,500	6,000	9,000	
1862 (35)	1,361,390	60.00	75.00	95.00	175.00	800.00

GOLD DOLLARS

	Quan. Minted	Fine	V. Fine	E. Fine	Unc.	Proof
1863.................(50)	6,250	$200.00	$300.00	$400.00	$650.00	$1,200
1864.................(50)	5,950	125.00	200.00	325.00	450.00	1,200
1865.................(25)	3,725	175.00	300.00	425.00	550.00	950.00
1866.................(30)	7,130	120.00	175.00	250.00	350.00	900.00
1867.................(50)	5,250	120.00	175.00	250.00	350.00	900.00
1868.................(25)	10,525	100.00	150.00	225.00	325.00	900.00
1869.................(25)	5,925	125.00	200.00	250.00	350.00	900.00
1870.................(35)	6,335	100.00	150.00	225.00	300.00	850.00
1870S.................	3,000	300.00	450.00	800.00	1,200	
1871.................(30)	3,930	100.00	150.00	225.00	300.00	850.00
1872.................(30)	3,530	100.00	150.00	225.00	300.00	850.00
1873 Closed 3.........(25) ⎫ 125,125		60.00	75.00	95.00	185.00	850.00
1873 Open 3.............⎭		60.00	75.00	95.00	175.00	
1874.................(20) 198,820		60.00	75.00	95.00	175.00	850.00
1875.................(20)	420	900.00	1,100	1,650	2,000	4,000
1876.................(45)	3,245	100.00	150.00	225.00	300.00	750.00
1877.................(20)	3,920	100.00	150.00	225.00	300.00	850.00
1878.................(20)	3,020	100.00	150.00	200.00	300.00	850.00
1879.................(30)	3,030	100.00	150.00	200.00	300.00	750.00
1880.................(36)	1,636	100.00	125.00	175.00	275.00	600.00
1881.................(87)	7,707	80.00	125.00	150.00	250.00	450.00
1882.................(125)	5,125	80.00	125.00	150.00	250.00	450.00
1883.................(207)	11,007	80.00	110.00	135.00	225.00	425.00
1884.................(1,006)	6,236	80.00	110.00	135.00	225.00	350.00
1885.................(1,105)	12,261	80.00	110.00	135.00	225.00	350.00
1886.................(1,016)	6,016	80.00	110.00	135.00	225.00	350.00
1887.................(1,043)	8,543	80.00	110.00	135.00	225.00	350.00
1888.................(1,079)	16,580	80.00	110.00	135.00	225.00	350.00
1889.................(1,779)	30,729	80.00	110.00	125.00	200.00	300.00

QUARTER EAGLES
($2.50 GOLD PIECES)

Authorized by the Act of April 2, 1792, they weighed 67.5 grains, 916⅔ fine until the weight was changed to 64.5 grains, fineness 899.225, by the Act of June 28, 1834. The Act of January 18, 1837 established fineness at .900. Most dates before 1834 are rare. The first issue was struck in 1796, most of which had no stars on the obverse.

Proofs of some dates prior to 1855 are known to exist, and all are rare.

CAPPED BUST TO RIGHT 1796-1807

Variety 1 — No stars
on obverse 1796 only

FINE—Hair worn smooth on high spots. E PLURIBUS UNUM weak but readable.
VERY FINE—Some wear on high spots.
EXTRA FINE—Only slight wear on hair and cheek.

Designer Robert Scot; weight 4.37 grams; composition: .9167 gold, .0833 copper; approx. diameter 20 mm; reeded edge.

	Quan. Minted	Fine	V. Fine	E. Fine	Unc.
1796 No stars on obverse...............963		$3,200	$5,750	$6,750	$9,000

QUARTER EAGLES

Variety 2 —
Stars on obverse
1796-1807

	Quan. Minted	Fine	V. Fine	E. Fine	Unc.
1796 Stars on obverse	432	$3,000	$5,500	$6,500	$9,000
1797	427	1,250	2,200	2,750	3,500
1798	1,094	1,200	2,000	2,500	4,750
1802, 2 over 1	3,035	550.00	925.00	1,250	2,400
1804, 13-Star reverse	} 3,327	600.00	925.00	1,250	2,200
1804, 14-Star reverse		600.00	950.00	1,350	2,200
1805	1,781	550.00	950.00	1,350	2,100
1806, 6 over 4	} 1,616	750.00	1,600	2,000	2,850
1806, 6 over 5		650.00	1,600	2,000	3,000
1807	6,812	475.00	750.00	950.00	1,500

CAPPED BUST TO LEFT, Large Size 1808

FINE—*E PLURIBUS UNUM and LIBERTY on headband readable but weak.*

VERY FINE—*Motto and LIBERTY clear.*

EXTRA FINE—*All details of hair are plain.*

Designer John Reich. Standards same as previous issue.

1808	2,710	2,000	4,250	5,500	7,500

CAPPED HEAD TO LEFT 1821-1834

Those dated 1829 through 1834 are smaller in diameter than the 1821-1827 pieces. They also have smaller letters, dates and stars.

Standards same as previous issue. Diameter changed to approximately 18.5 mm.

1826
over
25

1821	6,448	500.00	1,000	2,000	3,500
1824, 4 over 1	2,600	500.00	1,000	1,650	3,000
1825	4,434	600.00	1,200	1,650	3,000
1826, 6 over 5	760	700.00	1,400	2,000	3,500
1827	2,800	600.00	1,000	1,500	2,750
1829	3,403	450.00	800.00	1,400	2,500
1830	4,540	450.00	700.00	1,000	2,000
1831	4,520	450.00	700.00	1,000	2,000
1832	4,400	450.00	700.00	1,000	2,000
1833	4,160	450.00	700.00	1,000	2,000
1834 (Motto)	4,000	1,250	2,000	2,600	4,500

QUARTER EAGLES
CLASSIC HEAD TYPE, No motto on reverse 1834-1839

In 1834 the quarter eagle was redesigned. A ribbon binding the hair, bearing the word **LIBERTY**, replaces the Liberty cap. The motto was omitted from the reverse. In 1840 a coronet and smaller head were designed to conform in appearance with that of the larger gold coins.

FINE—*LIBERTY readable and complete. Curl under ear outlined but no detail.*
VERY FINE—*LIBERTY plain. Hair curl has detail.*
EXTRA FINE—*Small amount of wear on top of hair and below L in LIBERTY. Wear evident on wing.*

Mint mark location

Designer William Kneass; weight 4.18 grams; composition: .8992 gold, .1008 copper; diameter 18.2 mm; reeded edge.

	Quan. Minted	Fine	V. Fine	E. Fine	Unc.
1834 No motto	112,234	$100.00	$125.00	$175.00	$300.00
1835	131,402	100.00	125.00	175.00	300.00
1836	547,986	100.00	125.00	175.00	300.00
1837	45,080	110.00	140.00	185.00	325.00
1838	47,030	110.00	140.00	185.00	325.00
1838C	7,880	175.00	275.00	375.00	600.00
1839	27,021	110.00	140.00	185.00	325.00
1839C	18,140	150.00	225.00	325.00	550.00
1839D	13,674	175.00	300.00	400.00	600.00
1839O	17,781	120.00	175.00	250.00	400.00

1839, 9 over 8 varieties exist for P, C and D mints.

CORONET TYPE 1840-1907

  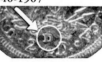

Mint mark location

Designer Christian Gobrecht; weight 4.18 grams; composition: .900 gold, .100 copper; diameter 18 mm; reeded edge.

1840	18,859	60.00	85.00	120.00	200.00
1840C	12,822	95.00	150.00	225.00	350.00
1840D	3,532	150.00	250.00	350.00	750.00
1840O	33,580	52.50	72.50	90.00	140.00
1841 Proof only	Shuford Sale 1968 Proof $18,000.00				
1841C	10,281	175.00	210.00	265.00	400.00
1841D	4,164	185.00	320.00	370.00	550.00
1842	2,823	135.00	260.00	310.00	400.00
1842C	6,729	135.00	185.00	225.00	350.00
1842D	4,643	145.00	225.00	285.00	525.00
1842O	19,800	50.00	75.00	90.00	125.00
1843	100,546	50.00	67.50	72.50	115.00
1843C Small date	26,064	165.00	475.00	725.00	1,500
1843C Large date		80.00	110.00	135.00	175.00
1843D Small date	36,209	95.00	125.00	160.00	275.00
1843O Small date	288,002	45.00	55.00	65.00	100.00
1843O Large date	76,000	75.00	115.00	130.00	210.00

QUARTER EAGLES

	Quan. Minted	Fine	V. Fine	E. Fine	Unc.
1844	6,784	$100.00	$150.00	$185.00	$300.00
1844C	11,622	110.00	145.00	175.00	260.00
1844D	17,332	95.00	125.00	150.00	300.00
1845	91,051	45.00	55.00	70.00	110.00
1845D	19,460	80.00	130.00	165.00	300.00
1845O	4,000	135.00	215.00	260.00	375.00
1846	21,598	45.00	57.50	70.00	110.00
1846C	4,808	140.00	225.00	285.00	450.00
1846D	19,303	95.00	150.00	185.00	295.00
1846O	66,000	45.00	55.00	80.00	125.00
1847	29,814	52.50	62.50	75.00	110.00
1847C	23,226	85.00	135.00	190.00	325.00
1847D	15,784	90.00	160.00	250.00	475.00
1847O	124,000	42.50	55.00	72.50	100.00
1848	7,489	325.00	575.00	800.00	1,250

CAL. above eagle on Reverse

Calif. Gold Quarter Eagle

In 1848 about two hundred and thirty ounces of gold were sent to Secretary of War Marcy by Col. R. B. Mason, Military Governor of California. The gold was turned over to the mint and made into quarter eagles. The distinguishing mark "CAL." was punched above the eagle on the reverse side, while the coins were in the die.

	Quan. Minted	Fine	V. Fine	E. Fine	Unc.
1848 CAL above eagle (2 Proofs known)	1,389	2,250	3,200	4,500	7,250
1848C	16,788	105.00	130.00	190.00	375.00
1848D	13,771	120.00	160.00	225.00	425.00
1849	23,294	40.00	52.50	80.00	130.00
1849C	10,220	90.00	135.00	185.00	325.00
1849D	10,945	115.00	185.00	240.00	375.00
1850	252,923	40.00	50.00	62.50	100.00
1850C	9,148	100.00	170.00	225.00	350.00
1850D	12,148	100.00	140.00	180.00	300.00
1850O	84,000	40.00	50.00	60.00	100.00
1851	1,372,748	40.00	45.00	55.00	100.00
1851C	14,923	110.00	150.00	240.00	450.00
1851D	11,264	120.00	160.00	250.00	450.00
1851O	148,000	40.00	50.00	60.00	100.00
1852	1,159,681	40.00	45.00	52.50	100.00
1852C	9,772	110.00	150.00	190.00	350.00
1852D	4,078	220.00	300.00	375.00	500.00
1852O	140,000	40.00	45.00	60.00	100.00
1853	1,404,668	40.00	45.00	55.00	100.00
1853D	3,178	325.00	450.00	600.00	1,200
1854	596,258	40.00	45.00	55.00	100.00
1854C	7,295	100.00	150.00	225.00	425.00
1854D	1,760	1,100	1,600	2,200	3,200
1854O	153,000	40.00	45.00	55.00	100.00
1854S	246		4,750	6,000	9,000

QUARTER EAGLES

	Quan. Minted	Fine	V. Fine	E. Fine	Unc.	Proof
1855	235,480	$40.00	$45.00	$60.00	$100.00	$4,400
1855C	3,677	275.00	375.00	485.00	800.00	
1855D	1,123	425.00	750.00	1,500	2,800	
1856	384,240	40.00	45.00	52.50	100.00	4,000
1856C	7,913	110.00	165.00	235.00	400.00	
1856D	874	750.00	1,500	2,750	5,000	
1856O	21,100	40.00	45.00	60.00	100.00	
1856S	71,120	40.00	45.00	70.00	125.00	
1857	214,130	40.00	45.00	55.00	100.00	2,750
1857D	2,364	325.00	450.00	600.00	900.00	
1857O	34,000	40.00	45.00	60.00	100.00	
1857S	69,200	42.50	55.00	75.00	125.00	
1858	47,377	40.00	47.50	57.50	100.00	1,900
1858C	9,056	145.00	185.00	240.00	425.00	
1859	39,444	40.00	45.00	55.00	100.00	1,250
1859D	2,244	260.00	375.00	480.00	900.00	
1859S	15,200	55.00	75.00	100.00	190.00	
1860 (112)	22,675	40.00	45.00	55.00	100.00	1,250
1860C	7,469	135.00	185.00	215.00	360.00	
1860S	35,600	50.00	80.00	110.00	200.00	
1861 (90)	1,283,878	40.00	45.00	52.50	100.00	1,250
1861S	24,000	45.00	55.00	75.00	175.00	

1862 Quarter Eagle
Overdate 2 over 1

	Quan. Minted	Fine	V. Fine	E. Fine	Unc.	Proof
1862, 2 over 1	} 98,543		—	—		
1862 (35)		40.00	45.00	55.00	100.00	1,400
1862S	8,000	80.00	120.00	165.00	425.00	
1863 Proofs only (30)	30					6,000
1863S	10,800	65.00	95.00	115.00	225.00	
1864 (50)	2,874	225.00	340.00	385.00	525.00	1,600
1865 (25)	1,545	265.00	365.00	425.00	600.00	1,600
1865S	23,376	40.00	50.00	75.00	175.00	
1866 (30)	3,110	135.00	210.00	250.00	400.00	1,200
1866S	38,960	40.00	47.50	60.00	110.00	
1867 (50)	3,250	125.00	175.00	215.00	400.00	1,100
1867S	28,000	42.50	55.00	70.00	115.00	
1868 (25)	3,625	110.00	145.00	190.00	350.00	1,300
1868S	34,000	42.50	55.00	75.00	135.00	
1869 (25)	4,345	85.00	120.00	145.00	250.00	1,300
1869S	29,500	42.50	55.00	65.00	110.00	
1870 (35)	4,555	80.00	110.00	140.00	240.00	1,100
1870S	16,000	47.50	60.00	75.00	140.00	
1871 (30)	5,350	80.00	120.00	150.00	260.00	1,000
1871S	22,000	60.00	75.00	85.00	130.00	
1872 (30)	3,030	110.00	150.00	185.00	300.00	1,000
1872S	18,000	50.00	60.00	70.00	115.00	
1873 Closed 3 (25)	} 178,025	40.00	47.50	60.00	100.00	1,100
1873 Open 3		40.00	47.50	60.00	100.00	

QUARTER EAGLES

	Quan. Minted	Fine	V. Fine	E. Fine	Unc.	Proof
1873S.....................	27,000	$42.50	$50.00	$60.00	$100.00	
1874................(20)	3,940	95.00	125.00	175.00	275.00	$1,300
1875................(20)	420	350.00	600.00	900.00	1,750	3,750
1875S.....................	11,600	50.00	85.00	115.00	200.00	
1876................(45)	4,221	100.00	130.00	165.00	275.00	1,100
1876S.....................	5,000	60.00	85.00	110.00	175.00	
1877................(20)	1,652	200.00	275.00	350.00	550.00	1,600
1877S.....................	35,400	40.00	45.00	55.00	100.00	
1878................(20)	286,260	40.00	45.00	50.00	100.00	1,200
1878S.....................	178,000	40.00	45.00	50.00	100.00	
1879................(30)	88,990	40.00	45.00	50.00	100.00	900.00
1879S.....................	43,500	42.50	52.50	60.00	100.00	
1880................(36)	2,996	135.00	175.00	200.00	300.00	1,100
1881................(51)	691	235.00	375.00	465.00	950.00	1,600
1882................(67)	4,067	135.00	175.00	225.00	350.00	1,100
1883................(82)	2,002	160.00	220.00	265.00	375.00	1,100
1884................(73)	2,023	160.00	220.00	265.00	375.00	1,100
1885................(87)	887	215.00	395.00	475.00	700.00	1,300
1886................(88)	4,088	90.00	125.00	175.00	300.00	800.00
1887................(122)	6,282	85.00	110.00	120.00	200.00	800.00
1888................(97)	16,098	50.00	65.00	80.00	125.00	750.00
1889................(48)	17,648	50.00	75.00	90.00	150.00	750.00
1890................(93)	8,813	75.00	90.00	110.00	165.00	750.00
1891................(80)	11,040	52.50	70.00	80.00	125.00	750.00
1892................(105)	2,545	100.00	135.00	160.00	300.00	750.00
1893................(106)	30,106	45.00	60.00	70.00	110.00	750.00
1894................(122)	4,122	75.00	110.00	130.00	200.00	750.00
1895................(119)	6,119	60.00	90.00	110.00	175.00	750.00
1896................(132)	19,202	40.00	60.00	70.00	110.00	750.00
1897................(136)	29,904	40.00	60.00	70.00	110.00	750.00
1898................(165)	24,165	40.00	60.00	70.00	110.00	650.00
1899................(150)	27,350	40.00	60.00	70.00	110.00	650.00
1900................(205)	67,205	40.00	60.00	65.00	100.00	600.00
1901................(223)	91,323	40.00	55.00	60.00	100.00	600.00
1902................(193)	133,733	40.00	50.00	57.50	100.00	600.00
1903................(197)	201,257	40.00	50.00	57.50	100.00	600.00
1904................(170)	160,960	40.00	50.00	57.50	100.00	600.00
1905*...............(144)	217,944	40.00	50.00	57.50	100.00	600.00
1906................(160)	176,490	40.00	50.00	57.50	100.00	600.00
1907................(154)	336,448	40.00	50.00	57.50	100.00	600.00

*Pieces dated 1905S are counterfeit.

INDIAN HEAD TYPE 1908-1929

The new type represents a departure from all preceding coin types in the United States series. Bela Lyon Pratt was the designer of this and the half eagle piece. The coin has no raised milling and the main devices and legends are incuse. Mint mark is on reverse left of fasces.

Designer Bela L. Pratt. Standards same as previous issue.

FINE—Knot in hair cord must show, small feathers on top of head will be faint.

VERY FINE—Hair cord knot distinct. Feathers at top of head clear. Cheekbone worn.

EXTRA FINE—Cheekbone, war bonnet and headband feathers slightly worn.

QUARTER EAGLES

	Quan. Minted	Fine	V. Fine	E. Fine	Unc.	Matte Proof
1908................(236)	565,057	$45.00	$50.00	$60.00	$100.00	$700.00
1909................(139)	441,899	45.00	50.00	60.00	75.00	800.00
1910................(682)	492,682	45.00	50.00	60.00	75.00	700.00
1911................(191)	704,191	45.00	50.00	60.00	75.00	700.00
1911D....................55,680		250.00	350.00	400.00	500.00	
1912................(197)	616,197	45.00	50.00	60.00	75.00	750.00
1913................(165)	722,165	45.00	50.00	60.00	75.00	750.00
1914................(117)	240,117	45.00	50.00	60.00	90.00	900.00
1914D...................448,000		45.00	50.00	60.00	75.00	
1915................(100)	606,100	45.00	50.00	60.00	75.00	900.00
1925D...................578,000		45.00	50.00	60.00	75.00	
1926......................446,000		45.00	50.00	60.00	75.00	
1927......................388,000		45.00	50.00	60.00	75.00	
1928......................416,000		45.00	50.00	60.00	75.00	
1929......................532,000		45.00	50.00	60.00	75.00	

THREE-DOLLAR GOLD PIECES
1854-1889

The three-dollar gold piece was authorized by Act of February 21, 1853. The coin was first struck in 1854. It was never popular and saw very little circulation.

The coin weighs 77.4 grains, .900 fine. The head on the obverse represents an Indian princess with hair tightly curling over the neck, head crowned with a circle of feathers, the band of which is inscribed LIBERTY. A wreath of tobacco, wheat, corn and cotton occupies the field of the reverse, with the denomination and date within it. No change of type was made during the life of this denomination.

In the year 1854 only, the word DOLLARS is in much smaller letters than in years 1855 through 1889. Mint mark is on reverse below wreath.

Designer James B. Longacre; weight 5.02 grams; composition: .900 gold, .100 copper; diameter 20.5 mm; reeded edge.

FINE—Top of headdress worn flat. Full LIBERTY. Beads above band partially worn.

VERY FINE—Eyebrow, hair about forehead and ear and bottom curl are worn smooth. Curled feather-ends have faint details showing.

EXTRA FINE—Only trace of wear above and to right of eye. Slight wear on top of curled feathers.

	Quan. Minted	Fine	V. Fine	E. Fine	Unc.	Proof
1854......................138,618		225.00	275.00	350.00	650.00	——
1854D......................1,120		1,100	2,000	2,600	3,500	
1854O......................24,000		225.00	275.00	350.00	650.00	
1855......................50,555		225.00	275.00	350.00	650.00	——
1855S......................6,600		250.00	325.00	450.00	750.00	
1856......................26,010		225.00	275.00	350.00	650.00	——
1856S*......................34,500		225.00	275.00	350.00	650.00	
1857......................20,891		225.00	275.00	350.00	650.00	——
1857S......................14,000		250.00	300.00	400.00	700.00	
1858......................2,133		300.00	425.00	550.00	1,000	3,000
1859......................15,638		225.00	275.00	350.00	650.00	1,650

*Small, medium and large S varieties exist.

THREE-DOLLAR GOLD PIECES

	Quan. Minted	Fine	V. Fine	E. Fine	Unc.	Proof
1860.................(119)	7,155	$250.00	$300.00	$450.00	$750.00	$1,500
1860S..(2,592 melted at Mint)	7,000	250.00	300.00	450.00	750.00	
1861.................(113)	6,072	225.00	275.00	350.00	650.00	2,000
1862.................(35)	5,785	225.00	275.00	350.00	650.00	2,000
1863.................(39)	5,039	250.00	300.00	450.00	750.00	2,000
1864.................(50)	2,680	300.00	400.00	550.00	900.00	2,000
1865.................(25)	1,165	300.00	400.00	550.00	1,000	2,000
1866.................(30)	4,030	250.00	300.00	450.00	650.00	2,000
1867.................(50)	2,650	250.00	300.00	450.00	750.00	2,000
1868.................(25)	4,875	250.00	300.00	450.00	650.00	2,000
1869.................(25)	2,525	250.00	300.00	450.00	750.00	2,000
1870.................(35)	3,535	250.00	300.00	450.00	650.00	2,000
1870S (Unique)..............2			——			
1871.................(30)	1,330	300.00	375.00	475.00	800.00	2,000
1872.................(30)	2,030	250.00	300.00	450.00	750.00	2,000
1873 Open 3...........(25)	25					4,000
1873 Closed 3 (All restrikes)........					2,500	3,000
1874.................(20)	41,820	250.00	300.00	450.00	650.00	2,500
1875 Proofs only.......(20)	20........R. L. Miles Sale 1968 $25,000					
1876 Proofs only.......(45)	45.........Charles Jay Sale 1967 $7,250					
1877.................(20)	1,488	400.00	700.00	1,000	1,350	3,500
1878.................(20)	82,324	250.00	300.00	450.00	650.00	2,400
1879.................(30)	3,030	250.00	350.00	450.00	850.00	1,800
1880.................(36)	1,036	275.00	375.00	500.00	900.00	1,800
1881.................(54)	554	400.00	600.00	850.00	1,300	2,500
1882.................(76)	1,576	275.00	375.00	475.00	850.00	1,600
1883.................(89)	989	325.00	425.00	525.00	950.00	1,600
1884.................(106)	1,106	325.00	425.00	525.00	950.00	1,600
1885.................(109)	910	350.00	450.00	650.00	1,000	2,300
1886.................(142)	1,142	325.00	425.00	550.00	900.00	1,600
1887.................(160)	6,160	250.00	300.00	450.00	750.00	1,500
1888.................(290)	5,291	250.00	300.00	450.00	750.00	1,250
1889.................(129)	2,429	250.00	300.00	450.00	800.00	1,250

FOUR-DOLLAR GOLD OR "STELLA"

These pattern coins were first suggested by the Hon. John A. Kasson, then U.S. Minister to Austria; and it was through the efforts of Dr. W. W. Hubbell, who patented the goloid metal used in making the goloid metric dollars, that we have these beautiful and interesting pieces.

There are two distinct types in both years of issue. Barber designed the flowing hair type, and Morgan the coiled hair. They were struck in gold, aluminum, copper and white metal. Only those struck in gold are listed.

	Proof			Proof
1879 Flowing hair (415)....	$10,000	1880 Flowing hair (15).....		——
1879 Coiled hair (10).......	——	1880 Coiled hair (10).......		——

HALF EAGLES — 1795-1929
($5.00 GOLD PIECES)

The half eagle was the first gold coin actually struck for the United States. The $5.00 piece was authorized to be coined by the Act of April 2, 1792 and the first type weighed 135 grains, 916⅔ fine. The weight was changed by Act of June 28, 1834 to 129 grains, 899.225 fine. Fineness became .900 by Act of January 18, 1837.

There are many varieties among the early dates caused by changes in the number of stars, style of eagle, overdates, and differences in the size of figures in the dates. Those dated prior to 1807 do not bear any mark of value. The 1822 half eagle is considered the most valuable regular issue coin of the entire United States series. Proofs of some dates prior to 1855 are known to exist, and all are rare. The half eagle was the only U.S. denomination struck in each of the seven mints.

CAPPED BUST TO RIGHT, SMALL EAGLE 1795-1798

This type was struck from mid-1795 to early 1798, when the small eagle reverse was changed to the large or "heraldic" eagle. Note that the 1795 and 1797 dates exist for both types, but the heraldic reverses of these dates were probably struck under emergency conditions in late 1798.

FINE—Hair worn smooth but with distinct outline. After 1797 E PLURIBUS UNUM is faint but readable.

VERY FINE—Slight to noticeable wear on high spots such as hair, turban, eagle's head and wings.

EXTRA FINE—Slight wear on hair and highest part of cheek.

Designer Robert Scot; weight 8.75 grams; composition: .9167 gold, .0833 copper; approx. diameter 25 mm; reeded edge.

	Quan. Minted	Fine	V. Fine	E. Fine	Unc.
1795 Small eagle*	8,707	$1,500	$1,800	$2,250	$3,500

*One variety has final s in STATES over D.

1796, 6 over 5	1797 - 15 Stars	16 Stars

1796, 6 over 5	6,196	1,400	1,800	2,750	3,500
1797, 15 stars	⎫ 3,609	1,400	2,200	3,400	4,600
1797, 16 stars	⎭	1,400	2,200	3,400	4,750
1798 Small eagle (6 known)		—	—	—	—

HALF EAGLES

CAPPED BUST TO RIGHT, HERALDIC EAGLE 1795-1807

	Quan. Minted	Fine	V. Fine	E. Fine	Unc.
1795 Heraldic eagle*		$2,000	$2,700	$4,400	$7,000
1797, 7 over 5*		1,500	2,400	3,300	4,500
1797, 16 star obverse*		—	—	—	
1798 Small 8		400.00	475.00	600.00	1,000
1798 Large 8, 13 star reverse	24,867	500.00	800.00	1,150	1,700
1798 Large 8, 14 star reverse		650.00	1,000	1,350	1,800
1799	7,451	475.00	600.00	800.00	1,200

*These three pieces are thought to have been struck in 1798.

1802 over 1	1803 over 2	Small 8	Sm. 8 over lg. 8

	Quan. Minted	Fine	V. Fine	E. Fine	Unc.
1800	37,628	500.00	600.00	750.00	1,000
1802, 2 over 1	53,176	500.00	600.00	675.00	900.00
1803, 3 over 2	33,506	500.00	600.00	675.00	900.00
1804 Small 8	30,475	500.00	600.00	675.00	900.00
1804 Small 8 over large 8		500.00	600.00	675.00	900.00
1805	33,183	500.00	600.00	675.00	900.00

Pointed 6,
8 & 5 Stars

Round Top 6,
7 & 6 Stars

	Quan. Minted	Fine	V. Fine	E. Fine	Unc.
1806 Pointed top 6	64,093	450.00	575.00	700.00	950.00
1806 Round top 6		450.00	575.00	700.00	950.00
1807	32,488	450.00	575.00	700.00	950.00

HALF EAGLES
CAPPED DRAPED BUST TO LEFT 1807-1812

Designer John Reich. Standards same as previous issue.

FINE—*LIBERTY readable but partly weak.*
VERY FINE—*Headband edges slightly worn. LIBERTY is bold.*
EXTRA FINE—*Slight wear on highest portions of hair. 80% of major curls are plain.*

	Quan. Minted	Fine	V. Fine	E. Fine	Unc.
1807.............................	51,605	$475.00	$575.00	$675.00	$900.00

1808 over 7		Normal Date			

	Quan. Minted	Fine	V. Fine	E. Fine	Unc.
1808, 8 over 7	} 55,578	425.00	500.00	575.00	750.00
1808............................		425.00	500.00	575.00	750.00
1809, 9 over 8	33,875	450.00	525.00	600.00	800.00

Small Date	Large Date	Small 5		Tall 5	
1810 Small date, small 5..........		850.00	1,300	2,250	——
1810 Small date, tall 5	} 100,287	450.00	550.00	625.00	800.00
1810 Large date, small 5..........		425.00	525.00	600.00	750.00
1810 Large date, tall 5		425.00	525.00	600.00	750.00
1811 Small 5.....................	} 99,581	425.00	525.00	600.00	750.00
1811 Large 5.....................		425.00	525.00	600.00	750.00
1812............................	58,087	450.00	550.00	625.00	750.00

CAPPED HEAD TO LEFT 1813-1834

		Fine	V. Fine	E. Fine	Unc.
1813............................	95,428	400.00	500.00	700.00	900.00
1814, 4 over 3....................	15,454	500.00	575.00	725.00	1,000
1815............................	635				7,500
1818 Normal dies.................		500.00	600.00	750.00	1,050
1818 STATESOF one word...........	} 48,588	500.00	600.00	750.00	1,050
1818, 5D over 50		500.00	600.00	750.00	1,050
1819............................	} 51,723	4,000	5,500	7,000	10,000
1819, 5D over 50				——	

HALF EAGLES

Curved-Base 2   Square-Base 2   Small Letters   Large Letters

	Quan. Minted	Fine	V. Fine	E. Fine	Unc.
1820 Curved-base 2, small letters...	} 263,806	$450.00	$725.00	$900.00	$1,400
1820 Curved-base 2, large letters...		500.00	800.00	1,100	1,750
1820 Square-base 2......................		500.00	800.00	1,100	1,750
1821..............................	34,641	1,000	1,800	3,250	5,500

1822   1825, 5 over 1   1825, 5 over 4

	Quan. Minted	Fine	V. Fine	E. Fine	Unc.
1822 (3 known).....................	17,796	—	—	—	—
1823..............................	14,485	750.00	1,000	1,650	2,400
1824..............................	17,340	2,600	3,750	6,000	9,000
1825, 5 over 1.....................	} 29,060	900.00	1,400	2,250	3,500
1825, 5 over 4.....................		—	—	—	—
1826..............................	18,069	1,250	2,250	3,100	4,250
1827..............................	24,913	2,600	3,750	6,000	8,500

1828, 8 over 7   Large Date   Small Date

	Quan. Minted	Fine	V. Fine	E. Fine	Unc.
1828, 8 over 7.....................	} 28,029	1,350	2,200	4,000	6,500
1828..............................		2,000	2,900	4,750	7,000
1829 Large date....................	} 57,442	—	—	—	—
1829 Small date....................		1970 California Sale $23,500			

The half eagles dated 1829 (small date) through 1834 are smaller in diameter than the earlier pieces. They also have smaller letters, dates and stars.

HALF EAGLES

Small 5D	Large 5D	12 Stars, Curved-Base 2	13 Stars, Square-Base 2

	Quan. Minted	Fine	V. Fine	E. Fine	Unc.
1830 Small 5 D.................	} 126,351	$700.00	$1,000	$1,500	$3,000
1830 Large 5 D.................		700.00	1,000	1,500	3,000
1831..........................	140,594	600.00	900.00	1,300	2,500
1832 Curved-base 2, 12 stars.......	} 157,487	—	—	—	—
1832 Square-base 2, 13 stars.......		1,500	2,400	3,300	5,000
1833..........................	193,630	650.00	950.00	1,500	2,750

4
Plain 4

4
Crosslet 4

1834 Plain 4.................	} 50,141	850.00	1,100	1,600	3,000
1834 Crosslet 4.................		850.00	1,100	1,600	3,000

CLASSIC HEAD TYPE 1834-1838

As on the quarter dollar of 1831, the motto E PLURIBUS UNUM was omitted from the new, reduced size half eagle in 1834, presumably for lack of space.

Designer William Kneass; weight 8.36 grams; composition: .8992 gold, .1008 copper; diameter 22.5 mm; reeded edge.

1834 Plain 4.................	} 658,028	90.00	125.00	275.00	550.00
1834 Crosslet 4.................		150.00	200.00	300.00	600.00
1835..........................	371,534	100.00	125.00	200.00	500.00
1836..........................	553,147	100.00	125.00	200.00	500.00
1837..........................	207,121	100.00	125.00	200.00	500.00
1838..........................	286,588	100.00	125.00	200.00	500.00
1838C.........................	17,179	250.00	450.00	675.00	1,200
1838D.........................	20,583	250.00	450.00	675.00	1,200

CORONET TYPE, no motto above eagle 1839-1866

Designer Christian Gobrecht; weight 8.36 grams; composition: .900 gold, .100 copper; diameter 21.6 mm; reeded edge.

FINE—*LIBERTY readable, but partly weak. Neck hair worn, but outlines clear.*

VERY FINE—*LIBERTY bold. Major lines show in neck hair.*

EXTRA FINE—*Neck hair details clear. Slight wear on top and lower part of coronet, and hair.*

Mint mark above date 1839 only.
Mint mark below eagle 1840-1908.

HALF EAGLES

	Quan. Minted	Fine	V.Fine	E.Fine	Unc.
1839, 9 over 8, curved date...... }	118,143				
1839 Normal date............... }		$60.00	$70.00	$90.00	$225.00
1839C...........................	17,205	150.00	250.00	350.00	600.00
1839D...........................	18,939	150.00	250.00	350.00	650.00
1840*...........................	137,382	60.00	70.00	90.00	175.00
1840C*..........................	18,992	125.00	150.00	185.00	450.00
1840D*..........................	22,896	125.00	150.00	185.00	450.00
1840O*..........................	40,120	100.00	125.00	150.00	400.00
1841............................	15,833	90.00	115.00	150.00	450.00
1841C...........................	21,467	125.00	175.00	225.00	425.00
1841D...........................	30,495	125.00	175.00	225.00	425.00
1841O (2 known).................	50	——	——		

*Scarce varieties of these pieces have uneven wide rims the size of 1834-1839 coins.

1842 Small Date   Small Letters   Large Letters

	Quan. Minted	Fine	V.Fine	E.Fine	Unc.
1842 Small letters.............. }	27,578	60.00	90.00	150.00	275.00
1842 Large letters............. }		60.00	90.00	150.00	275.00
1842C Small date............... }	28,184	100.00	150.00	200.00	600.00
1842C Large date............... }		100.00	125.00	160.00	375.00
1842D Small date............... }	59,608	100.00	125.00	160.00	375.00
1842D Large date............... }		150.00	350.00	450.00	650.00
1842O..........................	16,400	95.00	110.00	140.00	325.00
1843...........................	611,205	55.00	65.00	75.00	135.00
1843C..........................	44,201	90.00	125.00	175.00	325.00
1843D..........................	98,452	90.00	125.00	175.00	325.00
1843O Small letters............	19,075	60.00	75.00	90.00	225.00
1843O Large letters............	82,000	60.00	75.00	90.00	225.00
1844...........................	340,330	55.00	65.00	90.00	175.00
1844C..........................	23,631	95.00	125.00	160.00	350.00
1844D..........................	88,982	95.00	125.00	160.00	300.00
1844O..........................	364,000	60.00	80.00	100.00	250.00
1845...........................	417,099	60.00	75.00	85.00	125.00
1845D..........................	90,629	95.00	110.00	150.00	300.00
1845O..........................	41,000	85.00	110.00	150.00	300.00
1846...........................	395,942	60.00	70.00	80.00	125.00
1846C..........................	12,995	95.00	125.00	175.00	400.00
1846D..........................	80,294	95.00	125.00	175.00	350.00
1846O..........................	58,000	75.00	90.00	150.00	225.00
1847...........................	915,981	60.00	70.00	75.00	110.00
1847C..........................	84,151	90.00	115.00	150.00	250.00
1847D..........................	64,405	90.00	115.00	150.00	300.00
1847O..........................	12,000	85.00	125.00	175.00	300.00
1848...........................	260,775	60.00	70.00	80.00	120.00
1848C..........................	64,472	95.00	125.00	175.00	300.00
1848D..........................	47,465	95.00	140.00	195.00	325.00
1849...........................	133,070	60.00	70.00	80.00	125.00

HALF EAGLES

	Quan. Minted	Fine	V. Fine	E. Fine	Unc.	Proof
1849C	64,823	$95.00	$125.00	$175.00	$300.00	
1849D	39,036	95.00	125.00	185.00	325.00	
1850	64,491	60.00	70.00	80.00	110.00	
1850C	63,591	95.00	125.00	175.00	300.00	
1850D	43,984	95.00	125.00	175.00	325.00	
1851	377,505	55.00	65.00	80.00	110.00	
1851C	49,176	95.00	125.00	175.00	350.00	
1851D	62,710	100.00	135.00	185.00	325.00	
1851O	41,000	70.00	80.00	95.00	200.00	
1852	573,901	60.00	70.00	80.00	110.00	
1852C	72,574	95.00	135.00	185.00	325.00	
1852D	91,584	95.00	135.00	175.00	325.00	
1853	305,770	55.00	60.00	75.00	120.00	
1853C	65,571	95.00	125.00	175.00	325.00	
1853D	89,678	95.00	125.00	175.00	350.00	
1854	160,675	50.00	60.00	75.00	125.00	
1854C	39,283	95.00	125.00	175.00	300.00	
1854D	56,413	95.00	125.00	175.00	350.00	
1854O	46,000	95.00	115.00	150.00	260.00	
1854S Wolfson Sale	268			16,500	——	
1855	117,098	55.00	60.00	75.00	120.00	$3,500
1855C	39,788	95.00	125.00	175.00	300.00	
1855D	22,432	110.00	140.00	195.00	375.00	
1855O	11,100	135.00	180.00	225.00	400.00	
1855S	61,000	75.00	90.00	125.00	225.00	
1856	197,990	55.00	60.00	75.00	125.00	3,500
1856C	28,457	95.00	125.00	175.00	300.00	
1856D	19,786	125.00	150.00	175.00	350.00	
1856O	10,000	165.00	240.00	375.00	600.00	
1856S	105,100	60.00	70.00	80.00	120.00	
1857	98,188	50.00	60.00	70.00	120.00	3,500
1857C	31,360	95.00	125.00	175.00	300.00	
1857D	17,046	110.00	140.00	195.00	350.00	
1857O	13,000	100.00	125.00	165.00	350.00	
1857S	87,000	70.00	85.00	100.00	200.00	
1858	15,136	125.00	150.00	175.00	350.00	2,500
1858C	38,856	95.00	125.00	175.00	275.00	
1858D	15,362	110.00	150.00	175.00	350.00	
1858S	18,600	90.00	125.00	150.00	275.00	
1859	16,814	90.00	150.00	200.00	325.00	1,800
1859C	31,847	125.00	175.00	225.00	350.00	
1859D	10,366	150.00	210.00	260.00	450.00	
1859S	13,220	90.00	110.00	150.00	275.00	
1860	(62) 19,825	80.00	90.00	125.00	250.00	1,400
1860C	14,813	125.00	150.00	185.00	350.00	
1860D	14,635	135.00	175.00	250.00	425.00	
1860S	21,200	70.00	85.00	110.00	200.00	
1861	(66)688,150	60.00	70.00	80.00	120.00	1,000
1861C	6,879	350.00	450.00	650.00	1,000	
1861D	1,597	1,250	1,600	2,350	3,500	
1861S	18,000	75.00	90.00	125.00	250.00	
1862	(35) 4,465	150.00	225.00	300.00	450.00	1,000
1862S	9,500	125.00	175.00	225.00	450.00	

HALF EAGLES

	Quan. Minted	Fine	V. Fine	E. Fine	Unc.	Proof
1863.................(30)	2,472	$225.00	$300.00	$400.00	$750.00	$1,200
1863S.....................17,000		95.00	125.00	175.00	300.00	
1864.................(50)	4,220	200.00	250.00	325.00	650.00	1,600
1864S.....................3,888		300.00	450.00	850.00	1,400	
1865.................(25)	1,295	250.00	325.00	400.00	800.00	1,300
1865S.....................27,612		80.00	125.00	175.00	275.00	
1866S.....................9,000		125.00	150.00	175.00	500.00	

Variety 2 — Motto above eagle 1866-1908

FINE—All letters in motto IN GOD WE TRUST readable.

VERY FINE — Half of hairlines above coronet missing. Hair curls under ear evident, but worn. Motto and its ribbon sharp.

EXTRA FINE—Small amount of wear on top of hair and below L in LIBERTY. Wear evident on wing tips and neck of eagle.

		Fine	V. Fine	E. Fine	Unc.	Proof
1866.................(30)	6,730	175.00	250.00	300.00	475.00	900.00
1866S.....................34,920		125.00	250.00	300.00	475.00	
1867.................(50)	6,920	125.00	200.00	275.00	400.00	900.00
1867S.....................29,000		80.00	100.00	125.00	300.00	
1868.................(25)	5,725	125.00	175.00	225.00	350.00	1,000
1868S.....................52,000		80.00	100.00	125.00	300.00	
1869.................(25)	1,785	200.00	300.00	375.00	800.00	1,600
1869S.....................31,000		80.00	100.00	125.00	300.00	
1870.................(35)	4,035	125.00	175.00	225.00	350.00	1,300
1870CC.....................7,675		550.00	700.00	850.00		
1870S.....................17,000		75.00	110.00	175.00	250.00	
1871.................(30)	3,230	160.00	275.00	375.00	575.00	1,300
1871CC.....................20,770		175.00	250.00	350.00	750.00	
1871S.....................25,000		70.00	100.00	150.00	250.00	
1872.................(30)	1,690	275.00	425.00	600.00	750.00	1,400
1872CC.....................16,980		175.00	250.00	375.00	750.00	
1872S.....................36,400		65.00	100.00	175.00	275.00	
1873 Closed 3.........(25)	}112,505	60.00	70.00	80.00	120.00	1,200
1873 Open 3		60.00	70.00	80.00	120.00	
1873CC.....................7,416		200.00	300.00	400.00	675.00	
1873S.....................31,000		75.00	90.00	140.00	250.00	
1874.................(20)	3,508	160.00	300.00	375.00	525.00	1,300
1874CC.....................21,198		150.00	200.00	275.00	475.00	
1874S.....................16,000		60.00	70.00	100.00	160.00	
1875.................(20)	220		1,500	2,500	4,000	6,000
1875CC.....................11,828		175.00	275.00	400.00	600.00	
1875S.....................9,000		85.00	135.00	210.00	325.00	
1876.................(45)	1,477	250.00	350.00	475.00	650.00	1,200
1876CC.....................6,887		200.00	290.00	350.00	600.00	
1876S.....................4,000		100.00	150.00	225.00	375.00	
1877.................(20)	1,152	225.00	450.00	725.00	1,000	1,800
1877CC.....................8,680		225.00	300.00	400.00	600.00	
1877S.....................26,700		65.00	85.00	110.00	175.00	
1878.................(20)131,740		60.00	70.00	80.00	120.00	1,400

HALF EAGLES

	Quan. Minted	Fine	V. Fine	E. Fine	Unc.	Proof
1878CC	9,054	$450.00	$600.00	$750.00		
1878S	144,700	50.00	60.00	70.00	$110.00	
1879 (30)	301,950	50.00	60.00	70.00	110.00	$800.00
1879CC	17,281	125.00	200.00	275.00	400.00	
1879S	426,200	50.00	60.00	70.00	110.00	
1880 (36)	3,166,436	50.00	60.00	70.00	100.00	800.00
1880CC	51,017	80.00	100.00	140.00	250.00	
1880S	1,348,900	50.00	60.00	70.00	110.00	
1881, 1 over 0 ⎫		—	—	—		
1881 (42) ⎭ 5,708,802		50.00	60.00	70.00	110.00	700.00
1881CC	13,886	85.00	115.00	140.00	275.00	
1881S	969,000	50.00	60.00	70.00	110.00	
1882 (48)	2,514,568	50.00	60.00	70.00	110.00	700.00
1882CC	82,817	75.00	90.00	115.00	175.00	
1882S	969,999	50.00	60.00	70.00	110.00	
1883 (61)	233,461	50.00	60.00	70.00	110.00	700.00
1883CC	12,958	90.00	110.00	145.00	250.00	
1883S	83,200	50.00	60.00	70.00	100.00	
1884 (48)	191,078	50.00	60.00	70.00	100.00	1,200
1884CC	16,402	90.00	110.00	145.00	200.00	
1884S	177,000	50.00	60.00	70.00	100.00	
1885 (66)	601,506	50.00	60.00	70.00	100.00	700.00
1885S	1,211,500	50.00	60.00	70.00	100.00	
1886 (72)	388,432	50.00	60.00	70.00	100.00	600.00
1886S	3,268,000	50.00	60.00	70.00	100.00	
1887 Proofs only (87)	87					4,000
1887S	1,912,000	50.00	60.00	70.00	100.00	
1888 (95)	18,296	60.00	70.00	80.00	140.00	900.00
1888S	293,900	50.00	60.00	70.00	100.00	
1889 (45)	7,565	175.00	225.00	275.00	500.00	1,000
1890 (88)	4,328	200.00	250.00	325.00	500.00	1,000
1890CC	53,800	65.00	75.00	90.00	125.00	
1891 (53)	61,413	50.00	60.00	70.00	100.00	800.00
1891CC	208,000	60.00	70.00	80.00	125.00	
1892 (92)	753,572	50.00	60.00	70.00	100.00	600.00
1892CC	82,968	60.00	70.00	80.00	125.00	
1892O	10,000	350.00	550.00	700.00	950.00	
1892S	298,400	50.00	60.00	70.00	100.00	
1893 (77)	1,528,197	50.00	60.00	70.00	100.00	600.00
1893CC	60,000	50.00	60.00	70.00	125.00	
1893O	110,000	50.00	60.00	70.00	125.00	
1893S	224,000	50.00	60.00	70.00	100.00	
1894 (75)	957,955	50.00	60.00	70.00	100.00	700.00
1894O	16,600	65.00	80.00	100.00	140.00	
1894S	55,900	60.00	70.00	80.00	125.00	
1895 (81)	1,345,936	50.00	60.00	70.00	100.00	600.00
1895S	112,000	50.00	60.00	70.00	100.00	
1896 (103)	59,063	50.00	60.00	70.00	100.00	600.00
1896S	155,400	50.00	60.00	70.00	100.00	
1897 (83)	867,883	50.00	60.00	70.00	100.00	600.00
1897S	354,000	50.00	60.00	70.00	100.00	
1898 (75)	633,495	50.00	60.00	70.00	100.00	600.00
1898S	1,397,400	50.00	60.00	70.00	100.00	
1899 (99)	1,710,729	50.00	60.00	70.00	100.00	600.00
1899S	1,545,000	50.00	60.00	70.00	100.00	

HALF EAGLES

	Quan. Minted	Fine	V. Fine	E. Fine	Unc.	Proof
1900 . . . . (230)	1,405,730	$50.00	$60.00	$70.00	$100.00	$600.00
1900S	329,000	50.00	60.00	70.00	100.00	
1901 . . . . (140)	616,040	50.00	60.00	70.00	100.00	600.00
1901S	3,648,000	50.00	60.00	70.00	100.00	
1902 . . . . (162)	172,562	50.00	60.00	70.00	100.00	600.00
1902S	939,000	50.00	60.00	70.00	100.00	
1903 . . . . (154)	227,024	50.00	60.00	70.00	100.00	600.00
1903S	1,855,000	50.00	60.00	70.00	100.00	
1904 . . . . (136)	392,136	50.00	60.00	70.00	100.00	600.00
1904S	97,000	50.00	60.00	70.00	125.00	
1905 . . . . (108)	302,308	50.00	60.00	70.00	100.00	600.00
1905S	880,700	50.00	60.00	70.00	100.00	
1906 . . . . (85)	348,820	50.00	60.00	70.00	100.00	600.00
1906D	320,000	50.00	60.00	70.00	100.00	
1906S	598,000	50.00	60.00	70.00	100.00	
1907 . . . . (92)	626,192	50.00	60.00	70.00	100.00	600.00
1907D	888,000	50.00	60.00	70.00	100.00	
1908	421,874	50.00	60.00	70.00	100.00	

INDIAN HEAD TYPE 1908-1929

This type conforms to the quarter eagle of the same date. The incuse designs and lettering make this a unique series, along with the quarter eagle, in our United States coinage.

Designer Bela L. Pratt. Standards same as previous issue.

Mint mark position

FINE—The knot in hair cord must show but small feathers on top of head will be faint.
VERY FINE—Noticeable wear on large middle feathers and tip of eagle's wing.
EXTRA FINE—Cheekbone, war bonnet and headband feathers slightly worn. Feathers on eagle's upper wing show considerable wear.

The scarcer coins with mint marks well struck command higher prices.

						Matte Proof
1908 . . . . (167)	578,012	50.00	60.00	70.00	100.00	900.00
1908D	148,000	50.00	60.00	70.00	100.00	
1908S	82,000	80.00	140.00	210.00	400.00	
1909 . . . . (78)	627,138	50.00	60.00	70.00	100.00	900.00
1909D	3,423,560	50.00	60.00	70.00	100.00	
1909O*	34,200	150.00	200.00	300.00	450.00	
1909S	297,200	60.00	70.00	80.00	140.00	
1910 . . . . (250)	604,250	50.00	60.00	70.00	100.00	900.00
1910D	193,600	50.00	60.00	70.00	100.00	
1910S	770,200	50.00	60.00	70.00	100.00	
1911 . . . . (139)	915,139	50.00	60.00	70.00	100.00	900.00
1911D	72,500	70.00	90.00	160.00	250.00	
1911S	1,416,000	50.00	60.00	70.00	100.00	

*Beware spurious "O" mint mark.

HALF EAGLES

	Quan. Minted	Fine	V. Fine	E. Fine	Unc.	Matte Proof
1912 ....(144)	790,144	$50.00	$60.00	$70.00	$100.00	
1912S	392,000	50.00	60.00	70.00	100.00	
1913 ....(99)	916,000	50.00	60.00	70.00	100.00	$900.00
1913S	408,000	50.00	60.00	70.00	125.00	
1914 ....(125)	247,125	50.00	60.00	70.00	100.00	1,000
1914D	247,000	50.00	60.00	70.00	100.00	
1914S	263,000	60.00	70.00	80.00	125.00	
1915* ....(75)	588,075	50.00	60.00	70.00	100.00	1,200
1915S	164,000	60.00	70.00	80.00	125.00	
1916S	240,000	60.00	70.00	80.00	125.00	
1929	662,000	1,100	1,400	1,600	2,000	

*Pieces dated 1915D are counterfeit.

EAGLES ($10.00 Gold Pieces)

Coinage authority including specified weights and fineness of the eagle conforms to that of the half eagle. The small eagle reverse was used until 1797 when the large, heraldic eagle replaced it. The early dates have variations in the number of stars, the rarest date being 1798. Many of these early pieces show file scratches from the mint's practice of adjusting weight. No eagles were struck dated 1805 to 1837. Proofs of some dates prior to 1855 are known to exist, and all are rare.

CAPPED BUST TO RIGHT, SMALL EAGLE 1795-1797

Designer Robert Scot; weight 17.50 grams; composition: .9167 gold, .0833 copper; approx. diameter 33 mm; reeded edge.

FINE—Details on turban and head obliterated.

VERY FINE—Neck hairlines and details under turban and over forehead are worn but distinguishable.

EXTRA FINE—Definite wear on hair to left of eye and strand of hair across and around turban, also on eagle's wing tips.

	Quan. Minted	Fine	V. Fine	E. Fine	Unc.
1795	5,583	$1,100	$1,500	$2,250	$4,500
1796	4,146	1,000	1,500	2,100	4,250
1797 Small eagle	2,466	1,000	1,500	2,100	4,500

CAPPED BUST TO RIGHT, HERALDIC EAGLE 1797-1804

	Quan. Minted	Fine	V. Fine	E. Fine	Unc.
1797 Large eagle	12,089	900.00	1,200	1,500	2,250

EAGLES

1798 over 97 9 Stars Left, 4 Right	1798 over 97 7 Stars Left, 6 Right	1799

	Quan. Minted	Fine	V. Fine	E. Fine	Unc.
1798, 8 over 7, 9 stars left, 4 right	900	$1,450	$2,000	$3,000	$4,250
1798, 8 over 7, 7 stars left, 6 right	842	2,500	4,000	6,250	10,000
1799	37,449	600.00	800.00	1,050	1,650
1800	5,999	700.00	900.00	1,200	1,650
1801	44,344	650.00	850.00	1,100	1,650
1803	15,017	700.00	900.00	1,200	1,650
1804	3,757	950.00	1,250	1,550	2,200

CORONET TYPE, no motto above eagle 1838-1866

In 1838 the weight and diameter of the eagle were reduced and the obverse and reverse were redesigned. Liberty now faces left and the word LIBERTY is placed on the coronet. A more natural appearing eagle is used on the reverse. The value, TEN D., is shown for the first time on this denomination. Mint mark position is on the reverse below the eagle.

Designer Christian Gobrecht; weight 16.72 grams; composition: .900 gold, .100 copper, diameter 27 mm; reeded edge.

FINE—LIBERTY readable but may be slightly worn.

VERY FINE—Hairlines above coronet partly worn. Curls under ear worn but defined.

EXTRA FINE—Small amount of wear on top of hair and below L in LIBERTY. Wear evident on wing tips and neck of eagle.

1838	7,200	375.00	550.00	800.00	1,250
1839 Large letters	25,801	300.00	400.00	650.00	1,000

The Liberty head style of 1838 and 1839 (large letters) differs from that used for subsequent issues.

1839 Small letters	12,447	400.00	650.00	850.00	1,200
1840	47,338	60.00	70.00	80.00	250.00
1841	63,131	60.00	70.00	80.00	350.00
1841O	2,500	300.00	400.00	525.00	1,250
1842 Small date	} 81,507	60.00	70.00	80.00	200.00
1842 Large date		60.00	70.00	80.00	200.00
1842O	27,400	70.00	90.00	110.00	275.00

EAGLES

	Quan. Minted	Fine	V. Fine	E. Fine	Unc.	Proof
1843	75,462	$60.00	$70.00	$80.00	$150.00	
1843O	175,162	60.00	70.00	80.00	150.00	
1844	6,361	150.00	225.00	300.00	600.00	
1844O	118,700	70.00	80.00	90.00	175.00	
1845	26,153	70.00	80.00	90.00	175.00	
1845O	47,500	70.00	80.00	90.00	175.00	
1846	20,095	70.00	80.00	90.00	225.00	
1846O	81,780	70.00	80.00	90.00	175.00	
1847	862,258	60.00	70.00	80.00	150.00	
1847O	571,500	60.00	70.00	80.00	150.00	
1848	145,484	60.00	70.00	80.00	200.00	
1848O	35,850	60.00	70.00	80.00	200.00	
1849	653,618	60.00	70.00	80.00	175.00	
1849O	23,900	80.00	100.00	125.00	250.00	
1850	291,451	70.00	80.00	90.00	150.00	
1850O	57,500	75.00	85.00	100.00	250.00	
1851	176,328	60.00	70.00	80.00	150.00	
1851O	263,000	60.00	70.00	80.00	150.00	
1852	263,106	60.00	70.00	80.00	150.00	
1852O	18,000	80.00	120.00	150.00	350.00	
1853	201,253	60.00	70.00	80.00	150.00	
1853O	51,000	75.00	85.00	100.00	200.00	
1854	54,250	60.00	70.00	80.00	150.00	
1854O	52,500	75.00	95.00	110.00	260.00	
1854S	123,826	70.00	80.00	90.00	200.00	
1855	121,701	60.00	70.00	80.00	150.00	$6,000
1855O	18,000	100.00	140.00	200.00	500.00	
1855S	9,000	150.00	190.00	250.00	400.00	
1856	60,490	60.00	70.00	80.00	150.00	4,000
1856O	14,500	90.00	120.00	150.00	400.00	
1856S	68,000	60.00	70.00	80.00	200.00	
1857	16,606	100.00	140.00	180.00	400.00	4,000
1857O	5,500	240.00	350.00	450.00	750.00	
1857S	26,000	90.00	120.00	150.00	400.00	
1858*	2,521	3,000	4,000	5,000		——
1858O	20,000	90.00	120.00	175.00	400.00	
1858S	11,800	85.00	100.00	150.00	275.00	
1859	16,093	100.00	150.00	200.00	375.00	2,000
1859O	2,300	180.00	225.00	300.00	800.00	
1859S	7,000	150.00	200.00	275.00	475.00	
1860 (50)	15,105	80.00	90.00	125.00	250.00	2,000
1860O	11,100	80.00	90.00	150.00	300.00	
1860S	5,000	300.00	375.00	475.00	800.00	
1861 (69)	113,233	70.00	80.00	90.00	200.00	2,000
1861S	15,500	70.00	80.00	90.00	250.00	
1862 (35)	10,995	100.00	160.00	240.00	350.00	2,000
1862S	12,500	100.00	160.00	240.00	400.00	
1863 (30)	1,248	375.00	575.00	900.00	1,400	3,000
1863S	10,000	150.00	250.00	300.00	600.00	
1864 (50)	3,580	250.00	350.00	450.00	900.00	2,500
1864S	2,500	350.00	500.00	950.00		
1865 (25)	4,005	275.00	400.00	600.00	1,000	2,500

*Beware removed mint mark.

EAGLES

	Quan. Minted	Fine	V. Fine	E. Fine	Unc.	Proof
1865S All kinds..............	16,700	$300.00	$475.00	$850.00	$1,500	
1865S over inverted 186......	}8,500					
1866S.....................		175.00	275.00	400.00	700.00	

Variety 2 — Motto above eagle 1866-1907

FINE—All letters in LIBERTY are complete.

VERY FINE—Half of hairlines over coronet visible. Curls under ear worn but defined. IN GOD WE TRUST and its ribbon are sharp.

EXTRA FINE—Small amount of wear on top of hair and below L in LIBERTY. Wear evident on wing tips and neck of eagle.

Mint mark position is on the reverse below the eagle.

		Fine	V. Fine	E. Fine	Unc.	Proof
1866..............(30)	3,780	150.00	300.00	400.00	800.00	$2,500
1866S.....................	11,500	125.00	225.00	350.00	600.00	
1867..............(50)	3,140	150.00	225.00	325.00	500.00	2,200
1867S.....................	9,000	125.00	175.00	225.00	400.00	
1868..............(25)	10,655	100.00	125.00	175.00	300.00	2,500
1868S.....................	13,500	100.00	125.00	175.00	350.00	
1869..............(25)	1,855	275.00	425.00	575.00	800.00	2,500
1869S.....................	6,430	150.00	250.00	350.00	600.00	
1870..............(35)	4,025	225.00	325.00	450.00	700.00	2,500
1870CC...................	5,908	300.00	400.00	750.00		
1870S.....................	8,000	150.00	200.00	250.00	500.00	
1871..............(30)	1,820	225.00	325.00	575.00	800.00	2,500
1871CC...................	7,185	300.00	500.00	750.00		
1871S.....................	16,500	100.00	120.00	200.00	250.00	
1872..............(30)	1,650	250.00	350.00	550.00	700.00	2,500
1872CC...................	5,500	350.00	500.00	650.00	900.00	
1872S.....................	17,300	100.00	125.00	175.00	350.00	
1873..............(25)	825	600.00	1,000	1,600	2,500	3,000
1873CC...................	4,543	375.00	450.00	700.00	1,000	
1873S.....................	12,000	100.00	130.00	200.00	350.00	
1874..............(20)	53,160	70.00	80.00	90.00	150.00	2,500
1874CC...................	16,767	150.00	200.00	300.00	450.00	
1874S.....................	10,000	100.00	150.00	200.00	350.00	
1875 (Gilhousen Sale 1973) (20)	.120		10,500			—
1875CC...................	7,715	250.00	350.00	475.00	650.00	
1876..............(45)	732	350.00	650.00	950.00	1,250	2,500
1876CC...................	4,696	250.00	375.00	475.00	800.00	
1876S.....................	5,000	160.00	250.00	300.00	550.00	
1877..............(20)	817	500.00	900.00	1,250	2,000	3,000
1877CC...................	3,332	250.00	375.00	475.00	825.00	
1877S.....................	17,000	70.00	80.00	110.00	200.00	
1878..............(20)	73,800	70.00	80.00	90.00	120.00	2,000
1878CC...................	3,244	300.00	450.00	550.00	1,400	
1878S.....................	26,100	70.00	80.00	90.00	120.00	
1879..............(30)	384,770	70.00	80.00	90.00	120.00	2,000
1879CC...................	1,762	600.00	850.00	1,350	2,400	

EAGLES

	Quan. Minted	Fine	V. Fine	E. Fine	Unc.	Proof
1879O	1,500	$550.00	$675.00	$950.00	$1,400	
1879S	224,000	70.00	80.00	90.00	120.00	
1880 (36)	1,644,876	70.00	80.00	90.00	120.00	$1,600
1880CC	11,190	85.00	100.00	140.00	275.00	
1880O	9,200	70.00	90.00	150.00	225.00	
1880S	506,250	70.00	80.00	90.00	120.00	
1881 (40)	3,877,260	70.00	80.00	90.00	120.00	1,600
1881CC	24,015	100.00	125.00	150.00	250.00	
1881O	8,350	90.00	110.00	175.00	250.00	
1881S	970,000	70.00	80.00	90.00	120.00	
1882 (40)	2,324,480	70.00	80.00	90.00	120.00	1,600
1882CC	6,764	95.00	150.00	185.00	300.00	
1882O	10,820	70.00	90.00	125.00	200.00	
1882S	132,000	70.00	80.00	90.00	120.00	
1883 (40)	208,740	70.00	80.00	90.00	120.00	1,600
1883CC	12,000	85.00	125.00	165.00	275.00	
1883O	800	675.00	1,100	1,500	2,250	
1883S	38,000	70.00	90.00	125.00	225.00	
1884 (15)	76,905	70.00	80.00	90.00	120.00	3,000
1884CC	9,925	100.00	130.00	200.00	350.00	
1884S	124,250	70.00	80.00	90.00	120.00	
1885 (65)	253,527	70.00	80.00	90.00	120.00	1,500
1885S	228,000	70.00	80.00	90.00	120.00	
1886 (60)	236,160	70.00	80.00	90.00	120.00	1,500
1886S	826,000	70.00	80.00	90.00	120.00	
1887 (80)	53,680	70.00	80.00	90.00	120.00	1,500
1887S	817,000	70.00	80.00	90.00	120.00	
1888 (75)	132,996	70.00	80.00	90.00	120.00	1,500
1888O	21,335	70.00	90.00	120.00	200.00	
1888S	648,700	70.00	80.00	90.00	120.00	
1889 (45)	4,485	150.00	250.00	325.00	600.00	1,500
1889S	425,400	70.00	80.00	90.00	120.00	
1890 (63)	58,043	70.00	80.00	90.00	120.00	1,500
1890CC	17,500	80.00	95.00	125.00	275.00	
1891 (48)	91,868	70.00	80.00	90.00	120.00	1,500
1891CC	103,732	80.00	90.00	100.00	175.00	
1892 (72)	797,552	70.00	80.00	90.00	120.00	1,500
1892CC	40,000	80.00	90.00	100.00	175.00	
1892O	28,688	70.00	80.00	90.00	120.00	
1892S	115,500	70.00	80.00	90.00	120.00	
1893 (55)	1,840,895	70.00	80.00	90.00	120.00	1,500
1893CC	14,000	80.00	90.00	100.00	200.00	
1893O	17,000	80.00	90.00	100.00	200.00	
1893S	141,350	70.00	80.00	90.00	120.00	
1894 (43)	2,470,778	70.00	80.00	90.00	120.00	1,500
1894O	107,500	70.00	80.00	90.00	120.00	
1894S	25,000	70.00	80.00	100.00	250.00	
1895 (56)	567,826	70.00	80.00	90.00	120.00	1,500
1895O	98,000	70.00	80.00	90.00	120.00	
1895S	49,000	70.00	80.00	90.00	120.00	
1896 (78)	76,348	70.00	80.00	90.00	120.00	1,500
1896S	123,750	70.00	80.00	90.00	120.00	
1897 (69)	1,000,159	70.00	80.00	90.00	120.00	1,500

EAGLES

	Quan. Minted	Fine	V. Fine	E. Fine	Unc.	Proof
1897O	42,500	$70.00	$80.00	$90.00	$120.00	
1897S	234,750	70.00	80.00	90.00	120.00	
1898 (67)	812,197	70.00	80.00	90.00	120.00	$1,250
1898S	473,600	70.00	80.00	90.00	120.00	
1899 (86)	1,262,305	70.00	80.00	90.00	120.00	1,250
1899O	37,047	70.00	80.00	90.00	120.00	
1899S	841,000	70.00	80.00	90.00	120.00	
1900 (120)	293,960	70.00	80.00	90.00	120.00	1,250
1900S	81,000	70.00	80.00	90.00	120.00	
1901 (85)	1,718,825	70.00	80.00	90.00	120.00	1,250
1901O	72,041	70.00	80.00	90.00	120.00	
1901S	2,812,750	70.00	80.00	90.00	120.00	
1902 (113)	82,513	70.00	80.00	90.00	120.00	1,250
1902S	469,500	70.00	80.00	90.00	120.00	
1903 (96)	125,926	70.00	80.00	90.00	120.00	1,250
1903O	112,771	70.00	80.00	90.00	120.00	
1903S	538,000	70.00	80.00	90.00	120.00	
1904 (108)	162,038	70.00	80.00	90.00	120.00	1,250
1904O	108,950	70.00	80.00	90.00	120.00	
1905 (86)	201,078	70.00	80.00	90.00	120.00	1,250
1905S	369,250	70.00	80.00	90.00	120.00	1,250
1906 (77)	165,497	70.00	80.00	90.00	120.00	
1906D	981,000	70.00	80.00	90.00	120.00	
1906O	86,895	70.00	80.00	90.00	120.00	
1906S	457,000	70.00	80.00	90.00	120.00	
1907 All kinds (74)	1,203,973	70.00	80.00	90.00	120.00	1,250
1907D	1,030,000	70.00	80.00	90.00	120.00	
1907S	210,500	70.00	80.00	90.00	120.00	

INDIAN HEAD TYPE 1907-1933
Variety 1 — No motto on reverse 1907-1908

Augustus Saint-Gaudens, considered by many the greatest of modern sculptors, introduced a new high standard of art in United States coins evidenced by his eagle and double eagle types of 1907. The obverse of the eagle shows the head of Liberty crowned with an Indian war bonnet while an impressively majestic eagle dominates the reverse side. A departure from older standards is found on the edge of the piece, where 46 raised stars are arranged signifying the states of the Union, instead of a lettered or reeded edge. (48 stars 1912 and later.)

The first eagles struck had no motto IN GOD WE TRUST as did the later issues starting in 1908. President Theodore Roosevelt personally objected to the use of the Deity's name on coins. The motto was restored to the coins by Act of Congress in 1908.

Mint mark location is on the reverse at left of fasces.

FINE—*Feathers on bonnet show definite wear. Full LIBERTY.*

VERY FINE—*Bonnet feathers worn near band. Hair high points show wear.*

EXTRA FINE—*Slight wear on cheekbone and headdress feathers. Eagle's eye and left wing will show slight wear.*

EAGLES

Designer Augustus Saint-Gaudens. Standards same as previous issue. Edge 1907-1911: 46 raised stars; 1912-1933: 48 raised stars.

No Motto   **With Motto**

	Quan. Minted	Fine	V. Fine	E. Fine	Unc.	Proof
1907 "Wire edge" (rim), periods before and after •E•PLURIBUS•UNUM•........500					$2,500	$4,500
1907 Same, no stars on edge (unique)					—	
1907 Rounded edge, periods......42				R. L. Miles Sale 1968		$8,250
1907 No periods............239,406	$80.00	$90.00	$100.00	$150.00		
1908 No motto.............33,500	85.00	95.00	100.00	160.00		
1908D No motto..........210,000	80.00	90.00	100.00	150.00		

Variety 2 — Motto on reverse 1908-1933

		Quan. Minted	Fine	V. Fine	E. Fine	Unc.	Matte Proof
1908.............(116)		341,486	65.00	80.00	95.00	125.00	1,600
1908D...................		836,500	65.00	80.00	95.00	125.00	
1908S...................		59,850	85.00	110.00	160.00	375.00	
1909.............(74)		184,863	65.00	80.00	95.00	125.00	1,600
1909D...................		121,540	65.00	80.00	95.00	125.00	
1909S...................		292,350	80.00	90.00	100.00	150.00	
1910.............(204)		318,704	65.00	80.00	95.00	125.00	1,600
1910D...................		2,356,640	65.00	80.00	95.00	125.00	
1910S...................		811,000	70.00	85.00	100.00	140.00	
1911.............(95)		505,595	65.00	80.00	95.00	125.00	1,600
1911D...................		30,100	100.00	125.00	160.00	275.00	
1911S...................		51,000	100.00	125.00	160.00	285.00	
1912.............(83)		405,083	65.00	80.00	95.00	125.00	1,600
1912S...................		300,000	65.00	80.00	95.00	125.00	
1913.............(71)		442,071	65.00	80.00	95.00	125.00	1,600
1913S...................		66,000	85.00	95.00	110.00	150.00	
1914.............(50)		151,050	65.00	80.00	95.00	125.00	2,000
1914D...................		343,500	65.00	80.00	95.00	125.00	
1914S...................		208,000	65.00	80.00	95.00	125.00	
1915.............(75)		351,075	65.00	80.00	95.00	125.00	1,600
1915S...................		59,000	90.00	110.00	150.00	250.00	
1916S...................		138,500	90.00	110.00	150.00	225.00	
1920S...................		126,500	2,500	3,500	4,500	6,500	
1926...................		1,014,000	65.00	80.00	95.00	125.00	
1930S...................		96,000	2,000	2,500	3,000	4,500	
1932...................		4,463,000	65.00	80.00	95.00	125.00	
1933 (1973 Gilhousen Sale)..		312,500				15,000	

DOUBLE EAGLES ($20.00 Gold Pieces) — 1849-1933

This largest of all regular United States issues was authorized to be coined by the Act of March 3, 1849. Its weight was 516 grains, .900 fine. The 1849 double eagle is a unique pattern and reposes in the Mint collection. The rarest date obtainable is 1883. The 1861S reverse design by Paquet was withdrawn soon after striking. Very few specimens are known.

FINE—LIBERTY worn but readable. All hairlines show considerable wear.
VERY FINE—LIBERTY is bold. Jewels on crown defined. Lower half worn flat. Hair worn about ear.
EXTRA FINE—Trace of wear on rounded prongs of crown and down hair curls. Minor bag marks.

Designer James B. Longacre; weight 33.44 grams; composition: .900 gold, .100 copper; diameter 34 mm; reeded edge.

Mint mark location is below eagle.   1861S Paquet Reverse

	Quan. Minted	Fine	V.Fine	E.Fine	Unc.	Proof
1849	1		U.S. Mint Collection			——
1850	1,170,261	$150.00	$175.00	$225.00	$600.00	
1850O	141,000	150.00	175.00	225.00	600.00	
1851	2,087,155	125.00	140.00	200.00	400.00	
1851O	315,000	150.00	175.00	300.00	650.00	
1852	2,053,026	125.00	150.00	200.00	350.00	
1852O	190,000	150.00	200.00	300.00	500.00	
1853	1,261,326	125.00	150.00	175.00	275.00	
1853O	71,000	200.00	275.00	375.00	650.00	
1854	757,899	125.00	160.00	200.00	350.00	
1854O (1973 Gilhousen Sale)	3,250			12,000		
1854S	141,468	175.00	250.00	375.00	650.00	
1855	364,666	125.00	165.00	200.00	350.00	
1855O	8,000	425.00	600.00	750.00	1,000	
1855S	879,675	125.00	160.00	250.00	475.00	
1856	329,878	125.00	160.00	225.00	325.00	
1856O	2,250	4,250	5,500	6,250		
1856S	1,189,750	125.00	150.00	200.00	400.00	
1857	439,375	125.00	150.00	200.00	325.00	
1857O	30,000	200.00	350.00	450.00	750.00	
1857S	970,500	125.00	160.00	225.00	500.00	
1858	211,714	125.00	150.00	200.00	425.00	$5,000
1858O	35,250	250.00	400.00	575.00	750.00	
1858S	846,710	125.00	150.00	200.00	400.00	
1859	43,597	175.00	225.00	275.00	450.00	5,000
1859O	9,100	400.00	575.00	900.00	1,400	
1859S	636,445	125.00	150.00	200.00	350.00	
1860 (59)	577,670	125.00	150.00	200.00	300.00	4,000
1860O	6,600	700.00	950.00	1,300	2,000	
1860S	544,950	125.00	150.00	200.00	300.00	
1861 (66)	2,976,453	125.00	150.00	175.00	250.00	4,000

DOUBLE EAGLES

	Quan. Minted	Fine	V. Fine	E. Fine	Unc.	Proof
1861O	5,000	$450.00	$575.00	$950.00	$1,200	
1861S	768,000	135.00	150.00	200.00	325.00	
1861 — A.C. Paquet rev. (Ex. Rare).					——	
1861S — A.C. Paquet rev.						
(Tall letters)			2,500	3,500	5,000	
1862 (35)	92,133	175.00	240.00	325.00	550.00	$4,000
1862S	854,173	125.00	150.00	200.00	300.00	
1863 (30)	142,790	175.00	240.00	325.00	550.00	4,000
1863S	966,570	125.00	150.00	175.00	275.00	
1864 (50)	204,285	125.00	150.00	200.00	360.00	4,000
1864S	793,660	125.00	150.00	200.00	300.00	
1865 (25)	351,200	150.00	200.00	240.00	350.00	4,000
1865S	1,042,500	125.00	150.00	175.00	250.00	
1866S		375.00	525.00	650.00	1,100	

Motto above eagle, value TWENTY D. 1866-1876

	Quan. Minted	Fine	V. Fine	E. Fine	Unc.	Proof
1866 (30)	698,775	125.00	150.00	200.00	400.00	4,000
1866S	842,250	125.00	150.00	200.00	400.00	
1867 (50)	251,065	125.00	150.00	200.00	300.00	4,000
1867S	920,750	125.00	150.00	200.00	325.00	
1868 (25)	98,600	160.00	200.00	250.00	350.00	4,000
1868S	837,500	125.00	150.00	200.00	275.00	
1869 (25)	175,155	125.00	160.00	200.00	325.00	4,000
1869S	686,750	135.00	150.00	200.00	300.00	
1870 (35)	155,185	135.00	160.00	200.00	375.00	4,000
1870CC (1973 Gilhousen Sale)	3,789		20,000			
1870S	982,000	125.00	160.00	200.00	300.00	
1871 (30)	80,150	150.00	180.00	225.00	400.00	4,000
1871CC	14,687	500.00	650.00	1,000		
1871S	928,000	125.00	160.00	200.00	275.00	
1872 (30)	251,880	135.00	165.00	200.00	325.00	4,000
1872CC	29,650	200.00	375.00	500.00	750.00	
1872S	780,000	125.00	160.00	200.00	275.00	
1873 Closed 3 (25)	⎫ 1,709,825	300.00	450.00	650.00	900.00	4,000
1873 Open 3	⎭	125.00	150.00	175.00	250.00	
1873CC Closed 3	22,410	225.00	350.00	500.00	900.00	
1873S	1,040,600	125.00	150.00	175.00	250.00	
1874 (20)	366,800	125.00	150.00	175.00	225.00	4,000
1874CC	115,085	150.00	175.00	200.00	260.00	
1874S	1,214,000	125.00	150.00	175.00	250.00	
1875 (20)	295,740	125.00	150.00	175.00	250.00	5,000

DOUBLE EAGLES

	Quan. Minted	Fine	V. Fine	E. Fine	Unc.	Proof
1875CC	111,151	$140.00	$160.00	$190.00	$300.00	
1875S	1,230,000	125.00	150.00	175.00	225.00	
1876 ......(45)	583,905	125.00	150.00	175.00	225.00	$4,000
1876CC	138,441	140.00	160.00	190.00	300.00	
1876S	1,597,000	125.00	150.00	175.00	200.00	

TWENTY DOLLARS

	Quan. Minted	Fine	V. Fine	E. Fine	Unc.	Proof
1877 ......(20)	397,670	125.00	150.00	175.00	200.00	4,000
1877CC	42,565	160.00	210.00	300.00	425.00	
1877S	1,735,000	125.00	150.00	175.00	200.00	
1878 ......(20)	543,645	125.00	150.00	175.00	200.00	4,000
1878CC	13,180	225.00	300.00	375.00	600.00	
1878S	1,739,000	125.00	150.00	175.00	200.00	
1879 ......(30)	207,630	125.00	150.00	175.00	200.00	4,000
1879CC	10,708	300.00	400.00	550.00	1,000	
1879O	2,325	600.00	900.00	1,100	1,450	
1879S	1,223,800	125.00	150.00	175.00	200.00	
1880 ......(36)	51,456	135.00	160.00	200.00	275.00	4,000
1880S	836,000	125.00	150.00	175.00	200.00	
1881 ......(40)	2,260	750.00	1,000	1,400	2,000	5,000
1881S	727,000	125.00	150.00	175.00	200.00	
1882 ......(40)	630	750.00	1,450	2,400	3,500	5,000
1882CC	39,140	150.00	200.00	240.00	325.00	
1882S	1,125,000	125.00	150.00	175.00	200.00	
1883 Proofs only....(40)	40					12,000
1883CC	59,962	175.00	240.00	300.00	350.00	
1883S	1,189,000	125.00	150.00	175.00	200.00	
1884 Proofs only....(71)	71					10,000
1884CC	81,139	175.00	240.00	300.00	400.00	
1884S	916,000	125.00	150.00	175.00	200.00	
1885 ......(77)	828	900.00	1,400	2,000	2,500	6,000
1885CC	9,450	300.00	425.00	550.00	950.00	
1885S	683,500	125.00	150.00	175.00	200.00	
1886 ......(106)	1,106	1,000	1,500	2,400	4,500	5,500
1887 Proofs only...(121)	121					6,000
1887S	283,000	140.00	175.00	225.00	300.00	
1888 ......(105)	226,266	135.00	160.00	200.00	275.00	3,800
1888S	859,600	125.00	150.00	175.00	200.00	
1889 ......(41)	44,111	140.00	165.00	195.00	300.00	4,000
1889CC	30,945	150.00	200.00	250.00	400.00	
1889S	774,700	125.00	150.00	175.00	200.00	
1890 ......(55)	75,995	125.00	150.00	175.00	200.00	3,500

DOUBLE EAGLES

	Quan. Minted	Fine	V. Fine	E. Fine	Unc.	Proof
1890CC	91,209	$125.00	$160.00	$200.00	$300.00	
1890S	802,750	125.00	150.00	175.00	200.00	
1891 (52)	1,442	450.00	700.00	900.00	1,200	$3,500
1891CC	5,000	375.00	475.00	575.00	800.00	
1891S	1,288,125	125.00	150.00	175.00	200.00	
1892 (93)	4,523	350.00	550.00	800.00	1,100	3,500
1892CC	27,265	160.00	200.00	250.00	350.00	
1892S	930,150	125.00	150.00	175.00	200.00	
1893 (59)	344,339	125.00	150.00	175.00	200.00	3,000
1893CC	18,402	200.00	250.00	300.00	400.00	
1893S	996,175	125.00	140.00	160.00	185.00	
1894 (50)	1,368,990	125.00	140.00	160.00	185.00	3,250
1894S	1,048,550	125.00	140.00	160.00	185.00	
1895 (51)	1,114,656	125.00	140.00	160.00	185.00	3,250
1895S	1,143,500	125.00	140.00	160.00	185.00	
1896 (128)	792,663	125.00	140.00	160.00	185.00	3,000
1896S	1,403,925	125.00	140.00	160.00	185.00	
1897 (86)	1,383,261	125.00	140.00	160.00	185.00	3,000
1897S	1,470,250	125.00	140.00	160.00	185.00	
1898 (75)	170,470	125.00	140.00	160.00	185.00	3,000
1898S	2,575,175	125.00	140.00	160.00	185.00	
1899 (84)	1,669,384	125.00	140.00	160.00	185.00	3,000
1899S	2,010,300	125.00	140.00	160.00	185.00	
1900 (124)	1,874,584	125.00	140.00	160.00	185.00	3,000
1900S	2,459,500	125.00	140.00	160.00	185.00	
1901 (96)	111,526	125.00	140.00	160.00	185.00	3,000
1901S	1,596,000	125.00	140.00	160.00	185.00	
1902 (114)	31,254	150.00	175.00	200.00	300.00	3,000
1902S	1,753,625	125.00	140.00	160.00	185.00	
1903 (158)	287,428	125.00	140.00	160.00	185.00	3,000
1903S	954,000	125.00	140.00	160.00	185.00	
1904 (98)	6,256,797	125.00	140.00	160.00	185.00	3,000
1904S	5,134,175	125.00	140.00	160.00	185.00	
1905 (90)	59,011	150.00	175.00	200.00	300.00	3,000
1905S	1,813,000	125.00	140.00	160.00	185.00	
1906 (94)	69,690	150.00	175.00	200.00	300.00	3,000
1906D	620,250	125.00	140.00	160.00	185.00	
1906S	2,065,750	125.00	140.00	160.00	185.00	
1907 (78)	1,451,864	125.00	140.00	160.00	185.00	3,000
1907D	842,250	125.00	140.00	160.00	185.00	
1907S	2,165,800	125.00	140.00	160.00	185.00	

SAINT-GAUDENS TYPE

A few experimental pieces were struck having an extremely high relief. They are easily distinguished from the ones issued later for general circulation, which also have a very high relief.

The field of the rare experimental pieces is excessively concave and connects directly with the edge without any border, giving it a sharp knifelike appearance; Liberty's skirt shows two folds on the side of her right leg; the Capitol building in the background at left is very small; the sun, on the reverse side, has 14 rays, as opposed to the regular high relief coins that have only 13 rays extending from the sun.

11,250 high relief pieces were struck for general circulation. The relief is somewhat lower but both have the date 1907 in Roman numerals. Flat-relief double eagles were issued later in 1907 with Arabic numerals.

DOUBLE EAGLES

Proof

1907 Ex. high relief, plain edge (Unique)...................———
1907 Ex. high relief, lettered edge...................———

VERY FINE—*Minor wear on legs and toes. Eagle's left wing and breast feathers worn.*

EXTRA FINE—*Drapery lines on chest visible. Wear on right breast, knee and below. Eagle's feathers on breast and right wing are bold.*

Designer Augustus Saint-Gaudens. Standards same as previous issue. Edge: E PLURIBUS UNUM with words divided by stars.

	Quan. Minted	V. Fine	Ex. Fine	Unc.	Proof
1907 High relief, Roman numerals (MCMVII), wire rim.....	11,250	$875.00	$1,250	$2,000	$5,000
1907 Same, flat rim...........		875.00	1,250	2,000	5,000

Arabic Numerals

No Motto

1907 Large letters on edge (Proof only. Unique) ....———
1907 Small letters on edge......361,667	140.00	160.00	200.00
1908........................4,271,551	140.00	160.00	200.00
1908D........................663,750	140.00	160.00	200.00

With motto IN GOD WE TRUST, 1908-1933

Mint mark location is on obverse above date

Matte Proof

1908...................(101) 156,359	125.00	150.00	175.00	3,000

DOUBLE EAGLES

	Quan. Minted	V. Fine	Ex. Fine	Unc.	Matte Proof
1908D	349,500	$125.00	$150.00	$175.00	
1908S	22,000	250.00	350.00	750.00	

These coins have a border of 46 stars on the obverse from 1907 to 1911, and 48 stars from 1912 to 1933.

1909
9 over 8

	Quan. Minted	V. Fine	Ex. Fine	Unc.	Matte Proof
1909, 9 over 8	} 161,282	160.00	185.00	250.00	
1909 (67)		150.00	175.00	210.00	$2,750
1909D	52,500	165.00	250.00	500.00	
1909S	2,774,925	125.00	150.00	175.00	
1910 (167)	482,167	125.00	150.00	175.00	2,500
1910D	429,000	125.00	150.00	175.00	
1910S	2,128,250	125.00	150.00	175.00	
1911 (100)	197,350	125.00	150.00	175.00	2,750
1911D	846,500	125.00	150.00	175.00	
1911S	775,750	125.00	150.00	175.00	
1912 (74)	149,824	175.00	200.00	250.00	2,750
1913 (58)	168,838	125.00	150.00	175.00	3,000
1913D	393,500	125.00	150.00	175.00	
1913S	34,000	160.00	225.00	350.00	
1914 (70)	95,320	125.00	150.00	175.00	3,000
1914D	453,000	125.00	150.00	175.00	
1914S	1,498,000	125.00	150.00	175.00	
1915 (50)	152,050	125.00	150.00	175.00	3,500
1915S	567,500	125.00	150.00	175.00	
1916S	796,000	125.00	150.00	175.00	
1920	228,250	125.00	150.00	175.00	
1920S	558,000	1,650	2,250	3,500	
1921	528,500	2,500	3,000	4,000	
1922	1,375,500	125.00	150.00	175.00	
1922S	2,658,000	160.00	200.00	300.00	
1923	566,000	125.00	150.00	175.00	
1923D	1,702,250	125.00	150.00	175.00	
1924	4,323,500	125.00	150.00	175.00	
1924D	3,049,500	200.00	250.00	425.00	
1924S	2,927,500	225.00	325.00	450.00	
1925	2,831,750	125.00	150.00	175.00	
1925D	2,938,500	425.00	550.00	750.00	
1925S	3,776,500	300.00	350.00	500.00	
1926	816,750	125.00	150.00	175.00	
1926D	481,000	550.00	750.00	1,000	
1926S	2,041,500	235.00	275.00	450.00	
1927	2,946,750	125.00	150.00	175.00	
1927D (1973 Gilhousen Sale)	180,000			60,000	
1927S	3,107,000	850.00	1,100	1,750	
1928	8,816,000	125.00	150.00	175.00	
1929	1,779,750		1,800	2,750	
1930S	74,000		2,750	5,000	
1931	2,938,250		2,000	3,250	
1931D	106,500		3,000	6,000	
1932	1,101,750		2,500	5,000	

1933 None placed in circulation.

COMMEMORATIVE COINS

Commemorative coins have been popular since the days of the Greeks and Romans. In the beginning they served to record and honor important events and in the absence of newspapers they proved highly useful in passing along news of the day.

Many modern nations have issued commemorative coins and such pieces are highly esteemed by collectors. Yet no nation has surpassed our own country when it comes to commemorative coins and in this we have reason to be proud.

The unique position occupied by commemoratives in United States coinage is largely due to the fact that with few exceptions they are the only coins that have a real historical significance. The progress and advance of people in the New World are presented in an interesting and instructive manner on the commemorative issues. Such a record of facts artistically presented on our gold and silver memorial issues appeals strongly to the collector who favors the historical side of numismatics. It is the historical features of the commemoratives, in fact, which create interest among many people who would otherwise have little interest in coins.

Commemorative issues are considered for coinage by two committees of Congress — The Committee on Banking and Currency of the Senate, and the Committee on Banking and Currency of the House. Congress is guided to a great extent by the reports of these committees when passing upon bills authorizing commemorative coins.

These special coins are usually issued either to commemorate events or to help pay for monuments or celebrations that commemorate historical persons, places or things. The commemorative coins are offered in most instances by a commission in charge of the event to be commemorated, and sold at a price in advance of the face value of the piece.

During a half century over fifty different types of commemorative coins have been issued in the United States. A complete type set of commemorative half dollars consists of forty-eight pieces. The addition of mint mark varieties makes a total of 142 coins in the series.

No commemorative coins were struck from 1940 to 1945, and none since 1954.

Unless otherwise stated, the coinage figures given represent the total outstanding coinage. In many cases, larger quantities were minted but were not all sold. The unsold coins were usually returned to the mint and melted, although some were placed in circulation at face value.

Select unblemished brilliant uncirculated commemoratives are generally worth more than listed values.

Note: The Commemorative section following is arranged alphabetically.

ISABELLA QUARTER DOLLAR

In 1893 the Board of Lady Managers of the Columbian Exposition petitioned for a souvenir quarter-dollar. Authority was granted March 3, 1893. The coin known as the Isabella quarter was designed by C. E. Barber. These souvenir quarters were sold for $1.00. The obverse has the crowned bust of Queen Isabella of Spain. The kneeling female on the reverse with distaff and spindle is emblematic of woman's industry.

		Quan. Minted	Ex. Fine	Unc.
1893	Columbian Exposition, Chicago......... 24,214		$77.50	$165.00

LAFAYETTE DOLLAR

The heads of Washington and Lafayette appear on this commemorative issue, which was the first commemorative coin of one dollar denomination, and the first authorized United States coin to bear a portrait of one of our presidents. The dies were prepared by C. E. Barber. The statue on the reverse is similar to the monument of General Lafayette which was erected in Paris as a gift of the American people. The coins were sold by the Lafayette Memorial Commission for $2.00 each.

1900	Lafayette Dollar........................ 36,026	190.00	450.00

ALABAMA CENTENNIAL

The Alabama half dollars were authorized in 1920 for the centennial which was celebrated in 1919, but they were not struck until 1921. The coins, designed by Laura Gardin Fraser, were offered first during President Harding's visit to Birmingham, October 26, 1921. The St. Andrews cross, an emblem on the state flag, appears on a part of the issue between the figures 22 indicating the twenty-second state of the Union. The obverse has busts of W. W. Bibb, first governor of Alabama, and T. E. Kilby, governor at the time of the centennial. This is the first instance of the use of a living person's portrait on a United States coin.

2x2 in field

	Quan. Minted	Ex. Fine	Unc.
1921 Alabama Centennial, with 2 x 2 in field of obverse	6,006	$90.00	$235.00
1921 Alabama Centennial, no 2 x 2	59,038	70.00	185.00

ALBANY, NEW YORK CHARTER

The two hundred and fiftieth anniversary of the granting of a charter to the city of Albany was the occasion for a commemorative half dollar. The reverse design shows Governor Dongan, Peter Schuyler and Robert Livingston. The obverse has a beaver which is gnawing on a maple branch. Gertrude K. Lathrop of Albany was the designer.

1936 Albany, New York	17,671	50.00	110.00

BATTLE OF ANTIETAM

A souvenir half dollar was designed by William Marks Simpson and struck in 1937 to commemorate the seventy-fifth anniversary of the famous Civil War battle to thwart Lee's invasion of Maryland. The opposing generals McClellan and Lee are featured on the obverse while the Burnside Bridge, an important tactical objective, is shown on the reverse. The Battle of Antietam on September 17, 1862, was one of the bloodiest single-day battles of the war with total losses of about 25,000 men.

1937 Battle of Antietam 1862-1937	18,028	80.00	185.00

ARKANSAS CENTENNIAL

This souvenir issue marked the one hundredth anniversary of the admission of Arkansas into the Union. Edward Everett Burr designed the piece and models were prepared by Emily Bates of Arkansas. Although 1936 was the centennial year the first of several issues was brought out in 1935 from all three mints. During 1936 a new design was authorized by Congress. The late Senator Joseph T. Robinson consented to have his portrait placed on the obverse side of the coins which were struck in January 1937 at the Philadelphia Mint. The 1937 and 1938 issues were the same as those of 1935 except for the dates. They were sold by the distributors at $8.75 per set of three coins. The obverse shows accolated heads of an Indian chief of 1836 and an American girl of 1936.

		Quan. Minted		Unc.
1935	Arkansas Centennial	13,012		
1935D	Same type D mint	5,505	Set	$95.00
1935S	Same type S mint	5,506		
1936	Arkansas Centennial, same as 1935 — date 1936 on rev	9,660		
1936D	Same type D mint	9,660	Set	95.00
1936S	Same type S mint	9,662		
1937	Arkansas Centennial (same as 1935)	5,505		
1937D	Same type D mint	5,505	Set	100.00
1937S	Same type S mint	5,506		
1938	Arkansas Centennial (same as 1935)	3,156		
1938D	Same type D mint	3,155	Set	275.00
1938S	Same type S mint	3,156		
1939	Arkansas Centennial (same as 1935)	2,104		
1939D	Same type D mint	2,104	Set	500.00
1939S	Same type S mint	2,105		
	Single, type coin			32.50

BAY BRIDGE SAN FRANCISCO-OAKLAND

The opening of the San Francisco Bay Bridge was the occasion for a special souvenir fifty-cent piece. The designs were the work of Jacques Schnier, a San Francisco artist. A California grizzly bear dominates the obverse. The famous bridge is shown on the reverse. The coins were struck at the San Francisco Mint in November 1936. The bear depicted was Monarch II.

	Quan. Minted	Ex. Fine	Unc.
1936 San Francisco-Oakland Bay Bridge S mint	71,424	$27.50	$47.50

DANIEL BOONE
BICENTENNIAL

This coin, issues for which covered several dates, was struck to commemorate the two hundredth anniversary of the famous frontiersman's birth. The commemorative date, 1934, was removed after the first issue. The change of date to 1935 for the next year's coinage brought about the addition of 1934 above the words PIONEER YEAR. Coinage covered several years similar to the schedule for the Texas issues. The models for this coin were prepared by Augustus Lukeman. The obverse bears a portrait of Daniel Boone. The reverse shows Boone with Chief Black Fish.

		Quan. Minted		Unc.
1934	Daniel Boone Bicentennial	10,007		$42.50
1935	Same type	10,010		
1935D	Same type D mint	5,005	Set	110.00
1935S	Same type S mint	5,005		

1935	Daniel Boone Bicentennial same as 1934 but small 1934 added on reverse	10,008		
1935D	Same type D mint	2,003	Set	550.00
1935S	Same type S mint	2,004		
1936	Daniel Boone Bicentennial (same as 1934)	12,012		
1936D	Same type D mint	5,005	Set	110.00
1936S	Same type S mint	5,006		
1937	Daniel Boone Bicentennial (same as 1934)	9,810		
1937D	Same type D mint	2,506	Set	260.00
1937S	Same type S mint	2,506		
1938	Daniel Boone Bicentennial (same as 1934)	2,100		
1938D	Same type D mint	2,100	Set	425.00
1938S	Same type S mint	2,100		
	Single, type coin	E.F. $16.50		35.00

COMM. SILVER — Bridgeport, California, Cincinnati

BRIDGEPORT, CONNECTICUT CENTENNIAL

In commemoration of the one hundredth anniversary of the incorporation of the city of Bridgeport a special fifty-cent piece was authorized May 15, 1936. Henry Kreiss designed this coin which somewhat resembles the Connecticut Tercentenary issue. The head of P. T. Barnum, who was Bridgeport's best known citizen, occupies the obverse. An ultra-modernistic eagle dominates the reverse.

	Quan. Minted	Ex. Fine	Unc.
1936 Bridgeport, Conn., Centennial	25,015	$27.50	$57.50

CALIFORNIA DIAMOND JUBILEE

The California half dollar was designed by Jo Mora, a noted California sculptor. The obverse bears a kneeling figure of a forty-niner. The reverse shows a walking grizzly bear, the state emblem. The celebration for which these coins were struck marked the seventy-fifth anniversary of the admission of California into the Union. The jubilee was held in 1925.

	Quan. Minted	Ex. Fine	Unc.
1925S California Diamond Jubilee	86,594	22.50	47.50

CINCINNATI MUSICAL CENTER

Although the head of Stephen Foster, "America's Troubadour," dominates the obverse of this special issue the anniversary celebrated bears no relation to him. The coins, designed by Constance Ortmayer of Washington, D. C., were struck to commemorate the fiftieth anniversary in 1936 of Cincinnati as a center of music. The coins were struck at the three mints and were sold only in sets at $7.75, the highest initial cost of a new type.

1936 Cincinnati Musical Center	5,005		
1936D Same type D	5,005	Set	525.00
1936S Same type S	5,006		
Single, type coin			175.00

CLEVELAND GREAT LAKES EXPOSITION

A special coinage of fifty-cent pieces was authorized in commemoration of the centennial celebration of Cleveland, Ohio on the occasion of the Great Lakes Exposition held there in 1936. The designs were prepared by Brenda Putnam. Although half the coinage was struck in 1937 all were dated 1936. The obverse has a bust of Moses Cleaveland and the reverse displays a map of the Great Lakes region with a compass pointed at Cleveland. Nine Great Lakes cities are marked by stars.

		Quan. Minted	Ex. Fine	Unc.
1936	Cleveland, Great Lakes Exposition	50,030	$18.00	$32.50

COLUMBIA, SOUTH CAROLINA SESQUICENTENNIAL

Souvenir half dollars were authorized to help finance the extensive celebrations marking the sesquicentennial of the founding of Columbia in 1786. A. Wolfe Davidson designed the coin which was struck at all three mints and sold only in sets. The obverse bears the figure of Justice with sword and scales. At the left is the Capitol of 1786 and at the right the Capitol of 1936. A palmetto tree, the state emblem, is the reverse device.

1936	Columbia, S. C., Sesquicentennial	9,007		
1936D	Same type D mint	8,009	Set	290.00
1936S	Same type S mint	8,007		
	Single, type coin		60.00	95.00

COLUMBIAN EXPOSITION HALF DOLLAR

The first United States commemorative coin was the Columbian half dollar. C. E. Barber designed the obverse showing the bust of Columbus; and G. T. Morgan designed the reverse having a representation of Columbus' flagship the Santa Maria above two hemispheres. The coins were sold for $1.00 each at the World's Columbian Exposition in Chicago during 1893. A great many remained unsold and a substantial quantity was later released for circulation at face value.

1892	Columbian Exposition, Chicago	950,000	7.00	19.00
1893	Same type	1,550,405	6.00	17.50

COMMEMORATIVE SILVER — Connecticut, Delaware, Elgin

CONNECTICUT TERCENTENARY

In commemoration of the three hundredth anniversary of the founding of the Colony of Connecticut a souvenir half dollar was struck. Henry Kreiss designed the coin. The famous "Charter Oak" is the main device on the obverse. According to tradition the Royal Charter was secreted in the tree during the reign of James II who wished to revoke it. The Charter was produced after the king's overthrow in 1688 and the Colony continued under its protection.

		Quan. Minted	Ex. Fine	Unc.
1935	Connecticut Tercentenary	25,018	$60.00	$110.00

DELAWARE TERCENTENARY

The three hundredth anniversary of the landing of the Swedes in Delaware was the occasion for a souvenir issue of half dollars. The colonists landed on a spot which is now Wilmington and established a church which is the oldest Protestant church still used for worship. Their ship "Kalmar Nyckel" is shown on the obverse of the coin and the Old Swedes Church is on the reverse. Designs were chosen from a competition which was won by Carl L. Schmitz. This coin was authorized in 1936, struck in 1937 and dated 1938 on the obverse and 1936 on the reverse. The anniversary was celebrated in 1938 both in Sweden and America. A two kroner coin was issued in Sweden to commemorate the same event.

1936	Delaware Tercentenary	20,993	45.00	80.00

ELGIN, ILLINOIS CENTENNIAL

The one hundredth anniversary of the founding of Elgin was marked by a special issue of half dollars in 1936. The proceeds were devoted to financing a Pioneer Memorial statue, which is depicted on the reverse of the coin. The year 1673 bears no relation to the event but refers to the year in which Joliet and Marquette entered Illinois Territory. The designs were prepared by Trygve Rovelstad who also designed the Memorial.

1936	Elgin, Illinois, Centennial	20,015	35.00	75.00

COMMEMORATIVE SILVER — Gettysburg, Grant, Hawaiian

BATTLE OF GETTYSBURG

On June 16, 1936 Congress authorized a coinage of fifty-cent pieces in commemoration of the Battle of Gettysburg. The models were prepared by Frank Vittor, a Philadelphia sculptor. Portraits of a Union and a Confederate veteran are shown on the obverse. Two shields representing the Union and Confederate armies separated by a double-bladed fasces are on the reverse.

	Quan. Minted	Ex. Fine	Unc.
1936 Battle of Gettysburg 1863-1938............	26,928	$37.50	$77.50

GRANT MEMORIAL

This coin was struck during 1922 as a centenary souvenir of Ulysses S. Grant's birth. A star which appeared on the first issues was later removed, creating a second variety. The star has no particular significance. Laura Gardin Fraser designed both the Grant half dollar and gold dollar. The reverse shows a log cabin in Point Pleasant, Ohio, where Grant lived as a boy.

(Fake stars have flattened spot on reverse.)

1922 Grant Memorial. Star in obverse field.......	4,256	125.00	335.00
1922 Same, no star..........................	67,405	25.00	57.50

HAWAIIAN SESQUICENTENNIAL

This small issue was struck to commemorate the 150th anniversary of the rediscovery of the Hawaiian Islands by Captain James Cook in 1778. The design was sketched by Juliette May Fraser of Honolulu and executed by Chester Beach. Captain Cook is shown on the obverse and a native chief on the reverse. The coins were distributed in 1928 and sold for $2.00 each, the highest initial sale price up to that time.

1928 Hawaiian Sesquicentennial.................	9,958	600.00	1,000
1928 Hawaiian Sesquicentennial — sandblast proof presentation piece............	50		——

COMMEMORATIVE SILVER — Hudson, Huguenot, Iowa

HUDSON, NEW YORK SESQUICENTENNIAL

This souvenir half dollar marked the one hundred and fiftieth anniversary of the founding of Hudson, New York, which was named after the explorer Hendrik Hudson. The designs by Chester Beach show Hudson's flagship the "Half Moon" on the obverse and the seal of the City of Hudson on the reverse. Details of the seal include representations of Neptune with trident on a spouting whale and a mermaid blowing a conch shell.

	Quan. Minted	Ex. Fine	Unc.
1935 Hudson, N. Y. Sesquicentennial	10,008	$225.00	$500.00

HUGUENOT-WALLOON TERCENTENARY

Settling of the Huguenots and Walloons in the New World was the occasion commemorated by this issue. New Netherlands, now New York, was founded in 1624 by a group of Dutch colonists. The persons represented on the obverse were not directly concerned with the occasion, however. They are Admiral Coligny and William the Silent. The reverse shows the vessel "Nieu Nederland." G. T. Morgan prepared the models for this coin.

1924 Huguenot-Walloon Tercentenary	142,080	35.00	65.00

IOWA CENTENNIAL

This half dollar, commemorating the one hundredth anniversary of Iowa's statehood, was designed by Adam Pietz of Philadelphia. The obverse shows the Iowa state seal and the reverse has the first stone capitol building at Iowa City. This issue was sold

first to the residents of Iowa and only a small remainder to others. The entire issue was disposed of in a few weeks.

1946 Iowa Centennial	100,057	25.00	42.50

[200]

LEXINGTON-CONCORD SESQUICENTENNIAL

The two famous battles fought in 1775 are commemorated on this coin. A statue of the familiar Minute Man is depicted on the obverse, and the old Belfry at Lexington is the reverse device. Chester Beach designed the coin. The famous statue by Daniel Chester French located in Concord was used for the design.

	Quan. Minted	Ex. Fine	Unc.
1925 Lexington-Concord Sesquicentennial	162,013	$17.50	$40.00

LINCOLN-ILLINOIS CENTENNIAL

The obverse was designed by G. T. Morgan and the reverse by J. R. Sinnock. The obverse shows the head of Lincoln taken from the statue by Andrew O'Connor in Springfield, Illinois. The reverse is based on the Illinois State Seal. This coin was authorized to commemorate the one hundredth anniversary of the admission of Illinois into the Union, the first souvenir piece for such an event.

1918 Illinois Centennial	100,058	25.00	55.00

LONG ISLAND TERCENTENARY

This souvenir issue was authorized to commemorate the three hundredth anniversary of the first white settlement on Long Island which was at Jamaica Bay by Dutch colonists. The design was prepared by Howard Kenneth Weinman, son of the sculptor A. A. Weinman, who designed the regular Liberty standing type half dollar. Accolated heads depicting a Dutch settler and an Indian are shown on the obverse, while a Dutch sailing vessel is the reverse device. This was the first issue for which a date was specified (1936) irrespective of the year minted or issued.

1936 Long Island Tercentenary	81,826	17.50	32.50

COMMEMORATIVE SILVER — Lynchburg, Maine, Maryland

LYNCHBURG, VIRGINIA SESQUICENTENNIAL

The issuance of a charter to the city of Lynchburg in 1786 was commemorated in 1936 by a special coinage of half dollars. The models for the coin were prepared by Charles Keck. The obverse bears a portrait of Senator Carter Glass, a native of Lynchburg and former Secretary of the Treasury, who objected to the idea of using portraits of living men on coins. Despite his protests his likeness was incorporated on the coin. The reverse shows Liberty standing, with the old Lynchburg courthouse in the background.

		Quan. Minted	Ex. Fine	Unc.
1936	Lynchburg, Va., Sesquicentennial	20,013	$40.00	$95.00

MAINE CENTENNIAL

Congress authorized the Maine Centennial half dollar May 10, 1920, to be sold at the Centennial celebration at Portland. They were received too late for this event and were sold by the state Treasurer until all were sold. Anthony de Francisci modeled this coin according to specifications furnished him. The latin word DIRIGO means: I direct. The obverse device is the arms of the state of Maine.

1920	Maine Centennial	50,028	27.50	67.50

MARYLAND TERCENTENARY

The three hundredth anniversary of the founding of the Maryland Colony by Cecil Calvert (known as Lord Baltimore) was the occasion for this special coin. The profits from the sale of this issue were used to finance the celebration in Baltimore during 1934. Hans Schuler designed the coin which shows the facing head of Lord Baltimore on the obverse and the arms of Maryland on the reverse, reminiscent of the Maryland colonial pieces.

1934	Maryland Tercentenary	25,015	35.00	75.00

MISSOURI CENTENNIAL

The one hundredth anniversary of the admission of Missouri to the Union was celebrated at Sedalia during August, 1921. To mark the occasion Congress authorized the coinage of a fifty-cent piece. Robert Aitken designed the piece which shows the bust of a frontiersman on the obverse, and another frontiersman and Indian on the reverse. The first coins struck show 2★4 incused, indicating that Missouri was the twenty-fourth star in the flag. The type without the star was struck later, but was the first to be sold.

2★4 in field

		Quan. Minted	Ex. Fine	Unc.
1921	Missouri Centennial 2★4 in field of obverse	5,000	$185.00	$475.00
1921	Missouri Centennial, no 2★4	15,428	150.00	400.00

MONROE DOCTRINE CENTENNIAL

The motion picture industry promoted this issue in conjunction with a motion picture exposition in June 1923. The obverse shows the heads of James Monroe and John Quincy Adams who were identified with the Monroe Doctrine. The Western Hemisphere is portrayed on the reverse by two female figures. Chester Beach prepared the models for this coin.

1923S Monroe Doctrine Centennial	274,077	18.00	32.50

NEW ROCHELLE, NEW YORK

To observe the founding of New Rochelle in 1688 by French Huguenots, a special half dollar was issued in 1938. The title to the land which the Huguenots purchased from John Pell provided that a fattened calf be given away every year on June 20th. This will explain the appearance of the calf and figure representing John Pell on the obverse of the coin. The fleur-de-lis

COMMEMORATIVE SILVER — Norfolk, Oregon

which is shown on the reverse is adopted from the Seal of the city. Both sides of the coin were designed by Gertrude K. Lathrop.

		Quan. Minted	Ex. Fine	Unc.
1938	New Rochelle, N. Y. 1688-1938	15,266	$67.50	$145.00

NORFOLK, VIRGINIA BICENTENNIAL

To provide funds for the celebration of Norfolk's anniversary of its growth from a township in 1682 to a royal borough in 1736, Congress first passed a law for the striking of medals. The proponents, however, being dissatisfied finally succeeded in winning authority for half dollars commemorating the 300th anniversary of the original Norfolk land grant and the 200th anniversary of the establishment of the borough. William Marks Simpson and his wife Marjorie Emory Simpson designed the piece. The obverse shows the Seal of the City of Norfolk with a three-masted ship as the central device. The reverse features the Royal Mace of Norfolk presented by Lieutenant Governor Dinwiddie in 1753.

1936	Norfolk, Va., Bicentennial	16,936	55.00	115.00

OREGON TRAIL MEMORIAL

This memorial coin was struck in commemoration of the Oregon trail and in memory of the pioneers, many of whom lie buried along the famous 2,000 mile highway of history. James Earle Fraser and his wife, Laura Gardin Fraser, prepared the designs. The original issue was struck at Philadelphia and San Francisco in 1926. The coin was reissued in 1928 (released in 1933), 1933, 1934, 1936, and 1938. The 1933 half dollar was the first commemorative coin struck at the Denver Mint.

1926	Oregon Trail Memorial	47,955	20.00	40.00
1926S	Same type S mint	83,055	20.00	40.00
1928	Oregon Trail Memorial (same as 1926)	6,028		65.00
1933D	Oregon Trail Memorial, same type, D mint	5,008		110.00
1934D	Oregon Trail Memorial, same type, D mint	7,006		55.00
1936	Oregon Trail Memorial (same as 1926)	10,006		55.00
1936S	Same type S mint	5,006		95.00
1937D	Oregon Trail Memorial D mint (same as 1926)	12,008		50.00
1938	Oregon Trail Memorial (same as 1926)	6,006		
1938D	Same type D mint	6,005	Set	175.00
1938S	Same type S mint	6,006		
1939	Oregon Trail (same as 1926)	3,004		
1939D	Same type D mint	3,004	Set	350.00
1939S	Same type S mint	3,005		
	Single, type coin			37.50

PANAMA-PACIFIC EXPOSITION

This half dollar was designed by C. E. Barber. The exposition held in San Francisco in 1915 celebrated the opening of the Panama Canal. The coins were struck at the San Francisco Mint and were sold at $1.00 each during the exposition. The Panama-Pacific coins have the distinction of being the first commemorative coins to carry the motto. IN GOD WE TRUST appears above the eagle. A representation of Columbia with the golden gate in the background is the principal feature of the obverse.

	Quan. Minted	Ex. Fine	Unc.
1915S Panama-Pacific Exposition	27,134	$90.00	$265.00

PILGRIM TERCENTENARY

To commemorate the landing of the Pilgrims at Plymouth, Massachusetts in 1620, Congress authorized a special half dollar May 12, 1920. Cyrus E. Dallin, a Boston sculptor, executed the designs furnished him by the Commission. The obverse has a portrait of Governor Bradford. The reverse shows the "Mayflower." The first issue had no date on the obverse. The coins struck in 1921 show that date in addition to 1620-1920. There was a large coinage of both issues and not all were sold. A total of 128,000 were returned to the mint and melted.

1920 Pilgrim Tercentenary	152,112	17.50	35.00

1921 Same type	20,053	32.50	65.00

COMM. SILVER — Rhode Island, Roanoke, Robinson

RHODE ISLAND, TERCENTENARY PROVIDENCE

The three hundredth anniversary of Roger Williams' founding of Providence was the occasion for this special half dollar in 1935. The designs were the work of Arthur Graham Carey and John Howard Benson. The obverse shows Roger Williams in a canoe being welcomed by an Indian. The reverse has the anchor of Hope with a shield and mantling in the background. Although the founding of Providence was being celebrated, no mention of the city is to be found on the coin.

	Quan. Minted	Ex. Fine	Unc.
1936 Rhode Island Tercentenary	20,013		
1936D Same type D mint	15,010 Set		$115.00
1936S Same type S mint	15,011		
Single, type coin		$12.00	40.00

ROANOKE ISLAND, NORTH CAROLINA

A celebration was held in Old Fort Raleigh in 1937 to commemorate the three hundred and fiftieth anniversary of Sir Walter Raleigh's "Lost Colony" and the birth of Virginia Dare, the first white child born on the American Continent. A special half dollar was minted for the occasion which was designed by William Marks Simpson of Baltimore. The obverse bears a portrait of Sir Walter Raleigh and the reverse has a figure representing Eleanor Dare holding the child Virginia Dare.

1937	Roanoke Island, N. C., 1587-1937	29,030	32.00	67.50

ROBINSON-ARKANSAS CENTENNIAL

A new obverse design for the Arkansas Centennial coin was authorized by the Act of June 26, 1936. Senator Joseph T. Robinson is the subject for the new issue designed by Henry Kreiss. The reverse, designed by Everett Burr, was unchanged. The law specified a change in the reverse, because of the fact that the obverse side is that which bears the date. From a numismatic viewpoint, however, the side which has the portrait is usually considered the obverse. Thus in this instance, the side with the eagle device is considered the reverse.

1936	Arkansas Centennial (Robinson)	25,265	27.50	55.00

COMM. SILVER — San Diego, Sesquicentennial, Spanish Trail

SAN DIEGO-CALIFORNIA-PACIFIC EXPOSITION

Congress approved the coinage of souvenir half dollars for the exposition May 3, 1935. Robert Aitken designed the coin which was struck at the San Francisco Mint. The same type with date 1936 was struck at the Denver Mint, under authority of the special Recoinage Act of May 6, 1936, which specified that 180,000 pieces could be recoined with the date 1936 irrespective of the year of issue. The obverse displays a seated female with spear and a bear in the left background. The reverse shows the observation tower and the State of California building at the Exposition.

	Quan. Minted	Ex. Fine	Unc.
1935S San Diego, California-Pacific Exp. S mint...	70,132	$18.00	$40.00
1936D San Diego, California-Pacific Exposition D mint (same as 1935)	30,092	21.00	50.00

SESQUICENTENNIAL OF AMERICAN INDEPENDENCE

The one hundred and fiftieth anniversary of the signing of the Declaration of Independence was the occasion for an International Fair held in Philadelphia in 1926. To help raise funds for financing the fair special issues of half dollars and quarter-eagles were authorized by Congress. For the first time a portrait of a president appeared on a coin struck during his lifetime. President Coolidge and Washington are depicted on the obverse of the half-dollar. The reverse bears an accurate model of the Liberty Bell. John R. Sinnock, Chief Engraver of the United States mint, designed the sesquicentennial coins. The dies were in very low relief causing much loss of detail in the coin.

1926 Sesquicentennial of American Independence	141,120	17.50	37.50

OLD SPANISH TRAIL

This coin commemorated the four hundredth anniversary of the overland trek of the Cabeza de Vaca Expedition through the gulf states in 1535. L. W. Hoffecker designed the coin models which were prepared by

COMMEMORATIVE SILVER — Stone Mountain, Texas

Edmund J. Senn. The explorer's name literally translated means "head of a cow," therefore this device was chosen for the obverse. The reverse bears a yucca tree and a map showing the Old Spanish Trail.

		Quan. Minted	Ex. Fine	Unc.
1935	Old Spanish Trail 1535-1935	10,008	$190.00	$385.00

STONE MOUNTAIN MEMORIAL

The models for this coin were prepared by Gutzon Borglum. The first coins were struck at Philadelphia January 21, 1925, General Thomas "Stonewall" Jackson's birthday. General Robert E. Lee and Jackson, mounted, are shown on the obverse. The reverse has an eagle and the words MEMORIAL TO THE VALOR OF THE SOLDIER OF THE SOUTH. The funds received from the sale of this large issue of half dollars were devoted to the expense of carving figures of Confederate leaders and soldiers on Stone Mountain in Georgia. The carving was completed and dedicated in 1970.

1925	Stone Mountain Memorial	1,314,709	13.00	20.00

TEXAS CENTENNIAL

This issue commemorated the independence of Texas. The first of several dates was offered in 1934. The later dates were struck at all three mints. The models were prepared by Pompeo Coppini. The reverse shows

the kneeling figure of winged Victory, and on each side, medallions with portraits of General Sam Houston and Stephen Austin, founders of the Republic and State of Texas. The large five-pointed star behind the eagle on the obverse carries out the "Lone star" tradition.

1934	Texas Centennial	61,463		37.50
1935	Texas Centennial (same as 1934)	9,996		
1935D	Same type D mint	10,007	Set	100.00
1935S	Same type S mint	10,008		
1936	Texas Centennial (same as 1934)	8,911		
1936D	Same type D mint	9,039	Set	100.00
1936S	Same type S mint	9,055		
1937	Texas Centennial (same as 1934)	6,571		
1937D	Same type D mint	6,605	Set	125.00
1937S	Same type S mint	6,637		
1938	Texas Centennial (same as 1934)	3,780		
1938D	Same type D mint	3,775	Set	325.00
1938S	Same type S mint	3,814		
	Single, type coin		22.50	33.00

COMM. SILVER — Vancouver, Vermont, B. T. Washington

FORT VANCOUVER CENTENNIAL

Dr. John McLaughlin, shown on the obverse of this coin, built Fort Vancouver on the Columbia River in 1825. The sale of the coins at $1.00 each helped to finance the pageant staged for the celebration. Laura Gardin Fraser prepared the models for this coin which was minted in San Francisco. The S Mint mark was omitted. The reverse has a pioneer settler in buckskin suit with a musket in his hands. Fort Vancouver is in the background.

	Quan. Minted	Ex. Fine	Unc.
1925 Fort Vancouver Centennial	14,994	$65.00	$175.00

VERMONT SESQUICENTENNIAL

This souvenir issue commemorates the 150th Anniversary of the Battle of Bennington and the Independence of Vermont. Authorized in 1925 it was not coined until 1927. The models were prepared by Charles Keck. The obverse shows the head of Ira Allen, founder of Vermont. The reverse bears a catamount on a pedestal.

1927 Vermont Sesquicentennial (Bennington)	28,142	36.00	75.00

BOOKER T. WASHINGTON MEMORIAL

The great Negro educator was memorialized in this half dollar. Issued from all mints, it received wide distribution from the start. The reverse has the legend FROM SLAVE CABIN TO HALL OF FAME. His log cabin birthplace is shown beneath. Designed by Isaac Scott Hathaway, as was the Washington-Carver half dollar issued under the same authority.

COMM. SILVER — Washington-Carver

		Quan. Minted	Ex. Fine	Unc.
1946	Booker T. Washington	*1,000,546		
1946D	Same type D mint	200,113	Set	$22.50
1946S	Same type S mint	500,279		
1947	Same type as 1946	100,017		
1947D	Same type D mint	100,017	Set	45.00
1947S	Same type S mint	100,017		
1948	Same type as 1946	8,005		
1948D	Same type D mint	8,005	Set	62.50
1948S	Same type S mint	8,005		
1949	Same type as 1946	6,004		
1949D	Same type D mint	6,004	Set	100.00
1949S	Same type S mint	6,004		
1950	Same type as 1946	6,004		
1950D	Same type D mint	6,004	Set	80.00
1950S	Same type S mint	512,091		
1951	Same type as 1946	510,082		
1951D	Same type D mint	7,004	Set	65.00
1951S	Same type S mint	7,004		
	Single, type coin			7.00

*Minted; quantity melted unknown.

WASHINGTON-CARVER

Designed by Isaac Scott Hathaway, this coin shows the conjoined busts of two prominent Negro Americans. Booker T. Washington was a lecturer, educator, and principal of Tuskegee Institute. He urged training to advance independence and efficiency for his race. George Washington Carver was an agricultural chemist who worked to improve the economy of the south. He spent his life teaching crop improvement and new uses for soybeans, peanuts, sweet potatoes and cotton waste.

Money obtained from the sale of these commemoratives was to be used "to oppose the spread of communism among Negroes in the interest of national defense."

1951	Washington-Carver	110,018		
1951D	Same type D mint	10,004	Set	52.50
1951S	Same type S mint	10,004		
1952	Same type as 1951	2,006,292		
1952D	Same type D mint	8,006	Set	65.00
1952S	Same type S mint	8,006		
1953	Same type as 1951	8,003		
1953D	Same type D mint	8,003	Set	72.50
1953S	Same type S mint	108,020		
1954	Same type as 1951	12,006		
1954D	Same type D mint	12,006	Set	52.50
1954S	Same type S mint	122,024		
	Single, type coin			7.00

WISCONSIN TERRITORIAL CENTENNIAL

The one hundredth anniversary of the Wisconsin Territorial government was the occasion for a special half dollar issue. The original design was made by David Parsons, a University of Wisconsin student. Benjamin Hawkins, a New York artist, made changes to conform with technical requirements. The obverse has the Territorial Seal, which includes a forearm holding a pickaxe over a mound of lead ore, and the inscription 4th DAY OF JULY ANNO DOMINI 1836. The reverse shows a badger on a log typifying the early fur trade, and the state emblem.

		Quan. Minted	Ex. Fine	Unc.
1936	Wisconsin Centennial	25,015	$32.50	$65.00

YORK COUNTY, MAINE TERCENTENARY

A souvenir half dollar was authorized by Congress upon the three hundredth anniversary of the founding of York County, Maine. Brown's Garrison on the Saco River was the site of a town which was settled in 1636. The designs were made by Walter H. Rich of Portland. The reverse design shows a stockade and the obverse has an adaptation of the York County seal. The oversize border inscriptions have been the basis for much adverse criticism.

1936	York County, Maine Centennial	25,015	32.50	65.00

COMMEMORATIVE GOLD —
Grant, Lewis & Clark, Louisiana Purchase

GRANT MEMORIAL GOLD DOLLARS

Like the half-dollar commemorative coins the gold dollars were issued first with a star which was removed for the later issues. The designs by Laura Gardin Fraser are the same as for the half-dollar coinage.

		Quan. Minted	V. Fine	Ex. Fine	Unc.
1922	Grant Memorial Dollar with star	5,016	$140.00	$225.00	$425.00
1922	Grant Memorial Dollar w/out star	5,000	150.00	250.00	450.00

LEWIS AND CLARK EXPOSITION

The Lewis and Clark Centennial Exposition was held in Portland, Oregon in 1905. A souvenir issue of gold dollars was struck to mark the event with the dates 1904 and 1905. The two famous explorers are represented on each side of the coin which was designed by C. E. Barber. A bronze memorial of the Indian guide, Sacagawea, who assisted in the famous expedition, was erected in Portland, Oregon and financed by the sale of these coins.

1904	Lewis and Clark Exposition Dollar	10,025	190.00	350.00	675.00
1905	Lewis and Clark Exposition Dollar	10,041	175.00	325.00	600.00

LOUISIANA PURCHASE EXPOSITION

The first souvenir gold coins were authorized for the Louisiana Purchase Exposition held in St. Louis in 1904. There are two varieties of gold dollars — one with the head of Jefferson who was president when the Louisiana Territory was purchased from France; and the other President William McKinley who sanctioned the Exposition. The reverse is the same for each variety. The designs were by C. E. Barber.

*1903	Louisiana Purchase Jefferson Dollar	17,500	60.00	85.00	180.00
*1903	Louisiana Purchase McKinley Dollar	17,500	60.00	85.00	180.00

*Proofs exist of each type.

COMMEMORATIVE GOLD — McKinley, Panama-Pacific

McKINLEY MEMORIAL GOLD DOLLARS

The sale of the McKinley dollars aided in paying for a memorial building at
Niles, Ohio, the martyred president's birthplace. The obverse showing a profile
of McKinley was designed by C. E. Barber and the reverse with the memorial
building designed by G. T. Morgan.

		Quan. Minted	V. Fine	Ex. Fine	Unc.
1916	McKinley Memorial Dollar	9,977	$60.00	$80.00	$165.00
1917	McKinley Memorial Dollar	10,000	80.00	100.00	215.00

PANAMA-PACIFIC EXPOSITION

Charles Keck designed the gold dollar, the obverse of which has the head
of a man representing a Panama Canal laborer. Two dolphins encircle ONE
DOLLAR on the reverse.

1915S	Panama-Pacific Exposition Dollar	15,000	65.00	85.00	175.00

The quarter-eagle was the work of Charles E. Barber and George T. Morgan.
It was the first commemorative coin of this denomination. The obverse shows
Columbia with a caduceus in her left hand seated on a hippocampus typifying
the use of the Panama Canal. An American eagle with raised wings is shown
on the reverse.

1915S	Panama-Pacific Exposition $2.50	6,749	325.00	425.00	675.00

The fifty-dollar gold piece was designed by Robert Aitken and was issued in
round and octagonal form. The obverse bears the helmeted head of Minerva;
the owl, symbol of wisdom, is on the reverse. The octagonal issue has eight
dolphins in the angles on both sides. The devices are smaller on the octagonal
variety.

COMMEMORATIVE GOLD — Philadelphia Sesquicentennial

		Quan. Minted	Ex. Fine	Unc.
1915S	Panama-Pacific $50 Round	483		$9,000
1915S	Panama-Pacific $50 Octagonal	645		7,500

PHILADELPHIA SESQUICENTENNIAL—QUARTER EAGLES

The obverse of this special gold issue has a standing female figure symbolic of Liberty, holding in one hand a scroll representing the Declaration of Independence and in the other the Torch of Freedom. The reverse bears a representation of Independence Hall in Philadelphia. The coin was designed by J. R. Sinnock.

1926	Philadelphia Sesquicentennial $2.50	46,019	60.00	130.00

BIBLIOGRAPHY

Bullowa, David M. *The Commemorative Coinage of the United States 1892-1938.* New York, 1938.

Mosher, Stuart. *United States Commemorative Coins 1892-1939.* New York, 1940.

Slabaugh, Arlie. *United States Commemorative Coinage.* Racine, 1962.

PRIVATE OR TERRITORIAL GOLD COINS

The words "Private Gold," used with reference to coins struck outside of the United States Mint, are a general term. In the sense that no state or territory had authority to coin money, private gold simply refers to those interesting necessity pieces of various shapes, denominations and degrees of intrinsic worth which were circulated in isolated areas of our country by individuals, assayers, bankers, etc. Some will use the words "Territorial" and "State" to cover certain issues because they were coined and circulated in a Territory or State. While the state of California properly sanctioned the ingots stamped by F. D. Kohler as state assayer, in no instance were any of the gold pieces struck by authority of any of the territorial governments.

The stamped ingots put out by Augustus Humbert, the United States assayer of gold, were not recognized at the United States Mint as an official issue of coins, but simply as ingots, though Humbert placed the value and fineness on the pieces as an official agent of the federal government.

Private coins were circulated in most instances because of a shortage of regular coinage. In the western states particularly, money became so scarce that the very commodity which the pioneers had come so far to acquire was converted into a local medium of exchange.

Ephraim Brasher's New York doubloon of 1787 described on page 41 also falls into this class.

BIBLIOGRAPHY

Adams, Edgar H. *Private Gold Coinage of California 1849-1855*. Brooklyn, N.Y., 1913·
Adams, Edgar H. *Official Premium Lists of Private and Territorial Gold Coins*. Brooklyn, N.Y., 1909.
Griffin, Clarence. *The Bechtlers and Bechtler Coinage and Gold Mining in North Carolina 1814-1830*. Spindale, N.C., 1929.
Lee, Ed. M. *California Gold — Quarters, Halves and Dollars*. Glendale, Cal., 1932.
Lee, Kenneth W. *California Gold — Dollars, Half Dollars, Quarter Dollars*. Glendale, Cal., 1970.

TEMPLETON REID
Georgia 1830

Gold pieces dated 1830 were struck by Templeton Reid, a goldsmith and assayer, in Lumpkin County, Georgia. Reid's private mint was in Gainesville. In 1830 what is now Lumpkin County, except for a small eastern strip, was all in the Cherokee Indian Nation, or Cherokee County as it was called at that time, the Nation having been taken over in 1828 by the State of Georgia.

The designs and denominations of these coins were well known, but almost nothing has been learned about Templeton Reid. Denominations struck were $2.50, $5.00 and $10.00.

	Fine
1830 $2.50...	—
1830 $5.00...	—

TEMPLETON REID — GEORGIA

1830 TEN DOLLARS. . . . .

Unc.

(No Date) TEN DOLLARS — Waldorf Sale 1966 . . . . $29,000

TEMPLETON REID

San Francisco, California 1849

The later Templeton Reid issues were made in California in 1849. It is supposed that he moved his coining equipment to California when gold was discovered there. The California issues were in denominations of ten and twenty-five dollars. The twenty-five dollar issue is unique in design and denomination.

Fine

1849 TEN DOLLAR GOLD (Mint Collection) . . . . Unique

1849 TWENTY-FIVE DOLLARS GOLD. . . . . Unknown

The only specimen known of this piece was stolen from the Cabinet of the U.S. Mint on August 16, 1858. It was never recovered.

THE BECHTLERS

Rutherford County, N. C. 1830-1852

Two skilled German metallurgists, Christopher Bechtler and his son, August Bechtler, and later Christopher Bechtler, Junior, a nephew of Christopher the elder, operated a "private" mint at Rutherfordton, North Carolina. Rutherford county in which Rutherfordton is located was the principal source of the nation's gold supply from 1790 to 1840.

The coins minted by the Bechtlers were of only three denominations, but they cover a wide variety of weights and sizes.

THE BECHTLERS

The Bechtlers have the distinction of producing the first gold dollar in the United States. The government mint did not release the first regular series until 1849.

The inscription "Aug. 1, 1834" on one variety of the five-dollar piece has a special significance. The Secretary of the Treasury recommended to the Director of the Mint that the gold coins of the reduced weight bear the date "Aug. 1, 1834." Instead of this, however, a new U.S. gold design was used (the motto was omitted). Christopher Bechtler evidently acted on the official recommendation to avoid any difficulty with Treasury authorities.

CHRISTOPHER BECHTLER

	V. Fine	Ex. Fine	Unc.
ONE DOLLAR CAROLINA, 28 gr. N reversed........	$125.00	$175.00	$250.00
ONE DOLLAR N. CAROLINA, 28 gr., without star ...	425.00	650.00	850.00

| ONE DOLLAR N. CAROLINA, 30 gr. .... | 175.00 | 250.00 | 375.00 |
| $2.50 CAROLINA, 67 gr. 21 carats.............. | 375.00 | 450.00 | 600.00 |

$2.50 CAROLINA, 70 gr. 20 carats..............	400.00	500.00	700.00
$2.50 GEORGIA, 64 gr. 22 carats..............	400.00	500.00	700.00
$2.50 GEORGIA, 64 gr. 22 carats — even 22.......	700.00	900.00	1,200

$2.50 NORTH CAROLINA, 75 gr. 20 carats.			
RUTHERFORD in a circle. Border of lg. beads..	725.00	800.00	1,300
$2.50 NORTH CAROLINA, without 75 G	725.00	800.00	1,300

THE BECHTLERS

	V. Fine	Ex. Fine	Unc.
$2.50 NORTH CAROLINA, without 75 G, CAROLINA above 250 instead of GOLD.......			(Unique)
$2.50 NORTH CAROLINA, 20 carats on obv. 75 gr. on rev. Border finely serrated.......	$1,400	$1,750	——

5 DOLLARS CAROLINA, RUTHERFORD, 140 gr. 20 carats. Date August 1, 1834. Plain or reeded edges.......................	375.00	450.00	575.00
5 DOLLARS CAROLINA, 134 gr. 21 carats..........	375.00	450.00	550.00

5 DOLLARS GEORGIA, RUTHERFORD. 128 gr. 22 carats............................	425.00	550.00	750.00
5 DOLLARS GEORGIA, RUTHERF. 128 gr. 22 carats..	375.00	450.00	550.00
5 DOLLARS CAROLINA, RUTHERF. 140 gr. 20 carats. Date August 1, 1834........	375.00	450.00	550.00

Without
150 G

5 DOLLARS NORTH CAROLINA, 150 gr. 20 carats...	900.00	1,250	1,750
5 DOLLARS. Same as last variety without 150 G...	2,200	3,000	4,000

THE BECHTLERS

AUGUST BECHTLER
1842-1852

	V. Fine	Ex. Fine	Unc.
1 DOLLAR CAROLINA, 27 gr. 21 carats	$125.00	$175.00	$300.00
5 DOLLARS CAROLINA, 134 gr. 21 carats	325.00	400.00	550.00

| 5 DOLLARS CAROLINA, 128 gr. 22 carats | 300.00 | 385.00 | 500.00 |
| 5 DOLLARS CAROLINA, 141 gr. 20 carats | 350.00 | 475.00 | 600.00 |

(Restrikes in "proof" exist from original dies.)

NORRIS, GRIEG & NORRIS
San Francisco 1849

Edgar H. Adams considered this piece the first of the California private gold coins. A newspaper account dated May 31, 1849, described a five-dollar gold coin, struck at Benicia City, though with the imprint San Francisco. It mentioned the private stamp of Norris, Grieg and Norris. The initials N. G. and N. were not identified until 1902 when the coins of Augustus Humbert were sold.

	Fine	V. Fine	Ex. Fine	Unc.
1849 HALF EAGLE — Plain Edge	$350.00	$500.00	$800.00	$1,100
1849 HALF EAGLE — Reeded Edge	350.00	500.00	800.00	1,100

A recently discovered specimen is dated 1850, with STOCKTON beneath date.
1850 HALF EAGLE (Unique)..................................... ——

MOFFAT & CO.

San Francisco 1849-1853

The firm of Moffat and Company was perhaps the most important of the California private coiners. The assay office they conducted was semi-official in character. The successors to this firm, Curtis, Perry and Ward, later established the United States Branch mint of San Francisco.

In June or July, 1849, Moffat & Co. began to issue small rectangular pieces of gold owing to lack of coin in the locality, in values from $9.43 to $264. The $9.43, $14.25 and $16.00 varieties are the only types known today.

$14.25 Ingot 1849

The only specimen known of the $9.43 ingot is in the National Coin Collection.

$9.43 Ingot (Unique)... ——
$14.25 Ingot (Unique)... ——
$16.00 Ingot (Beware of spurious specimens cast in base metal)...... ——

The dies for the $10 piece were cut by a Bavarian, Albert Kuner. The words MOFFAT & CO. appear on the coronet of Liberty instead of the word LIBERTY as in regular United States issues.

	Fine	V. Fine	Ex. Fine	Unc.
1849 FIVE DOL. (All varieties)..........	$200.00	$300.00	$450.00	$750.00
1850 FIVE DOL. (All varieties)..........	200.00	325.00	525.00	875.00
1849 TEN DOL.	375.00	500.00	875.00	——
1849 TEN D.	550.00	800.00	1,300	——

United States Assay Office
AUGUSTUS HUMBERT
U. S. Assayer 1851

Augustus Humbert, a New York watch-case maker, was appointed United States Assayer, and he placed his name and the government stamp on the ingots of gold issued by Moffat & Co. The assay office was a temporary expedient to accommodate the Californians until the establishment of a permanent branch mint.

The fifty-dollar piece was accepted as legal tender on a par with standard U.S. gold coins and was known variously as a slug, quintuple eagle or five-eagle piece. It was officially termed an ingot.

MOFFAT — HUMBERT

LETTERED EDGE VARIETIES

	Fine	V. Fine	Ex. Fine	Unc.
1851 50 D C 880 THOUS., no 50 on Reverse. Sunk in Edge: AUGUSTUS HUMBERT UNITED STATES ASSAYER OF GOLD CALIFORNIA 1851	$2,200	$2,800	$4,000	——

Rev. Rays From Central Star

	Fine	V. Fine	Ex. Fine	Unc.
1851 50 D C Similar to last variety, but 50 on Reverse	2,400	3,000	4,500	——
1851 Similar to last variety, but 887 THOUS	2,400	3,000	4,250	——
1851 50 D C 887 THOUS., no 50 on Reverse	2,500	3,200	4,250	——
1851 50 D C 880 THOUS. Rev. Rays from Central Star (Unique)				——

MOFFAT — HUMBERT

REEDED EDGE VARIETIES

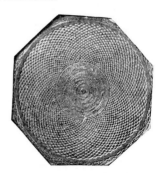

	Fine	V. Fine	Ex. Fine	Unc.
1851 FIFTY DOLLS 880 THOUS.				
"Target" Reverse...............	$1,600	$2,200	$2,900	——
1851 FIFTY DOLLS 887 THOUS.				
"Target" Reverse...............	1,500	2,000	2,750	——
1852 FIFTY DOLLS. 887 THOUS..........	1,650	2,300	3,000	——

The withdrawal of the discredited private coins of $5, $10 and $20 denominations as a result of the new U.S. Assay operations caused a new turn of affairs for Californians.

The fractional currency coins of almost every nation were pressed into service by the Californians, but the supply was too small to help to any extent. Moffat & Co. proceeded in January, 1852 to issue a new ten-dollar piece bearing the stamp MOFFAT & CO.

1852 TEN D. MOFFAT & CO. (Wide Date).	550.00	750.00	1,000	——
1852 TEN D. MOFFAT & CO. (Close Date).	450.00	650.00	900.00	——

	Fine	V. Fine	Ex. Fine	Unc.
1852 TWENTY DOLS. 1852 over 1........	$2,000	$2,800	$4,000	——

1852 TEN DOLS. 1852 over 1...........	325.00	425.00	700.00	——
1852 TEN DOLS......................	300.00	375.00	550.00	——

UNITED STATES ASSAY OFFICE OF GOLD
1852

The firm of Moffat & Co. dissolved and a new reorganized company known as the United States Assay Office of Gold, composed of Curtis, Perry and Ward took over the contract.

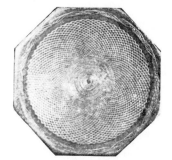

1852 FIFTY DOLLS. 887 THOUS..........	1,500	2,000	2,500	——
1852 FIFTY DOLLS. 900 THOUS..........	1,600	2,100	2,800	——

UNITED STATES ASSAY OFFICE

TEN DOLS   TEN D.

	Fine	V. Fine	Ex. Fine	Unc.
1852 TEN DOLS 884 THOUS	$300.00	$400.00	$600.00	$750.00
1853 TEN D. 884 THOUS	600.00	750.00	1,000	——

| 1853 TEN D. 900 THOUS | 550.00 | 700.00 | 1,000 | —— |

| 1853 TWENTY D. 884 THOUS | 1,250 | 1,800 | 2,200 | —— |

| 1853 TWENTY D. 900 THOUS | 300.00 | 425.00 | 525.00 | 750.00 |

U. S. ASSAY — MOFFAT

The last Moffat issue was the 1853 Twenty-dollar piece which is very similar to the U.S. Double Eagle of that period. It was struck after the retirement of Mr. Moffat from the Assay Office.

	Fine	V. Fine	Ex. Fine	Unc.
1853 TWENTY D.	$450.00	$600.00	$850.00	——

CINCINNATI MINING & TRADING CO.

The origin and location of this company are unknown.

	Fine	Unc.
1849 FIVE DOLLARS..................................	——	——
1849 TEN DOLLARS...................................	——	——

MASSACHUSETTS AND CALIFORNIA COMPANY
San Francisco 1849

This company was believed to have been organized in Northampton, Mass. in May 1849.

1849 FIVE D. — Waldorf Sale 1964........................Proof $8,750.00

MINERS' BANK
San Francisco 1849

The institution of Wright & Co., exchange brokers located in Portsmouth Square, San Francisco, was known as the Miners' Bank.

A ten-dollar piece was issued in the autumn of 1849, but the coins were not readily accepted because they were worth less than face value. The firm dissolved January 14, 1850. Unlike most issues, the gold in these coins was alloyed with copper.

	V. Fine	Ex. Fine	Unc.
(1849) TEN. D.	$2,000	$3,000	$4,000

J. S. ORMSBY
Sacramento 1849

The initials J. S. O. which appear on certain issues of California privately coined gold pieces represent the firm of J. S. Ormsby & Co. They struck both five- and ten-dollar denominations, all undated.

	Fine	Unc.
(1849) 5 DOLLS.	——	——
(1849) 10 DOLLS.	——	——

PACIFIC COMPANY
San Francisco 1849

The origin of the Pacific Co. is very uncertain. All data regarding the firm is based on conjecture.

Edgar H. Adams wrote that he believed that the coins bearing the stamp of the Pacific Company were produced by the coining firm of Broderick and Kohler. The coins were probably handstruck, with the aid of a sledgehammer.

PACIFIC COMPANY

1849 5 DOLLARS
Waldorf Sale, 1964
Ex. Fine.......$18,000.00

1849 10 DOLLARS
Waldorf Sale, 1964
Ex. Fine.......$24,000.00

F. D. KOHLER
California State Assayer 1850

The State Assay Office was authorized April 12, 1850. Governor Burnett appointed F. D. Kohler that year who thereupon sold his assaying business to Baldwin & Co. He served at both San Francisco and Sacramento Offices. The State Assay Offices were discontinued at the time the U.S. Assay Office was established Feb. 1, 1851.

Ingots issued ranged from $36.55 to $150.

	Fine
$36.55 Sacramento...........	——
$37.31 San Francisco........	——
$40.07 San Francisco........	——
Note: $40.07 stolen from the Mint Cabinet in 1858 and was never recovered.	
$41.68 San Francisco........	——
$45.34 San Francisco........	——
$50.00 San Francisco........	——
$54.09 San Francisco........	——

DUBOSQ & COMPANY
San Francisco 1850

Theodore Dubosq, a Philadelphia jeweler, took melting and coining machinery to San Francisco in 1849.

	Fine	Unc.
1850 FIVE D......	——	——
1850 TEN D.	——	——

BALDWIN & COMPANY
San Francisco 1850

George C. Baldwin and Thomas S. Holman were in the jewelry business in San Francisco and were known as Baldwin & Co. They were the successors to F. D. Kohler & Co., taking over their machinery and other equipment in May, 1850.

	Fine	V. Fine	Ex. Fine	Unc.
1850 FIVE DOL.	$800.00	$1,250	$2,000	———
1850 TEN DOLLARS — Horseman type...				$10,000

| 1851 TEN D. .... | 3,000 | 4,000 | ——— | ——— |

The Baldwin & Co. $20 piece was the first of that denomination issued in California.

Baldwin coins were believed to have contained about twenty-thousandths copper alloy.

	Fine	Unc.
1851 TWENTY D.	—	—

SCHULTZ & COMPANY
San Francisco 1851

The firm located in back of Baldwin's establishment conducted a brass foundry beginning in 1851. Judge G. W. Schultz and William T. Garratt were partners in the enterprise.

1851 FIVE D — Walton Sale 1963........................V. Fine $8,250
Waldorf Sale 1964..........................Fine   3,800

DUNBAR & COMPANY
San Francisco 1851

Edward E. Dunbar conducted the California Bank in San Francisco. Mr. Dunbar later returned to New York and organized the famous Continental Bank Note Co.

1851 FIVE D — Walton Sale 1963.......................Ex. Fine $11,250

WASS, MOLITOR & COMPANY
San Francisco 1852-1855

The gold smelting and assaying plant of Wass, Molitor & Co. was composed of two Hungarian patriots Count S. C. Wass and A. P. Molitor. They maintained an excellent laboratory and complete apparatus for analysis and coinage of gold.

Large Head, Pointed Bust

	Fine	V. Fine	Ex. Fine	Unc.
1852 FIVE DOLLARS Small head with rounded bust...............	$700.00	$1,000	$1,800	——
1852 FIVE DOLLARS Large head with pointed bust................	600.00	900.00	1,400	——

WASS, MOLITOR & COMPANY

The company struck five-, ten-, twenty- and fifty-dollar coins. In 1852 . addition to the five-dollar piece illustrated above they produced a ten-dollar piece similar in design to the five-dollar denomination. The difference is in the reverse legend which reads: s.m.v. (Standard Mint Value) CALIFORNIA GOLD TEN D.

Large Head   Small Head

	Fine	V. Fine	Ex. Fine	Unc.
1852 TEN D. Large Head	$400.00	$575.00	$875.00	——
1852 TEN D. Small Head	1,100	1,700	2,500	——

No pieces were coined in 1853 or 1854, but they brought out the twenty-dollar and fifty-dollar pieces in 1855. A considerable number of the fifty-dollar coins were made. There was a ten-dollar piece issued in 1855 also, with a somewhat different design of the Liberty head.

1855 TEN D.	825.00	1,200	1,900	——

Large Head   Small Head

1855 TWENTY DOL. Large Head	——	——	——	——
1855 TWENTY DOL. Small Head	1,250	2,100	——	——

WASS, MOLITOR & COMPANY

	Fine	V. Fine	Ex. Fine	Unc.
1855 50 DOLLARS....................	$3,000	$4,500	$5,750	——

KELLOGG & COMPANY
San Francisco 1854-1855

John G. Kellogg came to San Francisco October 12, 1849, from Auburn,
New York. At first he was employed by Moffat and Company, and remained
with that organization when control passed to Curtis, Perry and Ward. When
the United States Assay Office was discontinued December 14, 1853, Mr.
Kellogg became associated with G. F. Richter, who had been an assayer in
the government assay office. These two set up business as Kellogg & Richter
December 19, 1853.

When the U. S. Assay Office ceased operations a period ensued during which
no private firm was striking gold. The new San Francisco branch mint did
not produce coins for some months after Curtis & Perry took the contract
for the government. The lack of coin was again keenly felt by businessmen
who petitioned Kellogg & Richter to "supply the vacuum" by issuing private
coin.

Their plea was soon answered, for on February 9, 1854, Kellogg & Co.
placed their first twenty-dollar piece in circulation.

1854 TWENTY D.	350.00	425.00	550.00	——

The 1855 twenty-dollar piece is similar to that dated 1854. The letters on
the reverse side are larger and the arrows longer on one 1854 variety. There
are several die varieties of both issues.

KELLOGG & COMPANY

	Fine	V. Fine	Ex. Fine	Unc.
1855 TWENTY D.	$375.00	$450.00	$600.00	——

The firm dissolved late in 1854 and reorganized as Kellogg & Humbert. The latter partner was Augustus Humbert, for some time identified as U. S. Assayer.

Regardless of the fact that the branch mint was then producing coins, Kellogg & Humbert issued coins in 1855 in a quantity greater than before.

| 1855 FIFTY DOLLS. .... | —— | —— | —— | —— |

CALIFORNIA SMALL
DENOMINATION GOLD PIECES

California Gold quarters, halves and dollars were struck from 1852 to 1882, when the U. S. Government passed a law forbidding private coinage. The impetus of the gold rush created a shortage of "small change," and private companies supplied these coins for the 30-year period in direct proportion to the need.

Shapes were both octagonal and round, and the genuine coins bear one of the following — "cents," "Dol," "Doll" or "Dollar" on the reverse. Obverses are of three main types — Liberty Head, Indian Head and Washington Head. The reverses are also of three main types — Wreath, Beaded Circle and Eagle. Coins with the word "cents" or the Washington Head or the Eagle Reverse are more scarce and command premium prices of about twice regular values.

CALIFORNIA SMALL DENOMINATION GOLD PIECES

Typical Obverses   Typical Reverses

	V. Fine	Unc.	Proof*
25¢ Octagonal: Liberty head	$32.50	$42.50	$50.00
Indian head	32.50	42.50	50.00
Washington head	67.50	85.00	100.00
25¢ Round: Liberty head	32.50	42.50	50.00
Indian head	32.50	42.50	50.00
Washington head	67.50	85.00	100.00
50¢ Octagonal: Liberty head	35.00	45.00	52.50
Indian head	35.00	47.50	52.50
Liberty head with eagle rev.	70.00	85.00	100.00
50¢ Round: Liberty head	35.00	45.00	52.50
Indian head	37.50	47.50	55.00
Liberty head with eagle rev.	75.00	100.00	125.00
Arms of California	95.00	120.00	135.00
$1.00 Octagonal: Liberty head	80.00	115.00	130.00
Indian head	80.00	120.00	135.00
Liberty head with eagle rev.	150.00	175.00	200.00
$1.00 Round: Liberty head	425.00	550.00	750.00
Indian head	425.00	550.00	750.00

*Not actually struck as proofs, but proof-like in appearance and quality.
See bibliography on page 215.

OREGON EXCHANGE COMPANY
Oregon City, 1849
THE BEAVER COINS OF OREGON

Upon the discovery of gold in California there was a great exodus of settlers who joined in the hunt for the precious metal. Soon returning gold seekers offered their gold dust, which became the accepted medium of exchange. As in other western areas of that time the uncertain qualities of the gold and weighing devices tended to irk the tradespeople and petitions were made to the legislature for a standard gold coin issue.

On February 16, 1849, the legislature passed an act providing for a mint and specified five- and ten-dollar gold coins without alloy. Oregon City, the largest city in the territory with a population of about 1000, was designated as the location for the mint. At the time this act was passed Oregon had been brought into the United States as a territory by act of Congress. When the new governor arrived March second, he declared the coinage act unconstitutional.

The public-spirited people, however, continued to work for a convenient medium of exchange and soon took matters into their own hands by starting a private mint. Eight men of affairs whose names were Kilborne, Magruder, Taylor, Abernethy, Willson, Rector, Campbell and Smith set up the Oregon Exchange Company.

OREGON EXCHANGE COMPANY

The coins struck were of virgin gold as specified in the original act. Ten-dollar dies were made later, and were of finer design and workmanship.

	Fine	V. Fine	Ex. Fine	Unc.
1849 5 D............................	$2,000	$2,700	$3,800	——

1849 TEN D — Walton Sale, 1963.........................V. Fine $10,500

MORMON GOLD PIECES

Salt Lake City, Utah 1849-1860

The first name given to the organized Mormon Territory was the "State of Deseret," the last word meaning "honey bee." The beehive, which is shown on the reverse of the five-dollar 1860 piece, was a favorite device of the followers of Joseph Smith and Brigham Young. The clasped hands appear on most Mormon coins and exemplify strength in unity. "Holiness to the Lord" was an inscription frequently used.

Brigham Young was the instigator of the coinage system and personally supervised the mint which was housed in a little adobe building in Salt Lake City.

The mint was inaugurated late in 1849 as a public convenience.

	Fine	V. Fine	Ex. Fine	Unc.
1849 TWO AND HALF DO..............	$550.00	$750.00	$1,000	——
1849 FIVE DOLLARS..................	450.00	550.00	675.00	——

MORMON GOLD PIECES

1849 TEN DOLLARS. . . . . .Fine $20,000

1849 TWENTY DOLLARS. . . . . .V. Fine $9,000.00

The Mormon twenty-dollar piece was the first of that denomination to be coined in this country.

1850 FIVE DOLLARS

Fine	$475.00
V. Fine	575.00
Ex. Fine	700.00
Unc	1,750

1860 5D

V. Fine	$1,150
Ex. Fine	1,500
Unc	1,750

COLORADO GOLD PIECES

Clark, Gruber & Co. — Denver 1860-1861

Clark, Gruber and Co. was a well-known private minting firm in Denver, Colo. in the early sixties.

COLORADO GOLD PIECES
CLARK, GRUBER & CO. 1860-1861

	Fine	V. Fine	Ex. Fine	Unc.
1860 2½D	$350.00	$450.00	$525.00	$850.00
1860 5D	450.00	550.00	700.00	1,000

1860 TEN D	775.00	1,300	1,800	2,500
1860 TWENTY D			Ex. Fine	$7,500

The $2.50 and five-dollar pieces of 1861 follow closely the designs of the 1860 issues. The main difference is found in the legends. The reverse side now has CLARK GRUBER & CO. DENVER. PIKES PEAK is on the coronet of Liberty.

1861 2½D	300.00	425.00	550.00	800.00
1861 FIVE D	400.00	500.00	700.00	1,000
1861 TEN D	400.00	500.00	700.00	1,850

1861 TWENTY D	1,100	1,500	2,000	——

JOHN PARSONS & COMPANY
Tarryall Mines — Colorado 1861

Very little is known regarding the mint of John Parsons and Co., although it is reasonably certain that it operated in the South Park of Colorado, near Tarryall, in the summer of 1861.

Pikes Peak Gold

	Fine	Unc.
(1861) Undated 2½ D..............................	——	——
(1861) Undated FIVE D..............................	——	——

J. J. CONWAY & COMPANY
Georgia Gulch, Colorado, 1861

Records show that the Conway Mint operated for a short while in 1861. As in all gold mining areas the value of gold dust caused disagreement among the merchants and the miners. The firm of J. J. Conway & Co. solved this difficulty by bringing out their gold pieces in August, 1861.

(1861) Undated 2½ DOLL's — Waldorf Sale, 1964 .... Ex. Fine $13,500.00

	Fine	Unc.
(1861) Undated FIVE DOLLARS........................	——	——

(1861) Undated FIVE DOLLARS, Similar.
    Variety without numeral 5 on reverse—Marks Sale, 1972 ... $36,000

(1861) Undated
    TEN DOLLARS.. ——

UNITED STATES
BRONZE, NICKEL and SILVER TYPE COINS

———— •◆• ————

A 26-Year Study

If the hobby of coin collecting were to be compared to a dwelling place in which we comfortably live, type collecting would correspond to its foundation, walls, and roof. Within this framework all other collecting phases such as date series, commemoratives, proofs, etc., could be likened to the furnishings and amenities of a home.

For anyone who has not yet heard the term "type collecting," let us say simply that it implies interest in the different designs and denominations of a country's coinage. A collection in this category usually contains at least one of each design or type, and the American collector traditionally includes major varieties. The charts that accompany this text cover generally accepted types and varieties of United States coinage.

It is easy to see how a collector is almost certain to start his collecting career as a type collector, whether he realizes it or not. He does what comes naturally, assembling as many types and denominations as he can, and no matter how few or how many different kinds he acquires during his first months of collecting, he is nevertheless a type collector. A look at the charts as well as the forepart of this catalog will reveal the scarcity of some early types. Examples are the 1796 Draped Bust small eagle quarter, 1859 Laurel Wreath Indian cent, and first types of half dollars and dollars. It is fortunately normal to begin with the coins in your purse and work backward in time, so the early, scarce types should be no immediate problem. In fact, many of us never acquire every type.

So we engage in a rather simple, automatic game, sort of like putting the pieces of a puzzle together. As we reach out for obsolete types, we must be prepared to pay a premium in increasing ratio, especially when we pass the World War II period. At the same time we are challenged by the importance of quality and its price. But when we seek the obsolete denominations, such as two cents, three cents, and twenty cents, we are confronted with true scarcities because of special collector interest. In fact, acquiring types beyond 75 years puts one in the realm of serious collecting, but happily this area offers the best investment opportunities.

Along the way the average collector will go into other phases of numismatics long before completing his type set. These avenues of interest such as date series and proofs actually are an expansion of the basic type concept. This study, however, will confine itself to the type and major variety category and will hopefully serve as a guide to old and new collectors alike.

First of all, quality, or best available grade, is the watchword when buying any commodity. It is especially important when selecting coin types. In the listings covering the past twenty-six editions, we have quoted values for the uncirculated grade unless otherwise noted. In the earliest editions, FINE was a standard column head for 1700 and early 1800 date coins. We have adhered to a single grade from one edition to the next, and thus values for a few years are not listed. Grades other than uncirculated are labeled in the charts. Since we are not making any exact value-increase comparisons, the charts will serve only as generalized year-to-year average price changes (mostly upward) of components of a type set. It should be explained here that the values listed for any particular type may represent different dates in different editions. Thus, increases in value are not actually traceable, or in fact significant.

Among the long list of types are designs with as few as one date (1796 quarter, 1859 Laurel Wreath cent for example), some with only five or so dates (silver coins 1853-55 with arrows at date), and many with long date coverage (Liberty Seated quarter with about 100 dates and mint marks and Barber half dollars with 73, are examples). The number of base price coins of any type can vary from one, two, ten or more dates in any edition, all with an identical low price. Total quantity within a category thus has a strong influence on value, which coupled with age, popularity, and other factors, produces the price-growth variations this chart so clearly reveals. Sometimes collector interest and demand makes a switch. Here is an interesting example: The value listed in the first edition for the Half Cent Head Facing Right 1794-97 is listed at $12.50. Interestingly this represents only one date-variety, the 1795 Plain Edge, Punctuated date. 26 editions later the average low for the type is $130.00, but it is for a different coin, namely the 1797, 1 above 1, plain edge. In other types, one date continues to hold the low spot throughout and in others several share the lowest price position over the years. So it is not feasible to show investment growth specifically, but growth there is and in real terms; better, in fact, than the dollar gain for rare dates.

A study published in the *Whitman Numismatic Journal* of January 1967 revealed that the dollar investment gain is greater for select quality, lowest value dates in all but a few type categories. Those few exceptions are outright rarities, the one-date types with which we are familiar. This phenomenon was explained by the fact that common dates have more room in which to grow, while scarce dates start with high values and often price themselves out of the market in a few short years.

Beware the exception, however. The 1883 nickel without *cents* has had a long-delayed investment record for a single date simply because it was hoarded by thousands of people in the 1880's owing to widespread publicity.

The later types of United States regular issue coins are not included in the tables simply because there is little or no value difference over the twenty-six-year period. This is also true to a degree of Morgan and Peace dollars. Though their values have moved only slightly for the period, they are included nevertheless. These figures at least reemphasize that even at this late date we still have a rare opportunity to get in on some bargains in two by-gone types of our nation's coinage.

Edition/Year	HALF CENTS					LARGE CENTS						
	Fine 1793	Fine 1794-1797	Fine 1800-1808	1809-1836	1849-1857	Chain 1793	Wreath 1793	Fine 1793-1796	Fine 1796-1807	Fine 1808-1814	1816-1835	1835-1857
1st/1947	$45.00	$12.50	$2.00	$3.00	$4.00	$125.00	$60.00	$7.50	$3.00	$4.00	$3.50	$3.50
2nd/1948	50.00	15.00	2.00	4.00	4.00	125.00	60.00	9.00	3.00	4.00	5.00	3.50
3rd/1949	50.00	15.00	2.00	5.00	4.00	100.00	60.00	10.00	3.00	4.00	5.00	3.50
4th/1951-52	50.00	15.00	2.00	5.00	4.00	100.00	60.00	10.00	3.00	5.00	6.00	3.50
5th/1952-53	55.00	17.50	2.00	5.00	4.00	100.00	65.00	10.00	3.00	5.00	6.00	3.50
6th/1953-54	60.00	20.00	2.50	5.50	4.50	110.00	70.00	12.50	3.50	5.00	6.00	4.00
7th/1954-55	65.00	20.00	2.50	5.50	4.50	110.00	70.00	12.50	3.50	5.00	6.50	4.00
8th/1955	65.00	22.50	3.00	7.50	5.50	110.00	70.00	13.50	4.50	6.00	7.50	4.00
9th/1956	75.00	22.50	3.50	9.00	7.50	125.00	75.00	15.00	5.00	6.00	9.00	5.00
10th/1957	77.50	25.00	4.50	10.00	9.00	130.00	80.00	16.00	5.00	6.50	10.00	6.50
11th/1958	82.50	27.50	4.50	10.00	9.00	135.00	95.00	17.50	5.00	7.50	12.50	7.50
12th/1959	95.00	30.00	4.50	11.50	10.00	155.00	105.00	18.50	5.50	8.50	13.00	8.00
13th/1960	115.00	35.00	5.50	13.00	12.00	190.00	115.00	19.00	6.00	8.50	15.00	9.00
14th/1961	140.00	40.00	6.50	15.00	14.00	215.00	130.00	22.50	7.50	9.50	18.50	10.50
15th/1962	155.00	46.00	7.00	18.50	16.25	250.00	145.00	26.00	9.00	10.50	21.00	13.50
16th/1963	175.00	55.00	8.00	23.00	20.00	325.00	195.00	32.50	12.00	15.00	25.00	16.00
17th/1964	275.00	65.00	9.50	28.50	26.50	420.00	262.50	40.00	13.50	17.50	28.00	19.00
18th/1965	425.00	100.00	11.50	35.00	32.50	525.00	325.00	50.00	17.00	21.00	35.00	22.50
19th/1966	550.00	125.00	15.00	45.00	42.50	625.00	400.00	60.00	20.00	26.00	60.00	40.00
20th/1967	600.00	135.00	17.50	55.00	50.00	700.00	475.00	75.00	22.50	28.00	75.00	50.00
21st/1968	635.00	125.00	15.00	60.00	52.50	740.00	600.00	75.00	21.00	27.50	82.50	55.00
22nd/1969	650.00	125.00	17.50	60.00	55.00	700.00	600.00	80.00	21.00	29.00	85.00	57.50
23rd/1970	650.00	135.00	17.50	62.50	60.00	750.00	600.00	87.50	22.50	31.00	92.50	62.50
24th/1971	650.00	135.00	17.50	60.00	60.00	800.00	600.00	90.00	25.00	32.50	100.00	62.50
25th/1972	650.00	140.00	19.00	65.00	65.00	850.00	625.00	100.00	25.00	33.50	105.00	65.00
26th/1973	650.00	130.00	20.00	67.50	70.00	975.00	650.00	100.00	25.00	33.50	105.00	65.00

Edition/Year	SMALL CENTS				TWO CENTS	THREE CENTS NICKEL	FIVE CENTS NICKEL					
	1856–1858	1859	1860–1864	1864–1909	1864–1873	1865–1889	Rays 1866–1867	No Rays 1867–1883	No Cents 1883	Cents 1883–1912	Mound 1913	Plain 1913–1938
1st/1947	$5.00	$4.50	$1.00	$ .75	$1.00	$1.35	$12.50	$2.25	$ .50	$2.00	$ .75	$ .35
2nd/1948	6.00	5.50	1.00	.85	1.00	1.35	12.50	3.00	.50	2.50	1.00	.35
3rd/1949	6.00	5.50	1.00	.75	1.00	1.25	10.00	2.75	.50	2.75	1.00	.25
4th/1951-52	7.00	5.50	1.00	.75	1.00	1.25	10.00	2.75	.50	2.75	.75	.25
5th/1952-53	7.50	5.50	1.00	.75	1.50	1.50	10.00	3.00	.50	2.75	.90	.25
6th/1953-54	8.00	6.00	1.25	.85	1.60	1.50	11.00	3.50	.65	3.00	.90	.25
7th/1954-55	9.00	7.50	1.25	1.00	2.00	.75	12.00	4.00	.75	3.75	1.00	.25
8th/1955	10.00	8.50	2.00	1.25	2.50	2.00	13.50	4.50	1.00	4.50	1.25	.25
9th/1956	12.00	10.00	2.50	1.50	3.00	2.50	15.00	5.00	1.50	5.00	1.50	.35
10th/1957	13.50	12.00	3.00	2.25	3.75	3.00	16.00	5.50	1.85	5.50	1.75	.35
11th/1958	16.00	15.00	3.50	2.75	4.50	3.75	19.00	7.00	2.25	7.00	2.00	.50
12th/1959	24.00	25.00	4.50	3.25	5.50	4.00	25.00	7.50	2.75	8.00	2.50	.65
13th/1960	25.00	30.00	5.00	3.50	6.50	4.50	27.50	8.50	3.00	9.00	3.00	.75
14th/1961	30.00	35.00	6.00	4.25	7.50	5.00	27.50	9.50	4.00	9.00	3.50	.75
15th/1962	33.50	40.00	8.00	4.50	8.50	6.25	35.00	9.50	4.00	9.50	4.00	1.00
16th/1963	45.00	50.00	12.00	6.00	10.50	7.00	40.00	11.00	4.50	10.00	5.00	1.00
17th/1964	57.50	65.00	20.00	8.00	11.50	7.50	50.00	14.00	4.50	11.00	5.50	1.50
18th/1965	80.00	82.50	22.50	11.00	15.00	10.00	85.00	17.50	6.00	15.00	7.00	2.00
19th/1966	100.00	90.00	27.00	12.50	20.00	13.00	100.00	24.00	8.00	21.00	9.00	3.00
20th/1967	100.00	90.00	30.00	12.50	25.00	17.50	112.50	27.50	9.50	25.00	10.00	4.10
21st/1968	100.00	77.50	25.00	9.25	25.00	17.50	120.00	30.00	8.50	25.00	10.00	4.00
22nd/1969	110.00	80.00	25.00	9.25	25.00	17.50	120.00	30.00	8.50	25.00	10.00	4.00
23rd/1970	115.00	82.50	25.00	9.25	27.50	17.50	120.00	30.00	11.50	25.00	11.00	4.25
24th/1971	115.00	82.50	25.00	9.25	27.50	17.50	120.00	30.00	10.50	25.00	11.00	4.25
25th/1972	115.00	82.50	25.00	9.25	27.50	19.00	120.00	30.00	9.00	25.00	11.00	4.25
26th/1973	125.00	85.00	27.00	9.25	30.00	20.00	125.00	30.00	10.00	25.00	12.00	4.25

Edition/Year	THREE CENTS SILVER			HALF DIMES						Arrows	
	1851–1853	1854–1858	1859–1873	1794–1795	1796–1797	1800–1805	1829–1837	1837–1838	1838–1859	1853–1855	1860–1873
1st/1947	$3.00	$2.50	$1.50	—	—	—	$2.25	$4.50	$1.25	$1.25	$1.50
2nd/1948	3.25	2.50	1.50	$50.00	$80.00	$50.00	2.50	7.50	1.35	1.50	1.50
3rd/1949	3.50	2.75	1.75	45.00	80.00	50.00	2.50	7.50	1.25	1.50	1.25
4th/1951-52	3.50	2.75	1.75	45.00	80.00	50.00	2.50	8.00	1.25	1.50	1.25
5th/1952-53	3.50	2.75	2.00	50.00	80.00	50.00	3.00	9.00	1.75	2.00	1.75
6th/1953-54	4.00	4.00	3.00	50.00	90.00	50.00	3.50	11.00	2.25	2.50	2.25
7th/1954-55	4.50	5.00	3.50	55.00	110.00	65.00	3.50	12.50	2.50	3.00	2.25
8th/1955	5.00	6.00	5.00	55.00	110.00	65.00	4.50	15.00	3.00	4.00	3.00
9th/1956	5.50	7.00	5.50	65.00	120.00	75.00	5.00	20.00	3.50	5.00	3.50
10th/1957	6.00	7.00	5.50	75.00	125.00	80.00	5.00	25.00	3.50	5.50	3.50
11th/1958	7.50	8.00	6.50	100.00	135.00	100.00	6.00	32.50	4.50	5.50	3.50
12th/1959	8.50	9.00	8.50	150.00	140.00	135.00	7.50	45.00	5.00	6.50	4.50
13th/1960	9.00	11.00	9.50	175.00	190.00	175.00	8.50	52.50	5.50	8.00	5.00
14th/1961	10.50	14.00	11.00	200.00	215.00	215.00	9.75	65.00	6.50	9.50	6.50
15th/1962	12.00	17.50	12.00	260.00	275.00	260.00	11.50	72.50	7.50	11.00	7.00
16th/1963	15.00	22.50	14.50	410.00	375.00	325.00	20.00	95.00	10.00	13.00	9.25
17th/1964	17.50	27.50	22.00	500.00	500.00	450.00	25.00	150.00	13.00	16.00	12.50
18th/1965	21.00	35.00	26.50	650.00	800.00	600.00	35.00	175.00	14.00	20.00	14.00
19th/1966	27.50	44.00	32.00	750.00	1,000	775.00	50.00	225.00	18.00	27.50	25.00
20th/1967	32.50	50.00	36.00	800.00	1,000	800.00	55.00	250.00	27.50	35.00	27.50
21st/1968	37.50	55.00	42.50	875.00	1,150	900.00	65.00	250.00	32.50	40.00	32.50
22nd/1969	42.50	60.00	45.00	875.00	1,150	900.00	70.00	260.00	32.50	40.00	32.50
23rd/1970	48.00	68.50	52.00	950.00	1,250	925.00	77.50	285.00	40.00	45.00	40.00
24th/1971	50.00	65.00	52.50	950.00	1,325	1,025	82.50	275.00	40.00	50.00	40.00
25th/1972	55.00	70.00	55.00	950.00	1,325	1,075	82.50	275.00	40.00	50.00	40.00
26th/1973	55.00	70.00	55.00	1,000	1,325	1,075	87.50	275.00	42.50	50.00	42.50

Edition/Year	DIMES										TWENTY CENTS
	1796–1797	1798–1807	1809–1837	1837–1838	1838–1860	Arrows 1853–1855	1860–1891	Arrows 1873–1874	1892–1916	1916–1945	1875–1878
1st/1947	—										$4.00
2nd/1948	$125.00	$30.00	$2.75	$12.50	$2.50	$2.25	$1.25	$2.00	$2.00	$ .25	5.00
3rd/1949	125.00	30.00	2.75	13.50	2.50	2.50	1.50	2.50	2.00	.25	7.50
4th/1951-52	125.00	30.00	2.75	15.00	2.50	2.50	1.50	3.50	1.50	.20	6.00
5th/1952-53	125.00	35.00	2.75	15.00	2.50	3.00	1.50	3.50	1.50	.20	8.00
6th/1953-54	135.00	35.00	2.75	17.50	2.50	3.00	1.75	5.00	2.00	.25	10.00
7th/1954-55	145.00	40.00	4.00	20.00	3.00	3.50	1.75	5.00	2.25	.25	12.50
8th/1955	150.00	45.00	5.00	22.50	4.00	4.50	2.25	9.00	2.50	.25	15.00
9th/1956	175.00	45.00	6.00	25.00	4.50	5.00	2.75	9.00	3.00	.25	17.50
10th/1957	190.00	45.00	6.00	32.50	4.50	5.50	3.00	10.00	4.00	.30	20.00
11th/1958	220.00	55.00	7.00	40.00	5.00	5.50	3.00	14.00	4.50	.30	25.00
12th/1959	300.00	67.50	8.50	47.50	5.50	6.00	3.50	17.50	5.00	.30	25.00
13th/1960	400.00	75.00	9.00	60.00	7.50	6.00	4.00	20.00	5.50	.35	30.00
14th/1961	460.00	95.00	11.00	65.00	9.00	7.50	5.50	27.50	6.00	.35	35.00
15th/1962	525.00	110.00	12.50	87.50	10.00	9.00	6.00	32.50	8.00	.45	36.00
16th/1963	740.00	172.50	18.00	95.00	16.00	11.00	7.50	40.00	8.00	.45	42.50
17th/1964	1,000	230.00	24.50	122.50	18.00	13.00	8.00	47.50	9.00	.50	55.00
18th/1965	1,350	325.00	40.00	175.00	25.00	16.00	9.50	55.00	9.00	.60	70.00
19th/1966	1,550	450.00	60.00	200.00	35.00	22.50	14.00	60.00	9.00	.75	90.00
20th/1967	1,550	450.00	85.00	240.00	35.00	27.50	20.00	75.00	15.00	1.25	105.00
21st/1968	1,850	500.00	95.00	300.00	42.50	35.00	24.00	95.00	17.50	1.25	130.00
22nd/1969	1,850	500.00	110.00	325.00	42.50	42.50	30.00	110.00	17.50	1.50	145.00
23rd/1970	1,900	560.00	120.00	350.00	47.50	47.50	35.00	120.00	21.00	1.25	160.00
24th/1971	1,900	650.00	140.00	350.00	47.50	47.50	35.00	140.00	22.50	1.50	175.00
25th/1972	1,900	650.00	150.00	350.00	55.00	55.00	35.00	155.00	22.50	1.25	175.00
26th/1973	1,950	700.00	165.00	350.00	65.00	65.00	40.00	165.00	25.00	1.25	200.00

Edition/Year	QUARTERS 1796	1804–1807	1815–1828	1831–1838	1838–1865	Arrows Ray 1853	Arrows 1854–1855	1866–1891	Arrows 1873–1874	1892–1916	1916–1917	1917–1930
1st/1947	$100.00	$25.00	$12.50	$5.00	$1.75	$3.50	$2.00	$1.50	$3.00	$2.50	$2.75	$1.50
2nd/1948	125.00	27.50	13.50	5.00	2.00	3.50	2.00	2.00	3.50	2.75	2.75	2.00
3rd/1949	135.00	30.00	15.00	5.00	2.25	4.50	2.75	2.00	3.50	2.75	2.75	2.00
4th/1951-52	175.00	35.00	15.00	5.00	2.25	5.00	3.00	2.25	4.50	2.75	2.75	2.00
5th/1952-53	200.00	35.00	15.00	10.00	3.00	6.00	4.00	2.75	6.00	2.75	3.50	2.00
6th/1953-54	250.00	40.00	15.00	10.00	3.00	6.00	4.00	2.75	7.50	3.25	3.50	2.00
7th/1954-55	250.00	50.00	20.00	10.00	3.50	7.50	4.50	3.00	12.50	4.50	4.00	3.50
8th/1955	275.00	60.00	22.50	11.00	4.00	9.00	5.00	4.00	15.00	5.50	5.00	4.00
9th/1956	325.00	65.00	25.00	12.50	4.50	11.00	7.50	4.50	20.00	5.50	5.50	4.50
10th/1957	425.00	70.00	30.00	13.50	4.50	15.00	7.50	4.50	25.00	6.50	6.50	4.50
11th/1958	700.00	90.00	30.00	15.00	5.00	16.50	8.00	4.50	30.00	6.50	6.50	4.50
12th/1959	900.00	135.00	42.50	17.50	6.00	20.00	11.00	5.00	45.00	7.50	7.00	5.00
13th/1960	1,250	150.00	47.50	18.00	7.00	22.50	12.00	5.50	50.00	8.00	8.00	6.00
14th/1961	1,450	175.00	55.00	22.50	9.00	25.00	15.00	6.00	60.00	10.00	10.00	7.50
15th/1962	1,800	225.00	65.00	30.00	10.00	27.50	17.50	8.00	67.50	10.00	12.50	8.50
16th/1963	2,750	350.00	90.00	40.00	12.50	33.00	22.00	10.00	77.00	13.00	17.50	11.00
17th/1964	2,750	450.00	125.00	65.00	14.50	40.00	25.00	12.00	95.00	15.00	21.00	12.50
18th/1965	3,750	550.00	160.00	75.00	16.00	55.00	40.00	14.00	120.00	17.00	30.00	15.00
19th/1966	4,250	640.00	190.00	90.00	20.00	65.00	48.00	18.00	150.00	25.00	36.00	20.00
20th/1967	5,900	640.00	200.00	135.00	26.00	65.00	48.00	22.50	150.00	32.50	40.00	22.50
21st/1968	5,750	700.00	300.00	175.00	27.50	75.00	50.00	30.00	160.00	32.50	42.50	26.00
22nd/1969	5,750	750.00	350.00	200.00	35.00	200.00	65.00	35.00	175.00	35.00	45.00	30.00
23rd/1970	5,750	800.00	400.00	250.00	40.00	275.00	75.00	42.50	200.00	40.00	47.50	32.50
24th/1971	5,750	850.00	425.00	300.00	45.00	350.00	85.00	45.00	200.00	40.00	47.50	32.50
25th/1972	5,750	850.00	475.00	325.00	50.00	350.00	95.00	45.00	210.00	45.00	50.00	32.50
26th/1973	6,000	850.00	525.00	350.00	65.00	375.00	100.00	65.00	210.00	50.00	55.00	32.50

HALF DOLLARS

Edition/Year	Fine 1794–1795	Fine 1796–1797	1801–1807	1807–1836	1836–1837	1838–1839	1839–1866	Arrows Ray 1853	Arrows 1854–1855	1866–1891	Arrows 1873–1874	1892–1915
1st/1947	$17.50	$200.00	—	—	$5.00	$5.00	$3.00	$6.50	$3.00	$2.75	$3.75	$3.50
2nd/1948	20.00	225.00	—	$3.50	6.50	6.50	3.00	7.00	3.00	3.50	4.00	4.00
3rd/1949	18.50	225.00	$17.50	3.50	6.50	6.50	3.00	7.00	3.50	3.50	4.00	4.00
4th/1951-52	18.50	225.00	17.50	3.50	6.50	6.50	3.00	8.00	3.50	3.50	6.00	4.00
5th/1952-53	20.00	225.00	17.50	3.50	7.50	7.50	3.50	9.00	5.00	3.50	7.50	4.00
6th/1953-54	22.50	225.00	17.50	4.00	8.50	8.50	4.00	10.00	6.00	3.50	9.00	4.50
7th/1954-55	25.00	250.00	22.50	5.00	10.00	11.00	4.00	12.00	7.50	4.00	13.50	6.00
8th/1955	27.50	275.00	25.00	5.50	11.50	12.50	5.00	15.00	8.00	5.00	15.00	7.50
9th/1956	35.00	325.00	32.50	6.00	12.50	15.00	5.50	17.50	8.50	5.50	20.00	8.00
10th/1957	35.00	350.00	40.00	7.00	16.00	17.50	6.00	20.00	10.00	6.00	32.50	9.00
11th/1958	40.00	380.00	55.00	8.50	20.00	20.00	7.00	25.00	12.00	7.50	37.50	10.00
12th/1959	47.50	450.00	55.00	9.50	30.00	35.00	8.50	35.00	14.00	8.00	55.00	12.00
13th/1960	55.00	485.00	65.00	10.50	37.50	37.50	9.00	37.50	16.50	9.50	65.00	14.00
14th/1961	70.00	675.00	82.50	14.00	45.00	45.00	11.00	42.50	19.00	11.00	75.00	17.50
15th/1962	85.00	900.00	100.00	15.00	50.00	50.00	14.00	47.50	21.00	12.00	90.00	17.50
16th/1963	125.00	1,500	130.00	16.00	60.00	60.00	15.00	55.00	25.00	14.00	100.00	17.50
17th/1964	150.00	2,000	150.00	16.00	75.00	65.00	18.00	70.00	35.00	14.00	120.00	17.50
18th/1965	185.00	2,100	160.00	18.00	80.00	75.00	20.00	80.00	40.00	19.00	135.00	25.00
19th/1966	240.00	2,700	185.00	25.00	95.00	85.00	25.00	90.00	45.00	25.00	165.00	55.00
20th/1967	275.00	3,500	275.00	42.50	110.00	100.00	35.00	125.00	55.00	35.00	175.00	75.00
21st/1968	275.00	3,500	325.00	47.50	137.50	120.00	42.50	225.00	67.50	45.00	195.00	80.00
22nd/1969	275.00	3,500	375.00	52.50	160.00	140.00	55.00	275.00	75.00	52.50	220.00	90.00
23rd/1970	275.00	3,500	375.00	52.50	190.00	175.00	55.00	370.00	85.00	52.50	250.00	90.00
24th/1971	275.00	3,650	425.00	60.00	190.00	175.00	55.00	450.00	90.00	57.50	250.00	95.00
25th/1972	275.00	4,100	425.00	60.00	190.00	175.00	55.00	450.00	90.00	60.00	250.00	110.00
26th/1973	275.00	4,100	500.00	90.00	200.00	190.00	75.00	475.00	105.00	75.00	250.00	135.00

	HALF DOLLARS			SILVER DOLLARS								
Edition/Year	Obv. MM 1916–1917	Rev. MM 1917–1947	Franklin 1948–1963	1794–1795	1795–1798	1798–1803	1840–1865	1866–1873	8 Feathers 1878	Morgan 1878–1921	Peace 1921–1935	Trade 1873–1883
1st/1947	$6.00	$ .75	—	—	—	—	$10.00	$7.00	$5.00	$2.00	$2.00	$4.00
2nd/1948	6.00	.75	$ .75	—	—	—	10.00	8.50	5.00	2.00	2.00	4.50
3rd/1949	6.00	.75	.75	$135.00	$100.00	$75.00	12.00	9.50	4.00	2.00	2.00	5.00
4th/1951-52	7.00	.75	.75	150.00	125.00	75.00	12.00	11.00	4.00	2.00	2.00	6.00
5th/1952-53	8.50	1.00	1.00	150.00	125.00	75.00	15.00	12.50	4.00	2.00	2.00	7.50
6th/1953-54	10.00	1.25	1.00	150.00	125.00	75.00	16.50	15.00	5.00	2.00	2.00	8.50
7th/1954-55	12.50	1.25	1.00	150.00	125.00	75.00	18.00	16.50	5.00	2.00	2.00	9.00
8th/1955	15.00	1.25	1.00	150.00	135.00	85.00	21.00	17.50	5.00	2.00	2.00	11.00
9th/1956	17.50	1.50	1.00	160.00	140.00	100.00	22.50	18.50	5.00	2.00	2.25	12.50
10th/1957	20.00	1.50	1.00	200.00	175.00	120.00	25.00	18.50	6.00	2.00	3.00	14.00
11th/1958	20.00	1.50	1.00	250.00	250.00	120.00	27.50	18.50	10.00	2.00	2.50	14.00
12th/1959	24.00	1.50	1.00	300.00	250.00	120.00	35.00	21.00	10.00	2.00	2.50	15.00
13th/1960	25.00	1.60	1.00	325.00	250.00	125.00	38.00	26.00	10.00	2.00	2.50	17.50
14th/1961	27.50	1.75	1.00	400.00	275.00	150.00	45.00	35.00	10.00	2.25	2.50	20.00
15th/1962	30.00	1.75	1.00	500.00	325.00	150.00	45.00	35.00	10.00	2.25	2.50	20.00
16th/1963	30.00	1.75	1.00	750.00	500.00	160.00	45.00	35.00	10.00	2.25	2.50	20.00
17th/1964	30.00	1.75	1.00	750.00	500.00	175.00	45.00	35.00	6.00	2.25	2.50	20.00
18th/1965	35.00	2.25	1.15	950.00	600.00	230.00	52.50	35.00	23.00	2.00	2.00	25.00
19th/1966	50.00	5.00	1.15	1,100	875.00	325.00	57.50	45.00	20.00	2.50	2.50	35.00
20th/1967	62.50	5.50	1.15	1,200	1,000	425.00	67.50	60.00	20.00	2.50	2.00	45.00
21st/1968	75.00	5.00	1.00	1,200	1,000	525.00	80.00	75.00	11.00	2.50	2.00	65.00
22nd/1969	75.00	5.00	1.25	1,300	1,100	625.00	90.00	90.00	11.00	3.50	3.50	80.00
23rd/1970	85.00	6.25	1.60	1,300	1,300	700.00	100.00	110.00	15.00	4.00	4.00	95.00
24th/1971	85.00	6.00	1.60	1,600	1,500	775.00	120.00	125.00	15.00	4.00	4.00	100.00
25th/1972	92.50	6.00	1.50	1,700	1,500	775.00	130.00	125.00	14.00	4.25	4.25	110.00
26th/1973	92.50	6.00	1.50	2,000	1,700	950.00	150.00	150.00	15.00	5.00	4.75	130.00

LESHER REFERENDUM DOLLARS

Coined by Joseph Lesher in 1900 and 1901 at Victor, Colorado. Used in trade to some extent, and stocked by various merchants who redeemed them in goods. Coins were numbered and a blank space left at bottom of 1901 issues, in which were stamped names of businessmen who bought them. All are quite rare, many varieties extremely rare. Composition is .950 fine silver alloyed with copper.

1900

1901

	V. Fine	Unc.
1900 First Type, no business name	$275.00	$500.00
1900 A.B. Bumstead, with scrolls	235.00	400.00
1900 A.B. Bumstead, no scrolls	200.00	375.00
1900 Bank Type (5 known)	——	——
1901 Imprint Type, no name	250.00	450.00
1901 Imprint Type, various names	$225-$750	$350-$1,500

Feuchtwanger Cent 1837

Dr. Lewis Feuchtwanger produced a metal which was really a variety of German silver consisting of nickel, copper and some zinc. He suggested as early as 1837 to Congress that his metal be substituted for copper. He made some one-cent and three-cent trial pieces in this metal at that time.

Values: Cent..Fine $12.50; Ex. Fine $32.00   Three-Cent piece..V. Scarce

HARD TIMES
TOKENS
1834-1844

In addition to the coins issued by the United States government, numismatists include in their collections the Hard Times and Civil War tokens which circulated as money during two periods in this country's history when nearly all the minor coin was hoarded.

The Hard Times tokens were issued in the period 1834-1844 and are the size of the large U. S. cent. They were generally struck in copper and are of two general groups: political tokens whose theme centered around President Jackson's fight against the United States Bank, and those issued by merchants (tradesmen's cards). Many different varieties exist. The most common pieces are generally valued at $1.75 Good to $8.50 Ex. Fine.

CIVIL WAR TOKENS — 1861-1864

Civil War Tokens are generally divided into two groups: tradesmen's tokens, and anonymously issued pieces with political or patriotic themes. They came into existence only because of the scarcity of government coins and disappeared as soon as the bronze coins of 1864 met the public demand for small copper change.

From the outset of the Civil War, government cents were insufficient in number, widely hoarded and worth a premium over all other currencies. As a result of this scarcity of cent pieces, private copper coins were issued by many individuals. Their wide circulation was made possible by the scarcity of copper-nickel cents and the public dislike of fractional paper money.

The tradesmen's tokens were issued by various firms to provide change and advertise the dealers' wares. They usually bore an implied or an explicit promise of redemption in goods or money. The second type was simply unauthorized substitutes for government coins, produced at a profit by private manufacturers and put into general circulation through various agencies.

These tokens are of great variety in composition and design. A number were more or less faithful imitations of the copper-nickel cent. A few of this type have the word "NOT" in very small letters above the words "ONE CENT."

Many pieces, especially of the tradesmen token type, were individual in device and size, representing any caprice of design or slogan that appealed to the maker. Some were political or patriotic in character, carrying the likeness of some military leader such as McClellan or bearing such inscriptions as "Millions for contractors, not one cent for the widows." An estimated 50,000,000 or more of these pieces were issued. Approximately 10,000 different varieties have been recorded.

The legal status of the Civil War Tokens was uncertain. Mint Director Pollock thought they were illegal; however, there was no law prohibiting the issue of tradesmen's tokens or of private coins not in imitation of United States coins. A law was passed on April 22, 1864 prohibiting the issue of any one or two-cent coins, tokens, or devices for use as money, and on June 8 another law was passed which abolished private coinage of every kind.

	Fine	V. Fine	Unc.
Copper or Brass Tokens	$1.35	$2.50	$5.00
Nickel or German Silver Tokens	4.25	8.00	17.50
White Metal Tokens	3.00	6.50	13.00
Copper-Nickel Tokens	3.50	7.00	15.00
Silver Tokens	8.50	15.00	30.00

CONFEDERATE STATES OF AMERICA
Confederate 1861 Half Dollar

The half dollar struck by the Confederacy was unknown to collectors until 1879. A specimen of the coin and both dies were found in the possession of Dr. B. F. Taylor of New Orleans. Mr. E. Mason, Jr. of Philadelphia purchased Dr. Taylor's specimen and the reverse die and later sold them to J. W. Scott and Company of New York.

CONFEDERATE STATES OF AMERICA — 1861

Five hundred genuine 1861 half dollars from the New Orleans mint were acquired by J. W. Scott and Company. The reverses were planed off and then restamped with the Confederate die. These are known as restrikes. The restrikes have flattened obverses.

According to records only four originals were struck. These were made on a hand press. Original silver half dollar planchets were used, as well as the original obverse die. One of the coins was given to the Secretary of the Confederacy Memminger who passed it on to President Jefferson Davis for his approval. Another was given to Prof. Biddle of the University of Louisiana. Dr. E. Ames of New Orleans received a third specimen, the last being kept by Chief Coiner Taylor, who sold it later as mentioned above.

Lack of bullion prevented the Confederate government from proceeding with any coinage plans that might have been made.

J. W. Scott struck some tokens in white metal using the Confederate reverse die and a special die bearing the inscription

4 ORIGINALS STRUCK BY ORDER OF C. S. A. IN NEW ORLEANS 1861 *******
REV. SAME AS U.S. (FROM ORIGINAL DIE SCOTT)

Confederate Reverse   Scott Obverse

	Quan. Minted	V. Fine	Unc.
1861 HALF DOL. (Ex. Rare)	4	—	—
1861 HALF DOL. Restrike	500	$400.00	$800.00
1861 Scott Token, obverse. Confederate reverse	500	75.00	150.00

THE CONFEDERATE CENT

An order to make cents for the Confederacy was placed with Mr. Robert Lovett Jr., an engraver and die-sinker of Philadelphia, through a jewelry firm of that city. Fearing arrest by the United States government for giving assistance to the enemy, Mr. Lovett decided against delivering the coins to the Confederate government and hid the coins and dies in his cellar.

The original dies were later purchased by Capt. John W. Haseltine who made restrikes from the dies.

		Proof
1861 Cent Original (copper-nickel)	12	$2,200
1861 Cent Restrike (copper)	55	1,200
1861 Cent Restrike (gold)	7	2,800
1861 Cent Restrike (silver)	12	1,750

COINS AND TOKENS OF HAWAII

The first official coins of Hawaii were the copper cents of 1847 issued by King Kamehameha III. The five cent piece of 1881 and the eighth dollar piece of 1883 are patterns. In 1883 Kalakaua I issued silver dimes, quarters, halves and dollars bearing his bust and showing the Hawaiian coat of arms on the reverse. By 1937 most of these silver coins had been withdrawn and melted. The plantation tokens listed here were all used as small change on the Islands.

Ten Cents 1883

One Cent — 1847

	Quan. Minted	Fine	V. Fine	Ex. Fine	Unc.	Proof
1847 Cent	100,000	$40.00	$60.00	$90.00	$170.00	
1881 Five Cents			450.00	600.00	900.00	$1,200
1883 Ten Cents	250,000	13.00	27.50	65.00	170.00	450.00
1883 Eighth Dollar (12½¢)			500.00	800.00	1,200	1,500
1883 Quarter Dollar	500,000	12.00	15.00	20.00	50.00	400.00
1883 Half Dollar	700,000	18.00	30.00	60.00	120.00	400.00
1883 Dollar	500,000	75.00	90.00	150.00	400.00	600.00

HAWAIIAN TOKENS

Thomas Hobron Token —1879   Haiku Plantation — 1882

Wailuku Plantation — 1871   Wailuku Plantation — 1880

	Fine	V.F.	E.F.
Waterhouse Token 1862. Bust of Kamehameha IV	$100.00	$150.00	$400.00
Wailuku Plantation Token 1871	60.00	75.00	100.00
Wailuku Plantation Token 1880	70.00	85.00	100.00
Wailuku Plantation Token, Half Real 1880	75.00	100.00	150.00
Thomas Hobron Token 1879	35.00	45.00	70.00
Haiku Plantation Token	45.00	50.00	70.00
Grove Ranch Plantation Token 1886	75.00	100.00	135.00
Grove Ranch Plantation Token 1887	85.00	110.00	150.00

ALASKA RURAL REHABILITATION CORPORATION
TOKENS OF 1935

These tokens were issued by the U. S. Government for the use of the colonists of the Matanuska Valley Colonization Project to supply them with much needed Federal aid. They were redeemable only at the ARRC stores. The "Bingles," as they were called, were in use only about six months during 1935. 1936 after which they were redeemed for regular U. S. money and destroyed. They were issued on a basis of family dependents. Each token is the size of the corresponding U. S. coin with the exception of the one cent piece which is octagonal. The design is the same on both sides of each denomination.

Aluminum				Quan. Mtd.	V. Fine	Unc.
Quan. Mtd.	V. Fine	Unc.	50¢ 2,500	$25.00	$50.00
1¢ 5,000	$15.00	$25.00	$1.00 2,500	40.00	85.00
5¢ 5,000	15.00	25.00	Brass		
10¢ 5,000	15.00	25.00	$5.00 1,000	60.00	100.00
25¢ 3,000	20.00	35.00	$10.00 1,000	75.00	125.00

PHILIPPINES UNDER SOVEREIGNTY OF THE U.S.

The 1903-19 issues were struck at Philadelphia and San Francisco. 1920 and after were struck at Manila. Because of World War II the 1944-45 coins were minted at Philadelphia, Denver and San Francisco.

Bronze

	E.F.	Unc.
½ Centavo 1903-08 . . .	$1.00	$3.50
1 Centavo 1903-36 . . .	.75	2.50

PHILIPPINES UNDER SOVEREIGNTY OF THE U. S.

Copper-Nickel

	E.F.	Unc.
5 Centavos 1903-28...	$1.00	$3.00
5 Centavos 1918 Rev. of 20 Centavos (Mule)............	45.00	90.00

Reduced Size

5 Centavos 1930-35...	1.25	4.00

Silver

10 Centavos 1903-06...	1.75	4.50
20 Centavos 1903-06...	2.50	7.00
50 Centavos 1903-06...	7.50	15.00
1 Peso 1903-06.. ...	8.50	15.00

Size Reduced

10 Centavos 1907-35...	1.00	4.00
20 Centavos 1907-29...	2.50	6.00
20 Centavos 1928 Rev. of 5 Centavos (Mule)	20.00	60.00
50 Centavos 1907-21...	4.00	9.00
1 Peso 1907-12.......	6.00	12.00

Commonwealth Issues
Bronze

1 Centavo 1937-44...	.15	.40

Copper-Nickel

	E.F.	Unc.
5 Centavos 1937-41...	$1.00	$3.00

Nickel-Silver
Same Type as Cop.-Nic.

5 Centavos 1944-45...	.15	.35

Silver

10 Centavos 1937-45...	.20	.40
20 Centavos 1937-45...	.30	.50
50 Centavos 1944-45...	.80	1.00

Commemorative Issues — Establishment of the Commonwealth 1935

Gov. Gen. Murphy and Quezon

50 Centavos 1936...........	27.50
1 Peso 1936	50.00

Roosevelt and Quezon

1 Peso 1936	50.00

INDEX

INDEX — *Continued*